THE CRITICAL FLAW

HOW TO PROFIT AND PROTECT WEALTH IN HISTORY'S GREATEST OPPORTUNITY

ALAN P. CHAN, PHARM.D

E.J. INTERNATIONAL SAN FRANCISCO

First printing.

ISBN: 978-0-9890312-0-2

Photography by Cathy Kam Photography

Edited by Trisha Barnes.

Layout, manuscript design, and cover design by Corina Kellam.

Table of Contents

Preface: From the Author, Dr. Alan P. Chan, Pharm.D

*"Yes, I've found a flaw. I don't know how significant or permanent it is... a **flaw** in the model that I perceive as **the critical functioning structure** that defines how the world works."*

- Dr. Alan Greenspan, Former Federal Reserve Chairman, Congressional testimony October 23, 2008

Problems always create opportunities of equal magnitude, and the greatest investment opportunity in history will come from the greatest Critical Flaw in the history of our financial system. This is why and how:

In the age of global currency debasement via multi-Quantitative Easing mechanisms and increasing global debts pushing the world into a global fiscal cliff, history proves repeatedly that only physical gold and silver can revalue itself to account for all paper currencies and credit outstanding when the dollar currency bubble pops. An enormous wealth transfer is about to take place and you can choose to be part of it... or not.

Gold and silver have always and will always balance the "fiat" or paper money because people around the world have an innate sense of the intrinsic value of gold and silver. When paper money becomes too abundant and thus loses value, physical gold and silver revalues itself to account for paper currencies and credit outstanding. The value and purchasing power of gold and silver increases exponentially; hence, the greatest wealth transfers in history.

This book will educate you, offer historical evidence, and realistic approaches to take advantage of this enormous opportunity. To be successful, one must know history, as it tends to repeat itself in a similar manner. We cannot possibly know where we are and where we are going without knowing how we got here.

The Critical Flaw will equip you with all you need to become a successful precious metals investor, potentially increasing your net worth exponentially. *Enjoy.*

ENDORSMENTS FOR THE CRITICAL FLAW

"Well-argued and ultimately quite persuasive... With a straightforward, accessible writing style that conveys his obvious passion for the topic, Chan articulates important points of economic theory without becoming too abstract. He covers topics like inflation, quantitative easing, the "fiscal cliff," and the global debt crisis with clarity and purpose. - ELIZABETH MILLARD, *Foreword Clarion Reviews.*

"Dr. Chan's book is needed for today's financial times. His guide will help stop you from making bad investments, getting caught up in financial debt, and ultimately it will provide answers to the questions you have been subconsciously asking for years. *What's the true picture? How can I invest well in the long term? How best to protect my future? What happens during the next financial crash? How can I avoid the traps?*" – BILL CHAN, Corporate Advisory Chair of Seine Image International Co. Ltd.

"The Critical Flaw describes how true and seriously faulty the assumptions on which we built our financial world upon. Brimming with straightforward facts and strategies, anyone can use Dr. Chan's book to overcome the key fears and questions associated with investing in physical gold and silver." – ESTHER JIN, MSOD, *Private Wealth Manager.*

"Dr. Chan does a great job of taking complicated financial concepts and explaining them in a fresh and clear manner. He also offers up some thoughtful ideas on how to navigate today's volatile financial landscape." – BRIAN SAMSON, *Founder & CEO, HR for Startups.*

"If you want to deploy a section of your portfolio into precious metals, then this book is the invaluable tool you'll need in order to capitalize on accurate concepts and helpful tactics which will allow you to protect your assets against the next financial crash and to increase your wealth on the way. Indeed, "The Critical Flaw" is a must-read and belongs in the collection of every self-respecting investor." – RALUCA IONITA, *Co-Founder and Managing Director AYG Romania.*

"Dr. Chan paints a bleak picture about the current state of a flawed global financial system. Through shrewd investing and economic foresight, he takes us on a journey towards financial independence, free from the control of central banks and governmental monetary policy." – CASEY FONG, *Founder of Dreaming Emotion*

"Heartfelt, inspiring, simple and clear. The Critical Flaw reveals a new approach for investors who want to succeed in this new economic landscape. I loved it!" – SIMEON DACUMOS, *CEO & Creative Director of Simeon Dacumos Co.*

"Alan cuts straight to the chase on what you need to do to make the most of the serious opportunities that's coming our way." – DR. BRINDA KANSAGRA, D.D.S., *Dental Surgeon in Southern California.*

"This is not a theoretical book on how to succeed as an investor. The Critical Flaw is a call to action for anyone who wants to live and preserve life on your own terms without sacrificing your soul for the Federal Reserve." – DR. ANTONIO RODRIGUEZ, PHARM.D, *Kaiser Permanente Clinical Pharmacist.*

"A simple, straightforward, and honest book that I would highly recommend to anyone who is searching for tips to an easy and effective way to invest in gold and silver." – DR. PEGGY CHAN, PHARM.D, *Compond Pharmacist in Southern California.*

Foreword: Clarion Reviews

Taking its title from congressional testimony by Alan Greenspan, a former chairman of the Federal Reserve, this fascinating work on currency, global debt, and the gold standard presents a unique viewpoint that runs counter to prevailing economic pronouncements about investments. It offers compelling advice on how individuals can protect their financial health by acquiring precious metals.

In his 2008 testimony, Greenspan noted a flaw in the economic model he previously thought defined how the world works. Greenspan was referring to the ability of banks and markets to regulate themselves—an ideology he admitted was proven incorrect with the 2008 economic meltdown. In his first book, The Critical Flaw: How to profit and protect using wealth in history's greatest opportunity, Alan P. Chan asserts his belief that Greenspan's "critical flaw" presents enormous investment potential. Chan states that gold and silver, rather than traditional currency, will be part of an enormous wealth-transfer system and that those who recognize the potential shift will benefit.

As a former wholesaler of gold and silver, the author has a unique "inside" perspective. In presenting research and evidence of money's shaky foundation as an economic driver, Chan's insight is enthralling.

With a straightforward, accessible writing style that conveys his passion for the topic, Chan articulates important points of economic theory with clarity. His explanation and insight into inflation, quantitative easing, the "fiscal cliff," and the global debt crisis convey his vision and expertise.

This background information is crucial to understanding the author's main message: traditional investments are doomed to fail because the concentration of wealth is limited to central banks and government overseers which causes "the economy, society, and civilization to decline."

In Chan's view, only physical gold and silver will be valued in a broken economic system because, historically, prices of these precious metals rise during times of economic uncertainty and inflation.

When his real estate portfolio lost seventy-five percent of its value in 2008, Chan learned how dangerous these *"bubbles"* can be. In trying to recover from that major setback, he became an advocate for wealth protection in the form of precious metals. Subsequent years spent researching the financial system and macroeconomics resulted in his theories, which act as a clarion call to those with concerns about more financial bubbles in the future.

Although there are many who advocate hoarding of gold and silver coins in case of economic collapse, Chan is unique in providing an extensive history of past economic meltdowns and explaining the role of precious metals during different eras. This book serves not only as a background education in Economics, but teaches the reader to make informed decisions about current and future investments.

Particularly helpful is that Chan covers different types of gold and silver, so readers can begin purchasing with a strong knowledge of the unique attributes of items like collectible coins, gold bullion, and gold and silver stock. For example, he cautions against overzealous acquisition of collectible coins, since the value of those items is in their rarity, which won't be crucial during a time of economic collapse.

Well-argued and ultimately quite persuasive, Chan's comprehensive guide to precious-metals investment is likely to spark discussion about economic models and the gold standard's potential return. For concerned investors, The Critical Flaw offers a smart, unique informative option.

Elizabeth Millard

Chapter 1 – Money's Fractured Foundations

Reserve Banking and Interest Creation During Money Generation

---

"At the end, fiat money returns to its inner value - zero."

- Voltaire, French writer

Most of us have used money all of our lives, but have rarely stopped to think about what money really is. Because economic theory is sometimes difficult to understand, many people do not take the time to find out more about our currency and the best ways to earn it, keep it, and grow it. Whether your economics-phobia came from a bad teacher in elementary school, a boring college class, or a disdain of the wonky terms and learning curve when you're an economic *padawan*, chances are that if you're living and working in our complex society today, you already have all of the skills and abilities needed. The first step is to understand what money is and how it is used by banks and corporations: *"A History of Economics and Investing"* short course is in order.

What is money? Money is created when a loan is obtained, and it should be extinguished when the loan is repaid. Banks issue only a fraction of their deposits, but cumulative lending and borrowing create an illusion of more money being available than there actually is. Furthermore, the interest charged on loans ensures that the money supply has to expand continuously if all loans are to be repaid with interest.

With expansion of money or growth of the economy, prices rise as the increased supply of money erodes its purchasing power. As this cycle continues, the percentage of interest-to-inflation increases at the cost of real increase in production and productivity. This makes defaults and economic slowdowns inevitable.

The American foreclosure crisis shifted the control of collateral to banks. This system of money generation ensures a steady shift in wealth from the productive sector to the financial sector. Concentration of wealth and power in the hands of those who create and lend money – the banks and the government – causes the economy, society, and the civilization to decline.

History shows us that in the long run, when greed consumes everything, everybody loses. Most forecasters agree that what is needed to avoid an across-the-board loss is the responsible and shared use of resources, elimination of the concept of interest, and stabilization of the unit that is used to measure the value of goods and services.

The rate of this paradigm shift has increased dramatically with the recent creation of central banks and the government's fiscal intervention. In the meantime, the only safe and profitable investment to this shift has been gold and silver. They have risen in value as accounts based on the dollar have continued to fall.

A Quick Introduction to Monetary Systems

A ***monetary system*** is a system in which a government issues currency that is accepted as a medium of exchange in a particular country-economy or in the whole world, and creates mechanisms employed by a government or a group of governments to control and manage it. It typically consists of a central bank at the apex. Mints and other commercial banks are the other pieces in this apparatus.

The ***international monetary system*** is the institutional mechanism that determines the exchange rate among different currencies, facilitates international payments, and accommodates the movement of capital across international borders. This system developed with globalization – the increasing connectivity between different regions of the world wherein events in one part of the world produce consequences elsewhere.

Traditionally, coins made from precious metals such as gold and silver were widely used. These coins have a value of their own and continue to possess this value, even if they are not currently used for common purchases. Because gold and silver coins are quite difficult to carry, their use made buying and selling a difficult process.

Out of this difficulty emerged paper currency. The notes and coins do not have a value of their own, but are, nevertheless, used because they are easy to carry around – making buying and selling easier – and, most importantly, because they are a mutually acceptable medium of exchange.

Differences between Money, Currency, and Wealth

Money, currency, and wealth all seem the same to the casual observer and hobby economist. There are, however, subtle differences in these concepts, as well as the terms of the economy, economics, and finance. While some of these terms are very different, all are inherently connected.

An *economy* refers to all of the institutional mechanisms directly and indirectly related to production, distribution, exchange, and consumption of goods and services. *Economics* is the study of these institutional mechanisms. *Finance* involves all of the transactions that are conducted for obtaining and repaying loans.

Wealth is anything generally considered valuable in an economic system. Fundamentally and historically, it can be created only through the processing of natural resources by human labor. Wealth can be traded through purchases or sales with barter, the exchange of currency, and through the creation of money.

Currency is the concentrated form of wealth used for trading. We understand currency in the form of coins and paper notes, such as the American dollar, the euro, and pound sterling.

Definition of Money

Any legally and socially accepted medium of exchange used for the purchase of goods and services and for the settlement of debts can be considered money. Note the mention of the word *debt* in this definition: it has great implications. Currency notes and coins, precious metals, cows, grains, fruits, conch shells and the like – anything acceptable in a society as a medium of exchange through laws and norms – is money.

A more precise and illustrative definition of money would also include anything that is a claim on human labor, especially when the human labor has occurred previously or is expected to occur again in the future.

In essence, it's easy to see that money can be an abstract concept. It's often overlooked that money's only value is derived from the fact that it represents a value in the eyes of members of the society and economy. It may or may not actually and realistically possess the value. A $100 currency note is not actually worth $100 – it only represents a $100. This intangibility concept is at the root of its maneuverability.

The Economy-Money Link

In our civilization, money evolved out of the need for a common item that could be exchanged in trade. As hunter-gatherer and agrarian groups began to merge and establish societies, people began to exchange goods and services to survive and to make life more comfortable. The role of those new economies was to provide a framework for those exchanges to occur.

With limited resources, all needs could not be met. Factors of production, such as land, labor, capital, and enterprise – needed to convert resources into goods and services – were limited. The primary challenge before any economy is to produce the required goods and services while making the best use of resources.

There are two ways to measure performance of an economy: through standard of living and quality of life:

- **Standard of Living is** measured in terms of the **Gross Domestic Product (GDP).** It is the sum total of the value of all goods and services produced by all people within the geographical boundaries of a country within a certain period of time. The gross domestic product is usually measured over a year.

  A more representative measure – similar to the gross domestic product – is the **Gross National Product (GNP)**. It's the sum total of all goods and services produced by citizens of a nation in a certain duration, irrespective of their location. GNP is a national concept, compared to the geographical basis of GDP.

Inflation presents a major problem in measurement of GDP and GNP, as the standard of living can sometimes be seen to be rising, only because prices of commodities and services have gone up without any actual increase in production and productivity.

- **Quality of Life** can be seen in an economy through harder to measure terms. There are many intangible qualities, like peace and freedom, which bring personal happiness. Environmental quality, satisfaction, and consumer comfort cannot be precisely measured, but do add to quality of life and can be judged.

Types of Economies

Two broad categories of economies are manufacturing and resource extraction.

- **Manufacturers**

  Low-end manufacturers include China and Asian Tigers (South Korea, Singapore, Hong Kong, and Taiwan). India is similar because it provides low-end service exports. One job for the production of such goods produces two more jobs in support of the first one. Such support jobs are created in housing, medicine, and government.

  American consumers and businesses are the greatest importers of low-end goods and services. A boom in the U.S. increases demand for these goods and services and stimulates their exports from these countries, causing a massive boom in these economies.

  Conversely, when demand from the U.S. falls during slowdowns, these economies also face slowdowns.

  High-End manufacturers such as Germany and Japan make consumer goods like automobiles and electronics and industrial goods like construction equipment and machine tools. Exports to the U.S. benefit them, and so does the job multiplier effect.

Low-End manufacturers import high-end machine tools from Japan and Germany, and this is the reason Germany was the largest exporter in 2008 – at $1.53 trillion, according to the CIA World Factbook.

High-Enders will suffer a double impact. A slowdown in the U.S. will lower demand for high-end, as well as low-end, goods and services. When Low-Enders suffer from low demand from the U.S., they will stop purchasing from High-Enders. The U.S. will also stop importing high-end goods and services, as these include non-essential luxury items such as entertainment, electronics, and costly bed sheets.

- **Resource Extraction Economies** include wealthy countries such as Canada, Russia, and Australia, as well as those in Africa, the Middle East, South America, and, interestingly, China. These rely on exports of their resources such as oil, minerals, grains, and lumber to booming economies.

  They enjoy two-fold benefits: rising exports that also raise the prices of these in-demand, exported resources. Such a boom creates jobs, highly valued companies, and billionaire miners.

  Double boom turns to double doom when the bubble in the economy to which they export fails, like when the U.S. burst and falling exports caused a fall in prices of exports.

  When all is said and done, it is the elasticity of money supply under a fiat money regime that is at the root of the boom and bust cycle; this is what present day economies go through on a continual basis. Our governments and banks adhere to this fundamentally flawed system of money because it allows concentration of monetary power in their hands.

  The gold standard also demands fiscal discipline, and you cannot cheat on gold –cheating is something that defines many among the banking and the political world.

Furthermore, governments can use this monetary system to print inflationary money for so-called welfare programs, while inflation continues to be the chief anti-welfare agent.

Be that as it may, such situations present a blessing in disguise for the vigilant and the informed. We have already noted how smart investors have benefited from investing in gold in the early 1970s. You can do the same. After all, it is what our ancestors have been doing for ages.

As human communities evolved, the need arose for more goods and services to make community members' lives more comfortable. Naturally, one person cannot master the art of producing all commodities and services. This need led to the origination of the concept of *specialization* that goes hand in hand with division of labor.

Trade evolved out of the need to exchange goods that a person could produce for those commodities he could not create on his own. The more goods he produced, the more he could exchange them for those commodities he needed. With more commodities in his bag, his life became more comfortable. Therefore, he needed to use resources efficiently during production of goods he could make.

Barter – trading one good for another – was the original system of trade. It works when societies are small, people trust each other, and the volume and diversity of goods and services is limited.

There are two fundamental limitations of the barter system: the double coincidence of wants, and difficulty in calculating cost.

- **Double Coincidence of Wants** occurs when both exchangers have what the other person wants and both are ready for the exchange at the same time.

  For example, if one person has rice and needs wheat, and the other person has wheat and wants rice, only then can bartering occur between those two people.

- **Difficulty in Calculating Cost** of each item occurs when there is no standard to compare the quantity and quality of one commodity with those of another. For example, a question could arise regarding what amount of rice of a certain quality should be exchanged for a different amount of wheat of the highest quality. The process of assigning value to differing quantities or qualities of goods is bound to create friction.

The perishability of certain commodities further complicates valuation, as rotting commodities lose value and, many times, the onset of rot cannot be immediately known to the observer.

In large societies people don't know all community members, let alone trust them. Specialization is another feature of large, advanced societies where the members need extensive goods and services. This automatically creates the need for a greater number of exchanges between unknown people, where barter has limited applicability. Money evolved out of the need for a common item that could be exchanged with goods and services in a trade.

Functions of Money

In order to avoid the pitfalls of the barter system, all items used as money should serve three basic functions: serving as a medium of exchange, storing the value of the exchange, and serving as a unit of account.

- **Medium of Exchange** for goods and services. In a transaction, the value and the price of the goods and services should be referred to in terms of the unit of money. In this way, trading – buying and selling of goods and services – is simplified and removes bartering conflicts inherent in using other commodities.

- **Storing the Value** represented by it. Ideally, the value should not decline. This exemplifies why perishable goods cannot be used as money.

  Problems begin to occur when inflation enters the picture. Inflation is the depreciation of the value of money in relation to goods and services, and is a major factor among the foundational fault lines of the present system of creation and expansion of money.

- **Unit of Account** The value represented by money should be divisible and one unit of money should have a constant value. Diamonds are a good example of value, but not a good example of Unit of Account, since they are not realistically divisible into precise units and each unit is not equivalent to the other.

  Precise divisibility and equivalence of the unit allows fixing of prices of all goods and services in some multiple of the unit, and makes transactions simpler for the buyer and seller.

Another occasional function of money is to serve as a **standard of deferred payment** that is again linked to money being a store of value that, ideally, does not depreciate with time.

Characteristics of Money

Certain characteristics are required for money to serve its chief functions: acceptability, durability, optimum availability, and divisibility.

- **Acceptability** of the money is the litmus test for the type of currency that serves as money. Unless people of a certain society accept that type of currency, it has no value. When humans lived as pastorals, cows had great value and were, therefore, used as money and a person's wealth was counted in terms of the number of cows owned. Cows were their currency.

- **Durability** ensures that the value stored by the entity is maintained or even appreciates a little. Normally, humans like to store money or invest it so its value either remains constant or increases with time. This instinctive urge is based on saving for the rainy day – learning from experience that financial status can change for the worse at any time and that stored money comes in handy during such situations.

  Desired durability is the reason perishable commodities that lose value over time – such as food – are no longer acceptable as money. Thousands of years ago, when societies were not very advanced, food items could have been used as money because they were immediately consumed and because the needs of people were limited. In modern society, those guidelines would be inappropriate and ineffective.

- **Optimum Availability** ensures the entity used as money is relatively scarce and not easily reproducible by people, but at the same time not too scarce.

  If money was easily available, everyone would have a great deal of it and it would quickly lose its value. For the same reason, rocks and pebbles cannot be used as money, because they can be found everywhere.

  For example, it could be argued that chestnuts can be used as money, as they are relatively scarce, but they can also be easily grown and easily reproduced by people. If chestnuts were used as money, everyone would start growing them and soon there would be so many chestnuts around that the excessive supply would cause them to lose value, triggering inflation.

  Money should not be too scarce and should be available in sufficient quantity to comfortably enable all the exchanges in the economy.

  These balancing considerations related to availability are the reason notes and coins are minted by public authorities, and the process is strictly regulated to ensure that not everyone can create them. Furthermore, modern coins and notes have certain hallmarks that enable us to distinguish the genuine from the fake ones.

- **Transportability,** the ease with which currency can be transported, helps greatly in facilitating economic transactions. As societies advance, economic transactions and accounts become increasingly complex. Such complicated trading – buying and selling – cannot be undertaken through use of money that is difficult to carry around.

  As mentioned earlier, cows were just one of the large items used as money when humans lived in pastoral settings, and economic give and take was fairly simple. Today's complex economic transactions across great distances cannot be undertaken through exchange of cows, not to mention the problems we'd all have with wallets, purses, and cash registers.

Bank money – especially electronic funds and electronic fund transfers – have added a completely new dimension to the concept of portability of money. These days, complex exchanges of money across international borders can be completed quickly without any real physical exchanges.

- **Divisibility** is essential for the money to serve as a unit of account. Divisibility ensures that usable fractions of money can be created and values of all available goods and services can be described in terms of some multiple or some fraction of the basic unit of the money. For example, a banana can be priced at 20 cents (or one-fifth of one dollar), while a car can be priced at 20,000 times one dollar.

Types of Money

- **Commodity Money** uses commodities as a medium of exchange – with coins made from gold, silver, copper or other precious metals. These commodities have an intrinsic value – a value of their own – and can continue to possess the value even if they are not used in money transactions. In some parts of the world, tobacco or sea shells are still used as money.

  If the intrinsic value of the gold or silver coins used as money exceeded the face value – the value represented by them – people would tend to hoard these coins. This hoarding tendency is referred to as Gresham's Law and it tends to reduce the amount of money in circulation, thereby limiting economic activities.

  Forces of demand and supply, including the process of hoarding, tend to keep the face value equal to the intrinsic value. This keeps inflation in check but economic activity is seriously restricted – since the limited availability of coins is also limited by availability of precious coin metal and those hoarding tendencies.

- **Commodity Backed Money** is money that is backed by real commodities like gold and silver, and that can be exchanged for that commodity on demand. Gold Standard money is an example of commodity backed money wherein all notes or coins in circulation are backed by a certain amount of reserves of a certain commodity.

  The value of one unit of money is fixed in terms of the commodity that backs the money – for example, if $100 was considered equal to one ounce of gold. Anyone could exchange their money for gold and vice versa at any time even though those notes do not have any intrinsic value.

- **Fiat Money** does not have any intrinsic value, but derives its legitimacy from the fact that the government orders people to accept it as money and makes it illegal for anyone to reject its use as a medium of exchange. In the simplest of terms, it is money **not** backed by any commodities. Such money can take the form of notes and coins.

  Fiat is a Latin word that means 'let it be done.' In short, in reference to economics, fiat means an order from a competent authority. Fiat money, therefore, derives its legitimacy primarily from the backing provided to it by the government. This makes it acceptable to the people, and acceptability, as already explained, is the litmus test for the use of money.

  As long as people of the economy accept fiat money as a valid form of payment, it serves all of the necessary three functions: medium of exchange, store of value, and unit of account. Most present day economies use fiat money.

  Fiduciary Money is another name for fiat money. The term fiduciary means 'held in trust' and is derived from the Latin term '**fiducia,**' meaning confidence or trust. Confidence in the government and economy is the basis for the existence of such money.

  Fiat money is used because it is easy and inexpensive for the government to issue, and the government does not have to pledge valuable resources such as gold and silver to back it up. People also find it remarkably easy to use, and it serves all of its functions as long as the sun shines down benevolently on the economy. Because it is not backed by any actual commodities, governments tend to over-issue it. Increased supply causes inflation or depreciation of the currency in relation to the prices of goods and commodities. This is one of the focal points of the discussion, which will be covered in later sections.

- **Commercial Bank Money** refers to those funds held in demand deposits with commercial banks. Demand deposits are those bank accounts from which the account holder can withdraw funds whenever he or she likes, subject to reasonable restrictions. These types of accounts are more commonly known as savings and current accounts.

  These are different from time deposits accounts, where funds can be withdrawn, with interest, only after a certain period of time. If funds are withdrawn before the time deposit accounts mature, a penalty has to be paid.

  Funds from standard accounts can be withdrawn in person via checks, bank drafts, or debit cards, or through online fund transfers. The transfer of funds from one account to another for settlement of trade becomes very simple, quick, and efficient. Bank money does not have to be carried around as cash – checks and interbank money transfers settle the trade. The portability of money has been further enhanced by online money transfers allowing massive amounts to be transferred quickly from one corner of the globe to another in a very short period of time.

Creation and Extinction of Money

Now that we have the fundamentals of money under our belts, we can move on to other important points. How is money created and extinguished, and what are the consequences of such a process? More importantly, how do the economic cycles of boom and recession define the economic equations of power in this world?

In order to understand how money is created, we need to first understand the concept of **Fractional Reserve Banking (FRB).** If the sum of all deposits in a bank is $1,000, for example, banks can lend up to $900, or 90%, while the remaining stays with the bank as reserve. This is the concept of FRB: banks retain only a fraction of the total deposits as reserves.

All banks perform the basic function of accepting deposits from those with surplus funds and lending those surplus funds to others who need them for capital or for any other purpose. The banks charge interest at a greater rate on loans than the interest they provide to depositors on their deposited funds. The difference between the interest received and the interest paid is the profit of the bank.

How FRB 'Creates' Money

Suppose a person named Alan deposits $1,000 in Apple Bank. Banks can make money only by lending to someone. In accordance with fiscal regulations, Apple Bank can now lend 90%, or $900. Now, suppose $900 is loaned to a person named Britney who deposits this into another bank, named Bay Bank. Again, Bay Bank can lend $810, or 90% of $900.

The initial $1,000 has now 'increased' to representing $2,710 = $1,000 + $900 + $810.

The amount of money in circulation is $2,710, though only $1,000 was originally deposited. This process can be repeated, with the amount of money in circulation increasing with every step, until we find that the total money in circulation is <u>ten times</u> what was originally deposited into the first bank in this chain. Most of this money in circulation is debt that has to be returned to someone.

Thus, creation of money and debt go hand in hand. This example is only illustrative. Britney can deposit the loaned $900 in Apple Bank – or she can use, say, $500, and deposit the remaining $400 with any bank, Apple Bank or Bay Bank. The point of the matter is that through FRB, the amount of money in circulation increases, as does debt.

Between 93% and 95% of the need for money is created through such deposition lending in banks via the FRB process. The remaining 7% to 5% is created through dealings between the Federal Reserve and the Treasury.

FRB works only as long as:

- People have faith in the economy and in the banks, and do not want to withdraw all their funds at once. In times of economic distress, when people lose faith in the economy and make a run to withdraw all their funds from the bank, FRB fails.

- There are no defaults.

Talking about defaults brings us to the second part of this process. Because banks charge interest on all the funds they loan out, the amount of money that has to be paid back is greater than the amount that was originally loaned. Unless additional money is created by someone, the principal and the interest can never actually be repaid because there is just not enough money to go around.

Money has to be continuously created if the present system is to work. Interest, therefore, is a functional glitch in the system, and FRB is at the root of this need for the continuous creation of money. If interest was not charged, the money created when the loan originated would be extinguished when the loan is repaid.

Interest Creates Need for Generation of More Money

Suppose you borrow $100 at 10% interest. Where will the $10 come from? It comes from the printing of extra money.

Money required to repay the interest is not created when the loan is originated – only the amount of money borrowed as principal is created. The money required to pay the interest is created by the Federal Reserve, which is the central bank in the American economy. The heart of the matter is that when more and more money is created, its supply increases. In accordance with the rules of supply and demand, when supply of a certain commodity is greater than the demand for it, its value declines. With money creation, the value of money goes down in relation to goods and services, and its purchasing power declines. To put it simply, there is **inflation**, which creates price increase.

In such a state of affairs, default is inevitable. Default is also a product of fraudulent tendencies by certain unscrupulous borrowers. Because of default, banks require money themselves. The lender of last resort in the United States of America is the central bank of the economy, the Federal Reserve.

Actual Printing of Money

When Congress needs more money to lend out to these banks, it asks the Treasury Department to sell Treasury Bonds to large banks. These banks then sell these bonds to the Federal Reserve, and they simply print more money to make the purchase. This is possible because all money, especially fiat money that is not backed by commodities, is an abstract concept, as mentioned earlier.

Interest and FRB ensure that money created when a loan is issued is never extinguished, because more money has to be created to repay the interest and the principal. This means that growth of money, which we know as economic growth measured through the increase of the GDP, is always accompanied by inflation, the silent killer.

Power Equations Inherent in the Process of Money Creation

Economists always refer to the inevitability of economic cycles of high and low economic activity, something we respectively know as "boom time" and "slowdowns." Such cycles are a result of the perpetual need for creation of more money. These cycles ensure that traders, both buyers and sellers, always remain at the mercy of the banks and the government.

When the cycle of money creation continues, the percentage of interest-inflation in the GDP increases exponentially. Because of the increase, more and more of the GDP is composed of interest and accompanying inflation. GDP grows due to:

- An actual increase in the production of goods and services produced by everyone within the geographical boundaries of a country.
- Inflation, a result of increasing interest load.

Real increase of GDP, or the increase in GDP without inflation, naturally decreases when the money generation cycle continues.

The increased interest load also means that instability is inevitable because people will default. When this happens, banks have fewer funds to lend to other businesses. This situation, therefore, creates economic slowdowns when the interest load or debt is wiped out through bankruptcies and default.

Another consequence of default is foreclosure, or the confiscation of property that the borrower has pledged to the bank as a security against non-payment of his dues to the bank. Such property is referred to as collateral, and its confiscation by the bank leads to an increase in the assets owned by the bank.

In effect, this cycle of generation of money shifts the control of wealth toward those who control assets and the system of money creation: the banks and the government. Traders – all buyers and sellers, ranging from common people to entrepreneurs and giants of the business world – are perpetually under the control of banks and governments.

It is widely but quietly acknowledged that heavyweights and heads of the industrial world always get loan waivers worth billions of dollars sanctioned from the government each year. Of course, it happens behind closed doors. It would not come as a surprise if these basics of the money generation process were used as a bargaining tool by industrial heads.

But where does that leave the common trader – normal people and small entrepreneurs? The answer is simple: nowhere. They certainly do not have the collective bargaining power of the colossal *corporates* to secure loan waivers. Then again, middle and lower class people who work as employees are the first to face the full blast of economic slowdowns in the form of layoffs and pay cuts.

Corporates can bargain because they are street-smart, provide employment to millions of people, and because they have financial muscle. No government wants to be seen as responsible for massive job cuts by refusing to bail out influential industrialists. And so goes the practice that some job and pay cuts are essential to prevent the same from occurring on a much larger scale.

This does not solve the problem. Slowdowns are bad not just because of the job and pay cuts, but because they introduce uncertainty and instability in the minds of people, especially those at the bottom of the socio-economic ladder. This robs people of peace of mind, destroys livelihoods, and is at the root of numerous problems.

Apart from smaller traders without any bargaining power, the fact that this process is complicated ensures that laymen do not understand the fundamentals. The disease is left undiagnosed and people only demand treatment of the symptoms in the form of stimulus and bailout packages.

Needless to say, this plays into the hands of the real powers. Through such programs, government makes a big show of doing something to improve the economy while leaving the fundamentals untouched. Through this charade, they become benevolent heroes in the eyes of the people, helping those in misfortune whose misfortune they have created, partially or wholly.

Economic democracy is absent, as wealth and control of this wealth is concentrated in the hands of a few. Political democracy does not automatically ensure economic democracy unless people understand the fractured foundation of the present economic system.

One cannot play God or micromanage a complex economy. As concentration of wealth and power acquires epic proportions, economy and culture decline, finally leading to disintegration of civilizations. Mesopotamian, Egyptian, Greek, and Roman civilizations declined due to some of the same reasons. When the civilization itself is destroyed, what is left for the micro-managers to manage?

Suggestions and Recommendations

Considering the fundamental nature of the problem, a paradigm shift will be required, one that questions long-established concepts. Not all interest charged by banks is used for their operational expenses. A greater portion constitutes profit, a tax that slowly but surely tilts the balance in favor of the financial sector at the cost of the productive sector.

If we are to establish genuine economic democracy, here are a few scenarios:

- Conversion of the money creation process from the present interest load-based system to a fee-for-service basis. This would ensure that when the loan is repaid, the money created when it was loaned is extinguished. Yes, there will be the fee to be repaid, but it will be far less than the present high interest programs. Money would not be required to expand to keep the economy running. It would prevent inflation, currency depreciation, and resultant slowdowns.

- Stabilization of the value of the monetary unit by defining it in terms of time and effort. An hour as a unit of time is unchangeable. When the effort put in this time slot is codified, you get a standard and constant unit that does not depreciate like present day money does.

  This is based on the premise that traders are willing to produce goods and services by putting in effort for certain durations of time. Of course, it is not very easy to calibrate effort because it is based on qualities like experience, skill, education, equipment used, and hazards involved in production, some of which are not precisely measurable.

- Combination of ownership of assets with responsibility of their use and sharing with those who are less blessed with such resources. Those who are blessed with greater resources have the responsibility to use them morally and share them with the less fortunate.

  Although this sounds Utopian and questions the very concept of property ownership and enjoyment of owned assets, it is a reasonable way forward. In the final analysis, we belong to the earth – the earth does not belong to us. How the balance between rights and responsibility is achieved is a matter that needs to be worked out at the community and national level.

The above three suggestions are holistic and demand a complete overhaul of the system that may or not be possible in the near future. There is a possibility of a new monetary system being framed by the G-20 as the dollar continues to lose its status as the preeminent currency in the world.

Prices of gold and silver have started rising after a fifteen year period of constant rates. Despite demand being more than production, the secret sale of gold stocks by central banks of the Western World has bridged the demand-supply gap and maintained the prices. This has artificially maintained the value of the dollar against gold and enabled the U.S. to import more than it exports.

Now things have come to a stage where these banks can no longer part ways with their remaining gold, and this precious metal will only get scarcer. The World Gold Council reported an increase in demand for investment gold by 62% in 2011 alone. All of the economic indicators point toward one conclusion: the price of gold is headed up.

Over the long term, markets act like a weight balance and strike equilibrium in the supply/demand and the price situation. Gold and silver prices rise whenever there is expansion in the money supply, as markets react to depreciation of currency and attempt to account for fiat currencies outstanding. This has happened twice in the U.S. – once in the early 1930s and once in 1971.

In a way, this is economic democracy at work – the people determining the cost of gold and silver. This is the complete opposite of a few people determining the amount of money in circulation by manipulation of the monetary policy.

As the demand for gold brings down its availability, silver will be in demand. More importantly, these metals pass the litmus test for any entity used as money: acceptability. This is as close as you can get to beating the big fish at their own game.

Civilizations decline not so much because of external invasions, but from the rot that sets in from within. Those who do not learn from history are condemned to repeat it. The decline starts in the mind with the emotion of greed, personified by establishing control over resources, natural and synthetic, and exploiting them to the fullest without any thought of sharing.

What starts in the mind must be stopped there. Although it would be too radical to question the concept of property itself, is it unwise to question man's right to unlimited enjoyment without sharing? Suggested recommendations are lofty and appear quixotic, but can we allow history to repeat itself and destroy another civilization?

As an individual, one can start by investing in physical gold and silver. With the dollar losing its status as the preeminent currency in the world, the value of gold and silver will rise to account for massive fiat currency printing. It has already started increasing. Gold has been a valuable collectible for the last 6,000 years, and its scarcity ensures its continued high value. Additionally, these metals are accepted by everyone in the world.

For most of the existence of civilizations, economies have based their currencies on the gold standard, which was eventually either diluted or switched to a paper-currency standard. What caused this general shift? Typically, the reason was to finance wars or deal with economic slowdowns – the latter being a product of expandability of money supply under the paper-currency standard.

History also testifies that the average duration of a monetary system is between 30 and 40 years. The present monetary system in the U.S. is 40 years old (with its inception in 1971), and it's coming to the end of its lifespan. A change is, therefore, only around the corner. Again, history teaches us that gold and silver prices spike when money in circulation increases.

Economics and Politics

All of us know that money enables us to purchase things we need for survival and to make our lives more comfortable. Some things are also purchased as a mark of prestige or as collectibles. Even though money is such an integral part of our lives, most of us cannot define what money is, how it works, or why prices of commodities rise.

Even expert economists can have trouble defining money precisely and comprehensively. Ironically, this confusion continues to occur even though money is the core of all economic activities. The complexity of the concept of money has vast, tangible consequences that affect people around the world.

Economics and politics always go hand in hand, and the present system of money in this nation is the culmination of multiple experiments, many of which failed. Numerous events in history and many great minds have contributed to its making. Strong economic fundamentals and European decline in international politics made the dollar the prime currency worldwide for the greater part of the 20th century.

Progressive dilution of the connection between the dollar and gold reserves started eroding its purchasing power since 1913. Such paper currency standard separation was completed between 1971 and 1973, resulting in a more pronounced decline in the dollar. The paper currency standard has not only caused economic hardships, but it can be considered morally wrong because it defeats the noble aspirations of the framers of our Constitution and the founders of our nation.

As amply demonstrated by preceding economic crises, the current slowdown in the global economy poses a great challenge to the dollar's purchasing power. It knocks the bottom out of savings and certain investments, and thereby robs citizens' livelihoods, making life difficult.

Furthermore, the present monetary system is ill-equipped to deal with this quagmire. If anything, it will make matters worse through typical knee-jerk reactions. But changing the entire system is too cumbersome and too slow. What, then, are we as individuals to do in the meantime as the value of our savings declines with each passing day?

History is always full of answers for those who are ready to take the trouble and time to explore it. We know – from history – that whenever the value of money declines, the value of gold and silver appreciates. Investments in precious metals are precisely the answer to this pressing question unleashed by the present economic slowdown.

Evolution is the law of nature: all systems change gradually. When there is no evolution, there are revolutions, sudden and massive changes that create upheavals in history. Unsurprisingly, economics has been at the foundation of many a revolution, for the use of money affects the very livelihood of people. Economics and politics are, therefore, inherently linked.

Ever since the concept of property took root in the heart and mind of mankind, people have developed an urge to own more and more things. The concept of money naturally emerged out of this desire and out of the need to make buying and selling more convenient. Essentially, money serves as a medium of exchange and as a store of value.

For a greater part of the economic history of the world, because of their intrinsic value, precious metals such as gold and silver have served as money. Other currency such as paper money has been used because of convenience. Any item that is used as money needs to be acceptable to the people in the economy; this is the currency's acid test.

The development of money and the monetary system of the U.S. is a complex topic. It has to be seen in the context of global and domestic economic-political developments and international monetary systems prevalent at various periods of time. Only through a historical treatment can we find a degree of completeness to the process, enabling a better understanding of the present economically distressing times.

Evolution of money and banking in the United States of America paints a picture of a continuous struggle between the vested interests and the genuine representatives of public interest. The initial focus of monetary development brought by independence from British colonial control evolved to a different kind of development after the success of the revolutionary war.

Wars and periods of financial emergencies provided those vested interests with a pretext to establish and maintain control over the money in the country. All inflationary money-banking schemes brought on by hard times were designed by the financial elite to this end. It is interesting that the Constitution that represents the soul of the nation does not allow such inflationary schemes.

Despite the dominance of those vested interests, there were periods when the stock of public interest rose, as well. During President Andrew Jackson's time in office between 1829 and 1837 there was an increase in public interest; however, inflation control failed due to circumstances largely beyond anyone's control. Another period of exception occurred later in the 1880s.

A common feature of all wars and financial emergencies is a rise in gold prices, causing the value of gold reserves to equal and even exceed the value of the money in circulation. This occurred in 1934 and then again in the early 1980s. Despite their efforts, the selfish elite were not able to cheat on gold.

It is a time-tested technique that those who find ways to profit from all situations – like the elite, even during adversity – can benefit from appreciating gold. This means that as a common investor, you too can benefit from the present adversity – and adversity and challenges in the future – by holding gold investments.

Monetary and banking history in the United States is full of ups and downs. It is also integrally connected with political developments, domestic and foreign, making it very interesting. Most importantly, this study of the evolution of money in the United States, or for that matter anywhere else in the world, provides insight into the nature of money. That study also reveals lessons for the present and the future.

Money is largely an intangible concept for the simple reason that whatever is used as money – a medium of exchange – has to command acceptability from the people who use it. Tangible actions and decisions do influence the acceptability of money, and sometimes disastrous consequences can result when acceptability of the medium of exchange is altered.

Theories, Observations, and Trends Associated with Money and Banking

In order to better understand the history of money and banking, there is a need to also understand some concepts or theories related to money. Certain common political-economic trends have always been observed during the evolution of money, and these trends reveal the true nature of those at the helm of economic and political affairs in any country.

I. ***Gresham's Law*** postulates that when government compulsorily over-values one money and under-values another, the undervalued money disappears into hoards or leaves the country while the overvalued money floods into circulation.

Typically, Gresham's Law has always operated during bimetallism, benefiting from the system of using coins of more than one metal as money and the exchange ratio between same weights of different metals as fixed by law. It also operates when currency notes are overvalued in relation to gold or silver *by law*.

When this ratio is fixed without due regard to the market rate of exchange between these metals or between the metals and the currency notes, the value represented by the undervalued metal in the metal coins becomes less than its intrinsic value. It can become more profitable to hoard the coins or to export them to foreign lands for a better price.

II. ***The Austrian Theory of Business Cycle*** states that any expansion in credit loaned by banks creates conditions for a boom-bust economic cycle, even if prices do not rise during such a phase of credit expansion.

Expansion in credit inflates money supply and brings down the purchasing power of money. This in turn decreases confidence. Cheap credit also results in borrowing for excessive and speculative investment during an economic bubble.

It is inevitable that some investments go bad and some economically productive activities are stalled. This leads to default; businesses, followed by banks, go bankrupt. People rush to withdraw their deposits from failing banks, and investors – foreign and domestic – exchange money for gold and silver. Such an exchange, financially called *redeemability*, is possible when the bank reserves are maintained in gold and silver.

Banks then contract money supplies in order to refuse such an exchange – otherwise they would be stripped of their hard metal reserves – in coin or bullion. Sometimes banks are allowed to cancel redeemability and this further erodes confidence as well as the value of paper money. Such a contraction in money leads to a slowdown of economic activity.

III. ***The Taylor Rule*** asks for an increase in lending interest rates with increasing inflation. An inflation of 1% should be countered by a greater than 1% increase in lending rates to control inflation through contraction in money supply. Taylor's Rule is based only on price and output stability.

When central banks, through monetary policy, increase the rates at which they lend to commercial banks or increase the percentage of deposits that commercial banks are supposed to maintain with them, the amount of money in circulation drops. Credit becomes more expensive and borrowing decreases.

This is done to control inflation and bubbles when economic growth is believed to be unsustainably fast and because of speculative investment. By reversing this tactic during economic slowdowns, money supply increases, encouraging discretionary spending, creating demand for goods and services, and stimulating production, which leads to economic recovery.

With elastic money supply in a fiat money regime, increase and decrease of interest rates becomes a cyclic process, for lowering interest rates can encourage inflation and speculation along with economic growth. This has to be countered with increasing interest rates that can lead to slowdown and require a decrease in interest rates.

Increases and decreases in interest rates are usually targeted at specific sectors of the economy rather than at the entire economy, so bubbles and slowdowns in that sector can be specifically addressed. Effectiveness of monetary policy in curbing inflation is, however, limited by savings as we shall see later in the chapter.

IV. Miscellaneous Observations on Money and Banking

· *Fractional Reserve Banking,* wherein the reserves maintained by banks are a small fraction of the total amount of money that the banks lend out, is always inflationary. A 10% reserve requirement 'creates' additional money worth ten times the initial deposit. Reserves of 100%, however, are not inflationary.

· Interest is another functional glitch of the banking system. Because interest is charged on the principal amount, a total repayment necessitates a continuous expansion of the money supply. More money in circulation decreases the purchasing power of money, causing inflation.

· Inflation always benefits debtors, since when the debtor pays back the agreed amount of money, it is with depreciated purchasing power. This is the reason lenders often impose a gold clause in credit agreements wherein the loaned and repayment amount is in terms of weight of gold.

· Inflation acts as a tariff against imports since depreciation of a certain currency makes imports more expensive and exports cheaper.

· Inflationary money-banking schemes are always promoted by certain sectors of bankers, governments, politicians, investors, speculators, and capitalists.

More money comes in handy for greater investment and capital, and these powerful vested interests always use freshly printed money before it depreciates. Sections of the banking and political community are able to place their perpetual yoke on the rest of the society through such schemes.

· During wars and financial emergencies, governments are often bailed out financially by bankers, investors, and capitalists, who usually purchase government bonds from freshly printed money. It is an inherently inflationary process, using loaned gold and silver reserves.

Later, these bonds either become inflationary public debt or the purchasers are covertly provided with a financial red carpet. The latter is more lethal because it perpetuates the dominance of vested interest over public interest, and democracies become 'governments of the vested interests, by these interests, and for these interests.'

V. The combined effect of all economic factors and indicators has to be taken into consideration during the analysis of each particular economic situation. Excessive reliance on one or two factors or indicators can present a deceptive picture.

Moderate price rise is usually taken as an indicator of economic growth, while deflation normally implies economic slowdown or even recession and negative growth. Inflation is often the result of expansion of money supply, while deflation is the consequence of the opposite.

However, another scenario is that prices drop because the production of goods and services increases at a rate higher than the speed at which the money supply expands. This is a very positive development and usually happens in free capitalism situations. This happened during the 1880s in the United States and is in marked contrast to the 1929-1933 deflation popularly known as the Great Depression.

Again, all deflations do not produce the same effects, and neither can they be said to be a result of the same set of factors. Unlike the Great Depression – when there was a fall in real gross investment, real consumption, and real GNP – in the 1839 to 1843 period, investment fell while real consumption and real GNP *increased*.

This difference was due to downward flexibility in prices when money supply contracted with falling prices, but did not cripple production or standard of living – the opposite to what happened during Depression times, when the government imposed restrictions on falling wages and prices.

VI. Trending is an important way to identify economic changes and opportunities. The following trends are generally observed during the evolution of money:

· Sovereign state starts with honest money, like money in gold and silver coins or money that is completely backed by gold and silver.

· As the state develops, economically and socially, it undertakes public works and social programs that add to its expenditure.

· An increase in economic affluence of the state leads to appreciation of its political influence, and the state or principality becomes an empire. Power is probably the greatest intoxicant known to mankind, and a large military is needed to maintain this economic-political influence. This further adds to the expenditure of the state.

· War is the natural culmination of such a heavy investment in the military production apparatus. The old adage of 'if you want peace, prepare for war' holds true only to a certain point; beyond that, it leads to diminishing returns… for example, an armed conflagration that imposes colossal burden on the treasury.

· Funding wars requires the state to expand the money supply. This naturally leads to a decrease in the value or of the purchasing power of money, according to the rules of supply and demand. Such an expansion in money supply was observed at the outbreak of the First World War. This also occurs during war, as was the case with ancient wars during the Greek and Roman era. It even happens after the war, as a solution to economic imbalances of previous wars, as happened in France in John Law's era.

In the ancient and late medieval periods, when **specie** or coin money was the established medium of exchange, the coins were debased – that is, the content of gold or silver in coins was reduced to enable minting of more coins. Ever since paper money has taken root, governments simply print tons of notes to finance wars.

· Such an expansion of money supply is also witnessed when banks lend out more credit when the economy is expected to do well and businesses and investors are expected to make profits.

· Massive inflation results because the purchasing power of money has declined; a greater amount of money is required to purchase the same amount of goods and services than before.

· With money not maintaining its value, people invest in assets such as gold, silver, land and other tangible assets that are seen to be rising or expected to rise in comparison to currency.

Currency collapses and wealth is transferred to those shrewd enough to invest early in such assets; these assets start to command greater and greater prices.

Such periods also witness bankruptcies followed by confiscation of collateral by banks and other financiers. This transfers wealth from the productive sector to the financial sector.

As people form lines outside banks to withdraw their funds or to redeem and exchange notes for specie or bullion, banks have to contract the money supply in accordance with the Austrian Theory of Business Cycle or suspend redeemability of notes for specie.

Chapter 2 – We Didn't Learn from History

"The most effective way to destroy people is to deny and obliterate their own understanding of their history."

– George Orwell

It is worthwhile to note that the beginning of the end of European domination in international politics started with the end of the First World War. Europe was the nerve center of the war and underwent economic destruction and other destruction of epic proportions.

European decline was complete by the end of the Second World War, and that also marked the acceleration of the process of decolonization. Again, this points to the inherent two-way link between politics and economics and how the pressure of maintaining political influence – itself a product of increasing economic *affluence* – can ultimately destroy that influence.

Colonialism, Empires, Hegemony, and Decline

Political Colonialism –the practice of political control over foreign lands – was practiced by European powers in the late medieval and early modern periods. All types of colonialism are designed for economic benefits of the colonial power, which also ensures its political and sometimes cultural hegemony.

In part, colonialism was a consequence of the Industrial Revolution, the unprecedented and widespread use of machines that greatly increased production capacity. Sustaining increased production required tons of raw materials. Then the produce had to be sold, and this required assured markets.

Colonies could be a cheap and convenient source of raw materials, where the surplus production could also be easily dumped by manipulating the foreign trade policy of the colony – low duties for export of raw materials and import of finished products coupled with high tariffs for export of finished goods and import of raw materials. The high tariffs also discouraged industrial development in the colonies to keep them perpetually subservient.

A race for colonies was sparked among European powers that formed armed coalitions with other such powers and against other similar power groups. These coalitions and the global spread of colonial empires ensured that any conflict in Europe would lead to a global conflagration. Apart from other reasons, the two world wars were a result of this phenomenon that ultimately led to European decline.

Although the U.S. is not an empire in the traditional sense of the word, it does behave like an economic empire, looking for cheap resources, markets, and investment opportunities for its multinational giants. Also, the U.S. is widely believed to practice cultural colonialism – the systematic and inconspicuous promotion of the high consumption American lifestyle that in turn generates a demand for American-style goods and services.

U.S. aggression in Iraq – what some may even call the colonization of Iraq – is believed by many to be a quest for a cheap and easy supply of oil to maintain economic affluence. The U.S. is also the chief resident power in Afghanistan, the graveyard of foreigners, where the British and Soviets have been buried alive.

These wars, however, are causing a drain of valuable financial and other resources. The Bush administration aggravated matters by cutting taxes despite mounting war expenditure. Does this mean that a political-economic decline of the U.S. is around the corner, just as wars have destroyed the hegemony of European colonial powers before? The answer may not necessarily be affirmative.

Money and Banking in the United States

A. Before the American Revolution, 1600s to 1775

In keeping with the established principal of maintaining perpetual subservience within the Americas and serving the interest of the mother power, England wanted to limit development in her American colonies. As a colonizing power, England knew that money was at the heart of controlling new lands and the people who lived there, so British leaders worked hard to keep the American colonies dependent on English economic guidance. Monetary development was not only actively discouraged, but sabotaged to prevent the monetary union of the colonies. The English knew from experience that an independent economy would eventually lead to political union followed by demands for independence.

Encouraging the colonies to send raw materials to England, the English also discouraged the colonies from trading with one another. England was a major ocean trading power in the world at the time, and acquisition of more raw materials strengthened her hold over global commerce.

Toward the end of this period, another development in England necessitated greater English control over all her colonies – the need for more suppliers of raw materials as well as an increase in the quantity of those raw materials. The beginning of the Industrial Revolution brought a great demand for items to supply the machines that were beginning to be used on an unprecedented scale. This multiplied the production capacity, and greater amounts of raw material were required to utilize this capacity.

Monetary innovation was a result of throwing off the economic-political English yoke. The following were the chief developments in this period within the American colonies:

- **Country Pay Period 1632-92** when many agricultural products were declared as money. This was not any better than barter. The Spanish dollar was the most widely accepted currency in the American market, although English and French currencies, along with direct barter, were used for trading.

- **Massachusetts Gold Mint of 1652** was a brave and directed attempt that failed as the English acquired the gold coins and had them transported to England. The mint was declared a treachery and closed down.

- **Land Standard Currencies of 1675 to 1739** that were backed by the value of land were issued by many private land banks. Issue of currency is essentially the function of a central public authority, not of any private entity. This currency failed because it was not acceptable to people who regarded such private issue as unreliable.

- **1690 Bills of Credit** in Massachusetts were a kind of paper money that was a promise to accept the paper bills for all monies due to Massachusetts. It was neither backed by any solid assets, nor was it a promise to pay anything, as is the case with legal tender notes that have *'I promise to pay the bearer a sum of...'* printed on them.

  Despite not being made the legal tender that could *command* mandatory acceptance, these bills of credit were a huge success for the simple reason that people in Massachusetts and in other colonies did accept them. The bills of credit improved commerce and facilitated development. Unlike the earlier Massachusetts gold mint coins, these bills did not flow to England. This system eventually failed due to over issue that eroded their value.

- **The 1723 Land Standard Currency of Pennsylvania** was devised with assistance from Benjamin Franklin in order to provide a standard medium of exchange. The system was simple: paper money was *loaned into existence* for eight years at 5% interest with land pledged as collateral.

  This land-based currency system went one step further because sums gathered from repaid loans were loaned out to others and the interest was used for development. With funds available, taxes were reduced, in effect giving every individual in Pennsylvania a stake in its functional success.

A stellar feature of this period was the total absence of inflation. In the 110 years between 1665 and 1776, there was absolutely no price rise. If a person had saved $100, his great-grandchildren would still be able to use that amount to purchase the same amount of goods or services.

In keeping with the philosophy of colonialism, a 1763 law banned all paper money systems in the American colonies. This and other causes triggered the American War of Independence, when the political-economic history of the emerging nation as well as the emerging economy becomes very interesting.

B. From Revolution to Bank of North America, 1775-92

Raising finances for war, as mentioned, results in the authorities printing money. Three kinds of tools were used by the revolutionaries to raise money to fight the War of Independence:

· Continentals – paper dollars – were issued in 1775. This was the brainchild of Governor Morris, the scion of a New York-based aristocratic family. Continentals were in circulation for seven years, and were to be redeemed by future tax collections.

Although a $200 million cap was placed on the total number of continentals, $225 million was made between 1775 and 1779. Before the war, money in circulation was $12 million. By 1781, 168 paper dollars could be traded for 1 specie dollar. The English helped the depreciation of Continentals by releasing hoards of fake Continentals.

This express deterioration led to the origin of the phrase 'not worth a Continental.'

· Paper Certificates by the Federal and the State Governments were issued during the war as an alternative to Continentals. Soldiers were paid in Continentals, but farmers refused to accept them, hence the need for this alternative.

A total of $200 million of federal certificates was issued during the war. Post-independence, federal authorities conveniently allowed most of the Continentals and paper certificates to sink in, without making any attempt to redeem them, as promised.

· Loan Certificates worth $600 million were issued during the war to pay for the purchase of war supplies from merchants. These would have sunk in, as well, if not for Robert Morris, a wealthy Philadelphia merchant and the virtual economic and financial czar of the Continental Congress in the last years of the war. While some were redeemed at depreciated rates, the bulk of these certificates formed the peacetime debt for the federal government.

Robert Morris was highly influential around the time of American independence, and had centralization tendencies manifested in his demands for a strong federal government, taxing powers for the federal government, and a perpetual public debt burden on the shoulders of the taxpayers.

In sync with these tendencies, he got Congress to pass a bill in 1781 for the creation of the first central bank in America – the Bank of North America. Modeled on the Bank of England, this was also the first bank in the U.S. to operate on the principle of fractional reserves – the reserves were in specie and the currency notes issued by it were partially redeemable with specie.

The following rights were conferred on this bank:

· Monopoly rights to issue paper money that was accorded a status equal to that of specie.

· Depository of all Congressional funds.

In return, this central bank was to lend $1.2 million of newly created money to Congress for repayment of public debt. This debt was comprised of loan certificates purchased by wealthy merchants, which was ultimately to be repaid by the taxpayer.

However, the market perceived that notes of this bank were excessively printed, leading to their depreciation. By 1783, Morris sold off the 5/8 share of the government in this bank to private players, and all the government's debt to the bank was repaid. This bank was no longer the central bank. It became a private commercial bank.

Related provisions in the **Constitution** represented a balance between the centralizing tendencies of the Federalists, led by Alexander Hamilton, and distribution-of-powers model pushed by anti-Federalists. The former were bankers and merchants, while the latter were generally land-owning farmers.

There was a clear insistence on the right to *coin money rather than print money*. The latter is possible with fiat currency, when money can be created out of thin air by merely printing more notes. At the most, the Constitution allowed the government to *emit bills of credit* – to print paper money only if it were backed by solid assets like gold and silver.

C. Bimetallism to the Second Bank of the United States (BUS), 1792 -1833

With the Coinage Act of 1792, bimetallism was established in the United States. The dollar was defined in terms of both silver and gold – 371.25 grains of pure silver or 24.75 grains of pure gold. The mint ratio between silver and gold was fixed at 15:1 – 15 units of weight of silver were equal to one unit of weight of gold. This matched the silver to gold exchange ratio in the market at that time.

Bimetallism reflected Alexander Hamilton's desire to increase monetary supply by keeping both metals in circulation. Sooner or later, Gresham's law would apply, as it did in the late 1790s and in 1805, when the ratio was 15.5:1 and 15.75:1 respectively. Gold coins began to disappear and from 1810 to 1834, only silver coins, domestic and foreign, circulated in the U.S.

In 1793, Congress declared all foreign coins in the U.S. to be legal tender. Around 80% of U.S. coins in the year 1800 were foreign coins, and when such foreign coins were banned in 1857, undervalued Spanish dollars and fractional American half dollars also disappeared. With gold coins already out of circulation, the U.S. was left with fractional Spanish coins only.

Alexander Hamilton was a former crony of Robert Morris, and similarly believed in a strong, centralized federal government that had control over money in circulation. The Hamiltonian financial system and some parts of the Constitution manifested the desire of Federalists to fund federal and state public debt through federal taxation.

The First Bank of the United States, from 1791 through 1811, was Hamilton's idea to replace the failed Bank of North America. It was privately held, with only 20% of the bank owned by the government. It issued notes of the same status of specie and these notes were redeemable in specie. The bank also acted as a depository of public funds.

To emphasize the continuity from the Bank of North America, Thomas Willing – its former president and a former partner of Robert Morris – was made the president of the First Bank of the United States. The bank had a charter for 20 years.

By 1796, the bank had lent $6.2 million to the U.S. government by printing more money. The bank had a reserve ratio of 0.39 only and in the 1791-96 period wholesale prices rose by 72%. In the same period, speculation in government securities and real estate triggered formation of eighteen new commercial banks. By 1811, the number of state banks expanded to 117.

In 1811, The First Bank of the United States could not be re-chartered. It lost by a single vote in both houses because Jeffersonians had questioned the Constitutional right of the government to create a central bank. In 1819, the Supreme Court upheld this right on the grounds that such a right was implied in the Constitutional provisions.

During the War with England, between 1812 and 1815, there was an explosion in the money supply that followed an expansion in the number of both incorporated and unincorporated banks. Only in New England did banking continue along sound, conservative lines.

While specie reserves with banks declined, money supply increased and this brought down the reserve ratio from 0.27 to 0.17 in the 1811 through 1815 period. Payments to New England banks were made in such notes of depreciating value. And when New England insisted on redemption in specie, this exchangeability was canceled by law in 1814 and lasted until 1817.

Canceled redeemability *by law* was an extremely bad precedent that was regularly followed later in different parts of the U.S. in 1819, 1839, and in 1857. Ironically, banks insisted on observance of contractual obligations by debtors; banking was not free, like any other business where non-observance of contractual obligations can lead to penalties and forced closures.

Along with currency notes, there was a huge release of treasury notes during the war – $15.46 million by 1815. This further fueled inflation. There was a 35% increase in prices between 1811 and 1815. As always, Gresham's Law caused undervalued specie to flow to New England and then outside the country.

Canceled redeemability in an era of inflation, high transportation cost, and slow communication caused notes to increasingly depreciate with increased distance from the issuing bank. This led to the emergence of money brokers who collected depreciated notes and had them redeemed for specie at issuing banks. Journals called 'bank note detectors' were published by these brokers to let people know the true value of state bank notes.

Bankers responded with wildcat banks located in areas where money brokers found it difficult to travel. Interestingly, locals blamed money brokers for the collapse of their friendly, neighborhood banks. Many states made laws against redeemability with money brokers, so notes could be redeemed by note owners only, and even this exchange was not guaranteed.

Neither did the courts offer any relief to note holders, including money brokers who sued banks for not redeeming, because courts could only implement the law. Such state action was necessary to maintain the value of their notes or what remained of the value, but it amounted to treating the symptoms, not the disease.

Redemption was so difficult because people were either stockholders with banks or their debtors – the former did not want to redeem notes, as banks would fail, and the latter were afraid. Those who were neither and still tried to redeem notes were treated as enemies of the state.

Instead of getting the numerous banks to redeem notes for specie and liquidate those that could not, thereby bringing specie back into circulation and eliminating inflation, the **Second Bank of the United**

States with 20% government ownership was launched. The bank could issue national paper currency redeemable in specie, purchase public debt, and act as a depository to public funds.

This **Second Bank of the United States, 1816-33,** was pushed through by Treasury Secretary Alexander Dallas, a close friend of Stephan Girard and John Jacob Astor, merchants respectively from Philadelphia and New York, who had purchased war debt bonds and wanted to recover their investment. William Jones, the bank's president, was a friend of Girard and Astor. The situation had interesting parallels to Robert Morris' Bank of North America loan certificates situation towards the end of the revolution.

Another round of inflationary printing of money started as money supplies increased by 40.7% during 1816-18. This facilitated a boom due to speculative investments in real estate, farms, turnpike construction, slaves, and farm improvement. This boom was also the reason the first indoor stock exchange – the New York Stock Exchange – was established in March 1817, and why investment banking started.

Undervalued specie was flowing out and the Bank of the United States played tough after sacking William Jones. It imported specie and insisted on payment in specie from debtor state banks, something it had avoided so far in view of state banks being run by powerful friends of the former president. During 1818-19, the total money supply contracted by 28.3% and the number of state banks declined, followed by bankruptcies, defaults, and deflation.

D. Jacksonian Movement, Suffolk Bank, and Civil War 1833-65

The much misunderstood Jacksonian Movement was in favor of hard money and elimination of fractional reserve banking. The Second Bank of the United States was led by Andrew Jackson, Senator Thomas Benton of Missouri, and James K. Polk of Tennessee. It eventually led to Martin Van Buren forging the Democratic Party in the 1820s.

Their beliefs were libertarian in that they wanted to limit the role of government interference. They believed in free markets and the separation of the government from banking. They wanted the government to confine itself to upholding rights of private property, and were strictly against subsidies or monopoly privileges to any business group.

Andrew Jackson was elected president in 1829 and used his veto in 1833 to abolish central banking. Public treasury deposits were shifted from the Bank of the United States to numerous other state banks called 'pet banks.' This was followed by 57% inflation in wholesale prices between 1833 and 1837 as the money supply increased from $155 million to $267 million.

It was widely believed that decentralization of public deposits and the removal of the restraining force of the Bank of the United States over the state banks caused this inflation. This belief was strengthened by the fact that there was virtually no wholesale inflation during 1823-33 when the Second Bank of the United States was in operation. This is not the whole truth.

The Bank of the United States regime between 1823 and 1833 inflated, rather than restrained, the expansion of the money supply that rose from $81 million to $155 million. Wholesale prices did not rise because there was a proportionate increase in production of goods and services that absorbed this financial expansion.

During 1823-33, specie in the country was stable at around $32 million. Between 1833 and 1837, it expanded to $73 million for the following reasons:

· There was a huge influx of silver coins from Mexico, a result of the Santa Anna regime in Mexico inflating paper money in relation to silver coins to finance deficits. This stopped in 1837 when Mexico adopted a proper exchange ratio.

· The silver exported to China declined as the Chinese preferred opium over silver.

Increased specie led to an increase in money supply in accordance with the principle of fractional reserve banking (FRB). This was something the movement promised to eliminate, but did not – or could not – for which the Jackson administration can be rightfully blamed.

Monetary expansion does lead to speculative investments. The Specie Circular of 1836 that required public land payment to be made in specie only stopped the speculative investments into Western public lands, and was a step in the direction of putting the U.S. finances on a purely specie basis. However, it led to further depreciation of money as confidence waned.

Boom was followed by bust as the Bank of England contracted credit in England that decreased the demand for U.S. cotton exports in 1837: money supply contracted from $276 million down to $232 million in one year. Wholesale prices fell by 30%.

Partial revival was seen in 1838 as Britain eased credit. This was followed by an expenditure overdrive by states on public works funded by the cotton boom, funds from the Bank of England, and budget surplus distributed by the federal government in 1836. Another collapse was inevitable and occurred in 1839 as cotton prices fell again.

Unsound banks, debts, and investments were liquidated during the 1839-1843 deflation, as money supply fell from $240 million to $158 million and prices fell by 42%. State debts increased. Unlike what happened between 1929 and 1933, when real gross investment, real consumption, and real GNP respectively fell by 91%, 19%, and 30%; between 1839 and 1843 investment fell by 23% while real consumption and real GNP *increased* respectively by 21% and 16%.

Downward flexibility in prices between 1839 and 1843 explains this lack of similarity. When money supply contracted, prices fell but did not cripple production or standard of living, as happened during the period from 1929 to 1933 when government imposed restrictions on falling wages and prices.

After Jackson, President Van Buren established a Treasury System. No bank or pet banks were to control monetary policy or to function as a depository, and federal funds would be maintained at its own treasury or sub-treasury branches. This system lasted until 1861.

Achievements of Jacksonians:

· Paid off federal debt for the first and last time in U.S. history.

· Lowered tariffs.

· Abolished central banking – the major inflationary culprit.

· Partially succeeded in eliminating paper money of less than $20 denomination by imposing a federal tax on them. When these notes lost value, average Americans who used these suffered the most.

· Through the 1834 Coinage Acts, they drove out depreciated notes by adopting a proper gold to silver exchange ratio and legalizing foreign specie.

Sudden discovery of gold mines in California, Russia, and Australia in 1850s drove down the price of gold as the mint ratio decreased to 15.32:1 by 1860. Silver coins disappeared, and this presented a problem because small denomination coins in silver could not be replaced by relatively valuable gold coins. This led to the influx of illegal bank notes of small denominations.

While adhering to *de jure* bimetallism, Congress in 1853 shifted to a *de facto* gold standard, with slightly debased silver coins of lower denomination. This meant that silver coins were not undervalued and stayed in circulation, and the problem was solved by 1854.

The 'Free Banking' concept was promoted by the Whig party in the 1840's. They wanted to fight the money printing restriction imposed on banks by Democrats. This free banking was not free in the economic sense, wherein there is free entry into banking. Banks are neither regulated nor subsidized, and are penalized or forced to close down when they fail to redeem in specie.

Eighteen out of thirty-three states adopted such a 'free' banking concept before the Civil War. Characteristics of free banks included:

· Freedom of regulations.

· Maintained government bonds as reserve and, therefore, were encouraged to monetize debt which encouraged state governments to be in debt, leading to a vicious debt monetization-inflation cycle.

· Periodically suspended specie redemption.

· Got their notes to be accepted as taxes.

Whigs also promoted usury laws opposed by Democrats. Usury fostered risky, speculative lending. These experiments, however, led to certain banking-related improvements, most notably the Suffolk Bank System.

Suffolk Bank (1818-20, 1824-58) was established in 1818 to play the role of a money broker, clearing house type bank – redemption of country bank notes (vis-à-vis city bank notes) for specie for a fee. A variety of notes and the uncertainty of their true value were inhibiting commerce and trade.

Despite its failure in 1820, Suffolk Bank reestablished redemption operations in 1824. The bank teamed up with six other banks to form the Associated Bank and raised $300,000 for this express purpose. By 1838, Suffolk Bank was the only bank through which all bank notes were being redeemed by other banks in New England.

Using this leverage to influence country banks, it cut down time and inconvenience needed for redemption, which led to certainty in the value of country bank notes that aided commerce and trade. The general public also felt confident about notes. Country Bank's efforts to stall Suffolk Bank in the state legislature and in the Massachusetts Supreme Court failed.

Suffolk made heavy profits through redemption and other related activities. At its peak in 1858, it redeemed $400 million while its salary bill was only $40,000. Its redemption services were much cheaper than those provided by the government. New England became the most stable banking area in the U.S., and no bank suspended specie redemption until 1857.

Success bred arrogance, and Suffolk behaved rudely with many member banks. By the mid-1850s, the political center of gravity had shifted outside of Boston to areas dominated by country banks, and the **Bank for Mutual Redemption** emerged as a strong competitor in 1858.

Suffolk tried to force this competitor bank out of business by refusing to deal with any banks that had links with it. Country banks sided with the Bank for Mutual Redemption, and Suffolk stopped redeeming activities in October 1858.

The laxity of the new redeemer could have brought Suffolk back into business but for the Civil War in 1861, and the 1863 National Banking Acts that made currency issue a government monopoly. The Suffolk phenomenon demonstrated the capacity of private banks as safe, efficient, and inexpensive clearing houses that can limit the over-issue of paper money in a free market.

The **Civil War** introduced numerous changes to the American banking and monetary system:

· Central banking became a function of the federal government.

· The U.S. was put on an irredeemable fiat currency that lasted for two decades. It fueled inflation and set an egregious precedent for the post-1933 and post-1971 periods.

War expenditure increased from $66 million in 1861 to $1.3 billion in 1865, and bonds were issued to raise funds. Currency notes called greenbacks were repeatedly issued during the war and these were made legal tender. Treasury Secretary Salmon Chase, a former Jacksonian, took steps to prevent depreciation of greenbacks but ended up doing the opposite by:

· Requiring banks to pay in specie for bonds, causing banks to suspend specie payments in December 1861 and undervaluing gold, leading to its disappearance.

· The elimination of greenback convertibility to specie.

· The elimination of the gold market to prevent the rise of gold prices in relation to greenbacks.

· Sale of treasury gold to bring down gold prices.

· Sale of U.S. foreign exchange (Forex) reserves in pounds to bring down pounds and to bring down the price of imported British gold.

· The elimination of the gold payment clause.

With greenbacks depreciating continuously, silver, nickel, and copper pennies became undervalued and disappeared into hoards and foreign lands. Finally, in 1864, the issue of debased bronze pennies addressed the greenback shortage.

Gold coins did not disappear from California because banks, businesses, legislators, judges, and newspapers closed rank against greenbacks. Many of these steps were successfully followed by the state of Oregon.

Between 1860-65, the total money supply in the U.S. increased from $745.4 million to $1.773 billion, and wholesale prices rose by 110.9% in the same period. Greenback legislation was mainly authored by Republican Elbridge Spaulding, the Chairman of the House Ways and Means Sub-Committee, who himself was a Buffalo banker.

Contrary to the administration's claim, the issue of greenbacks was not inevitable because these financed only $431.7 million of the total wartime deficit of $2.614 billion, and the war went on even after the issue was suspended after 1863. Increased taxes and government bonds raised most of the war funds. The issue was necessary as the government was apprehensive of a rise of the price and the interest payments on these bonds.

Jay Cooke and his brother were close friends of Salmon Chase and lobbied hard to make Chase the Treasury Secretary. Salmon Chase made Jay Cooke & Co. the sole underwriter of all the public war debt. Cooke then sold these bonds to the public and sort of invented the art of public relations and mass propaganda for the sale of bonds.

During the war, he bought and sold almost $2 billion worth of bonds.

Wartime emergency was used to prepare ground for the **National Banking System** by the Cooke brothers. The control of the states over banking was shifted to Washington and a few Wall Street banks. While the effects of inflationary greenbacks were eliminated in 1879 when specie payments were resumed, those of the National Banking System are still felt.

This system had high capital requirements – between $50,000 and $200,000 – and consisted of three sets of national banks:

· **Central Reserve City Banks** in New York that only maintained 25% reserves in vault cash – in gold, silver, and greenbacks.

· Reserve **City Banks** in cities with over 50,000 population that maintained 25% reserves – half as vault cash and half as demand / checking deposits with the central reserve city bank.

· Country **Banks** were all other national banks and maintained 15% reserves – 40% as vault cash and the remaining 60% as demand deposits with the central reserve city banks or the reserve city banks.

Limitations on money expansion of earlier state banks included demands for redemption in specie by the general public and other banks wanting to clear checks issued by them. Now, banks at each rung could expand the money supply on the basis of reserves maintained with it by a bank in the lower rung – $1 million vault cash with a country bank expanded total credit by all three bank levels by $9.6 million.

Reserve requirements are a sound way to limit expansion of bank credit, but setting a lower reserve ratio by law can result in all banks adhering to lower reserves. Without a legal limit, free competition will lead to banks maintaining higher reserves. Any limit less than 100% is always inflationary.

A 10% tax imposed on all state bank notes in 1865 effectively outlawed all such notes, and the number of state banks and the total value of notes issued by them fell rapidly. Later, state banks revived as subordinates of national banks and had to maintain reserves at these banks. In effect, they became a fourth layer of the national banking system and further added to inflation.

Vested interests were at work in the National Banking System: Chase wanted an assured market for government bonds for raising war finances, and Cooke, as the monopoly underwriter, wanted a market for his bonds. National banks purchased bonds and issued notes to pay for them. Employing their propaganda machine, the Cooke brothers pushed through national bank legislation despite democratic opposition.

E. Post-Civil War, 1865-79

Because inflation makes imports more expensive, serving as surrogate tariff, and because it benefits borrowers, the powerful steel manufacturing lobby led by Henry Carey, gold speculators, heavily indebted railroad companies, and other manufacturers supported the greenback.

Greenbacks were declared unconstitutional by the U.S. Supreme Court in 1870, much to the chagrin of Chief Justice Salmon Chase. Democratic judges voted against greenbacks, and Republican judges voted for them. This was reversed in 1871 when two vacancies allowed the Chief Justice to conveniently bring in pro-greenback judges.

Between 1865 and 1873, the number of national and state banks increased. The total deposits with both of these banks increased from $835 million to $1.964 billion. The financial panics of 1873, 1884, 1893, and 1907 were a result of excessive deposit creation during financial prosperity. However, money supply did not contract after these panics, it merely stagnated.

Only after the Democrats swept Congress in 1874 was there a semblance of unanimity on monetary matters, in the form of the Resumption Act of 1875 that resulted in specie resumption through the following actions:

· The U.S. government was to start the purchase of gold with government bonds in order to redeem greenbacks at pre-war rates on January 1, 1879. Gold purchase was necessary, as there was not enough specie with banks to balance the inflated greenback supplies.

· The $300 million limit on national bank notes was eliminated.

· There was an 80% contraction of greenback supplies, but these could be issued again.

Cooke originally favored contraction of greenbacks in 1866, as he was afraid of the falling value of his bonds. By the late 1860s, however, Cooke had received a 47 million acre land grant for railroad expansion and needed an expanding money supply to finance building railroads through the Northern Pacific Railroad.

The speculative railroad bubble busted in 1873 when Jay Cooke & Co. declared bankruptcy as the overextended Northern Pacific sunk. This touched off the panic of 1873 that lasted until 1879. But was it really a depression, as interpreted by the falling prices of 3.8% per annum between 1869 and 1879?

Consider this: between 1869 and 1879, money national product, real national product, and real product per capita, respectively increased per annum by 3%, 6.8%, and 4.5%. Money supply increased from $1.964 billion to $2.221 billion between 1873 and 1878.

Falling prices were a result of slow expansion of the money supply that in free capitalism leads to an increase in production of goods and services at a faster rate than the rate at which money is created – a positive development. The 1873 crisis resulted in bankruptcies of over-inflated banks and railroads.

Silver was expected to fall below the long-held mint ratio of 15.5:1 as Europeans were shifting to a gold standard and silver mines were being discovered in the western United States. Congress hastily passed two bills in 1873 and 1874 to discontinue minting of silver dollars and to demonetize silver coins above $5.

These bills were perfectly timed as silver fell below 16:1 in 1874 and hit 32:1 in 1894. There were, however, three problems:

· The increased silver production made miners call for purchase at higher than market rates.

· The agrarian crisis made farmers demand free minting of silver to pay off debts.

· The hasty action in passing the bills made it look suspicious.

Furthermore, laws prevented an influx of cheap silver that would be similar to over-issuing currency notes. These conditions found an outlet in the form of the 1876 to 1879 agitation for free coinage in silver, particularly in the western silver mining region, and this agitation almost blocked the return to the gold standard in 1879.

Ultimately, the administration was able to secure resumption of payments in gold, but only after making the Bland Allison Silver Purchase Act of 1878, which mandated the treasury purchase $2,000,000 to $4,000,000 of silver per month.

F. The Classical Gold Standard Period: 1879 to 1913

This was the period when the leading economies of the world were on a classical gold standard with 100% reserves. Currencies were defined by their weight in gold, providing stable exchange ratios between the different currencies. That was good for long term business and investment plans. Despite financial booms and busts, total inflation in this period was virtually zero.

Economic balance was maintained under this standard. A country in economic boom imported more. Payment in gold made gold flow out of the country, and the money supply contracted as gold was the basis of the money supply. This led to deflation and economic slowdown.

The demand for imports fell, and so did prices, making exports cheaper. This created greater demand for exports, and gold flowed back in the country and increased the money supply. Value of the gold-based currency was always changing within a narrow range, in step with changes in gold reserves.

For the U.S., the 1879-96 period is remarkably similar to the 1873-1879 period, when real tangible wealth per capita, real net national product, per capita net national product, and money supply grew while prices fell.

Price deflation under the gold standard after 1879 was less than in the era before the gold standard, which means the gold standard is not associated with deflation. Absence of sustained inflation and a rise in savings and in capital formation led to a real rise in wages in the 1880s.

This decade also saw yields on long term U.S. bonds decrease to the 3-3.5% range, the same range in Holland in the 17th century and in England in the 18th-19th century, when these colonial powers were at the peak of their economic prowess. With resumption starting in 1879, greenbacks were trusted. Foreigners were ready to hold dollars, so gold inflows began.

Many regard the 1880s as the best period of U.S. economic history because of the increase in labor productivity, due to increased capital investment in business establishments, farms, cultivated area, farm production, farm productivity, and farm wages.

There was, however, a slight deflation in 1884 when money supply contracted to $3.15 billion from $3.19 billion in 1883. The Brand Allison Silver Purchase Act of 1878 created stockpiles of silver, as gold was undervalued and flowed abroad as foreign investors doubted the willingness of the U.S. government to stay on the gold standard.

Free Silver agitation raised its head again in the 1890s. The Sherman Silver Purchase Act of 1890 doubled the silver purchase obligations by the Treasury. In view of the increased production of silver, inflationary silver monometallism and the disappearance of undervalued gold, the depletion of the nation's gold reserves was inevitable.

Inflationary high tariffs and soft money promoted by the 1890

McKinley Tariff Act and the imposition of a stiff fee on export of gold bars by the Treasury in 1891 to prevent the outflow of gold caused further loss of confidence in the American gold standard. Even the abortive Free Silver Coinage Bill in 1892 rang alarm bells in the investor community.

Foreign investors lost confidence in the dollar's purchasing power and made a run on gold. Banks imposed gold clauses in loans and mortgage agreements, bank runs demanding specie began as many fractional reserve banks collapsed, and numerous banks, especially in the West and the South, suspended specie payments.

The panic was on. The stock market crashed just two months after Grover Cleveland – a Democrat and a hard money enthusiast – assumed presidency. Between 1892 and 1893, the total money supply fell by 6.3%. By the end of 1893, the panic ended as the Sherman Act was repealed.

Confidence in the gold standard was threatened by the Silver Agitation of 1895, but that was countered by the Treasury purchasing gold from the banking syndicate led by J.P. Morgan and August Belmont. Things settled down further as pro-gold Republicans won the 1897 presidential polls.

G. Federal Reserve, Gold Exchange Standard, and the Interwar Period, 1913-44

During the 1907 Stock Market Panic, it is widely known that New York banks called money trusts were causing such crashes to buy stocks cheaply and then selling these at windfall profits when such sudden purchases increased prices. J.P. Morgan played the role of lender of last resort, triggering vociferous calls for government action rather than private favors.

In 1908, the National Monetary Commission under chairmanship of Senator Nelson Aldrich went to Europe and spent $300,000, roughly equal to present day $6 million. He spent two years in consultation with English, French, and German central banks.

On his return, Aldrich secretly consulted with New York bankers – people he was supposed to investigate, not consult. The result was the Aldrich Plan Currency Report, which became the basis of the Federal Reserve, the U.S.' central bank, and the new currency system.

The Aldrich Plan was backed by Republicans but could not passed through Congress, as Republicans were a minority. After minor changes in 1913, the Aldrich Plan with induced Congress to transfer its Constitutional right to coin money to the Federal Reserve.

As already mentioned, interest and fractional reserve banking are fundamental flaws – every time Congress and large banks need money, they avail a loan from the Federal Reserve, which simply prints more money to this end.

Every single dollar in circulation is, therefore, 'borrowed into existence' by Congress and the banks. Interest ensures that total repayment will require a continuous, inflationary expansion of money supply. Total repayment, however, is made impossible as this process promotes fiscal indiscipline.

Interestingly, **income tax** was **created** through the Sixteenth Amendment **in the same year of 1913**. Before that, government expenditure was managed through import duties and excise and production taxes. Because the government could never make a total payback to the Federal Reserve, it created the income tax to raise repayment funds. Effectively, all of us still pay for the continuation of this system: a never-ending rabbit hole of money expansion and inflation.

Expenses from the **First World War** caused Europeans to abandon the gold standard and print inflationary paper money. War exports to Europeans that were paid back in gold caused the U.S. gold reserves to increase by 60%. When European allies could no longer pay in gold, the U.S. extended credit. Once the U.S. joined the war in 1917, its national debt increased from $1 billion in 1916 to $25 billion by 1919.

An oversupply of money in the world made a return to the classical gold standard impossible. There was just not enough gold in the world to balance the cash in circulation without devaluation of currency, and governments were not ready for devaluation. Gold cannot be cheated on, something that governments never fully understand.

The U.S. possessed 40% of the world's gold, while Europeans had wads of U.S. dollars received as war loans. Therefore, a pseudo-gold standard called **gold exchange standard** evolved:

· The U.S. dollar, the British pound, and gold were made the reserve currencies by the world's central banks.

· The dollar and the pound could be redeemed for gold.

In the U.S., 40% of gold reserves were maintained, and currency in circulation was worth 2.5 times the value of gold reserves held by the Federal Reserve. Fractional reserves act like an inverted pyramid of expanding money that is bound to collapse. Combined with fractional reserves of commercial banks, another more unstable inverted pyramid is imposed atop the original unstable inverted pyramid.

Domestically, before the Federal Reserve, banks with 10% fractional reserves could hold $20 in reserves and loan out another $180 to create total money of $200. With the fractional reserve system in place at the Federal Reserve, $20 with the central bank could create $50 with the 40% reserve requirement. Then the second layer of banks could create a total of $500 (10 x $50: 10% reserves) from this $50.

Foreign central banks could use dollars as reserves instead of gold. $20 with the Federal Reserve created $50 in circulation – if this $50 was borrowed by another central bank, it could issue $125 ($50 x 2.5: 40% reserves) in its currency. Commercial banks in this country could hold $125 in reserves and create a total of $1,250 ($125 x 10: 10% reserves).

The Real Reserve Ratio, or the real money that could be paid out against their currency, became only 1.6% ($20 divided by $1,250).

Pyramids worked well in the early days, but increased cash

availability causes commercial banks to issue more credit. Now, credit was availed more for purchasing consumer goods such as automobiles and non-farmland real estate vis-à-vis commercial loans for productive business activities of the pre-1913 period.

Credit availability also facilitated an investment boom. People stopped saving and started investing in stocks and real estate, both of which were rising in tune with the increased demand created by loans now available for purchase.

However, value of a brokerage account depends on the perception of the market about the investment, and that, unlike money in savings account, can change overnight. This is similar to what people did during the housing bubble – treated their homes and its appreciating value as their savings account.

A credit boom and a credit-based economy are based on the perception of people and traders. If people believe the economy will maintain a positive performance, they borrow for spending and for investment, and the economy flourishes. When they have doubts, things go wrong the way they did in the **Great Depression,** symbolized by the **1929 stock market crash**.

A result of the interaction of numerous national and international factors, the Great Depression was the worst economic crisis the world had ever seen. Real gross investment, real consumption, and real GNP respectively fell by 91%, 19%, and 30%. Stock prices fell by 80%, manufacturing by 46%, wholesale prices by 30.8% and consumer prices by 24.4%. Worse, unemployment jumped to between 25% and 30%.

The following causes are generally held responsible for the deflation in 1929-33:

· The Federal Reserve had increased discount rates, the rates at which it lends to commercial banks. This was done to mop up excess liquidity caused by excessive printing of money to finance the First World War. This had created partial deflation in the U.S.

· Excessive production in agriculture and industry, a product of the booming economy of the 1920s, added to the deflation.

· In unregulated businesses, in keeping with *laissez faire* policy, profits were not distributed fairly to the working and service classes who did not have funds to buy the produced goods and services. This reduced demand.

The result of these circumstances depreciated the stock of overproducing companies. Investors who had invested in such companies lost heavily, followed by bankruptcies and foreclosures.

· Internationally, the French returned to the gold standard in 1928 and deliberately undervalued the franc so that gold flowed into France according to Gresham's Law. Undervaluation also increased French exports.

However, France did not increase money supplies with increased gold reserves in order to restrain inflation. This also restrained economic activity and added to international deflation.

· When American economic aid dried up to war-ravaged Europe, European economies faced slowdowns followed by protectionist tariff walls against international trade that dropped by 50%.

Distrust inspired by the First World War was enough to prevent any cohesive international action against this crisis.

Money is created when funds are loaned and money is destroyed with loan repayment, bankruptcies, foreclosures, and during bank runs. Between 1930 and 1933, one-third of the money in the U.S. contracted. Deflation was further aggravated by bank runs. For every $1 deposited in a bank, 10% fractional reserve banking creates $9 worth of loans. During bank runs, every $1 withdrawal liquidates $9 of loans.

Fractional reserves also mean that people had little cash and large deposits, while banks had low reserves and too much credit that was about to go bad. Failure of the 62 branches of the Bank of the United

States in December, 1930, caused a chain reaction failure of 352 banks with over $370 million deposits in that very month. Deposit insurance was a largely unheard system, and many lost their life's savings.

To aggravate matters, Great Britain went off the gold standard in September. Fears that the U.S. would do the same and print money to get out of deflation caused a run on Treasury gold by many foreign central banks. *Barron's* March 1933 issue aptly observed: "Stages of deflation since 1929 have been the flight of wealth from securities to bank deposits to currency and thence to gold."

When Roosevelt assumed presidency in 1933, he took the following measures to deal with the situation:

· From 1933 to 1934, the dual standard was introduced: gold for foreign exchange and silver for Americans.

· March 1933: A bank holiday was declared, and banks were prevented from paying out gold coin after resuming operations. All forex operations were frozen.

· April 5, 1933: Private ownership of gold was banned and all private gold was handed over to the Federal Reserve in return for federal notes.

· April 20, 1933: No U.S. citizen could buy or trade in foreign currencies or transfer currencies to accounts outside the U.S.

· May 1933: The president was empowered to devalue the dollar up to 50%. Federal Reserve notes and coins were given the status of 'lawful money' or 'fiat money.'

· On June 5, 1933, the 'gold clause' in contracts was outlawed and no one could demand gold in lieu of any due payment, since gold was not supposed to be in private hands.

Gold clauses were inserted into contracts at the end of the Civil War in 1865 to protect lenders who were being paid back in depreciated greenback dollars for the loans given out in gold-backed dollars.

This clause mandated payment in gold or an amount of currency equal to the 'weight of gold' value at the onset of the contract. Most government contracts had this clause and dollar devaluation would increase the cost of government obligations.

· Gold Reserve Act of January 30, 1934: the Federal Reserve was given ownership of all the gold it had collected. The Act also devalued the dollar from $20.67 per ounce of gold to $35 per ounce.

In effect, this meant a 40% devaluation of the Federal Reserve notes that were redeemable in silver. Between 1933 and 1963, Federal Reserve notes were redeemable in silver. During the discussions on this act, Senator Thomas Gore of Oklahoma famously remarked, "Why, that's just plain stealing, isn't it, Mr. President?"

Less than 22% of the privately-held gold was turned over to the Federal Reserve, and no one was prosecuted for wrongfully owning gold. The victims were the law abiding citizens who had turned over their gold in exchange for Federal Reserve notes and suffered 40% devaluation of these notes.

Devaluation of the dollar did make exchanging dollars for gold more expensive for foreign central banks and stopped the gold run. Another effect of devaluation was that the *value of gold reserves became equal to the value of money in circulation* in 1934, as under the classical gold standard. The U.S. could have gone back to the classical gold standard, but that requires governments and banks to demonstrate fiscal discipline.

The U.S. was rescued from the Great Depression from a trade surplus and influx of gold during 1934-37 – both a result of dollar devaluation and the looming WWII:

· Devaluation made the U.S. exports cheaper, creating a trade surplus. Gold prices went up by 70% – from $20 an ounce to $35 an ounce. Under the gold exchange standard, foreign currencies could buy 70% more American goods and services.

· Undervaluation in comparison to gold made gold flow into the U.S., as foreigners and gold miners could get more dollars by selling gold. These dollars could then be used for paying for goods imported from the U.S.

· When Germany annexed Austria in 1938, Europe panicked and investments from Europe were diverted to the U.S. Also, European consumer goods factories were used for war production, so everyday items for Europeans had to be sourced from the U.S., which stimulated the U.S. economy, and payments were made by Europeans in gold.

The U.S. profited from destruction in Europe. By 1945, the U.S. possessed two-thirds of the world's monetary gold reserves and produced two-thirds of the world's electricity and half of the world's coal. A huge manufacturing base was created out of war production for Europe. The U.S. now represented 40% of the world's GDP with a hugely favorable trade balance; however, that created an unsustainable international trade imbalance.

H. Bretton Woods System, 1944-71

This system was designed to create a system of international payments for sustainable international trade that would prevent:

· Huge fluctuations in currency exchange rates.

· Sudden depreciation of currency.

Such developments create international trade payments imbalances that may be followed by tariff walls against international trade, as happened during the Great Depression.

All currencies were to have a fixed exchange ratio with the dollar. The value of the dollar was fixed at $1/35^{th}$ an ounce of gold, or $35 per ounce of gold. Only dollars could be exchanged for gold. All central banks except the Federal Reserve were to hold dollars as monetary reserves instead of gold; they could also hold gold if they had any left.

There were two problems with the Bretton Woods System:

· The fractional reserve ratio between the value of gold reserves with the Federal Reserve and the value of dollars in circulation was not set; the U.S. could print any number of dollars.

· In the International Open Gold Market, U.S. citizens traded gold, which operated in parallel with the Bretton Woods Gold Market and depreciated dollars against gold.

Deficits created to fund the **Vietnam War – the Deficit War** – were financed by printing dollars. This was the first war that U.S. citizens were not asked to make financial sacrifices apart from paying taxes; there were no war bonds or transformation of the consumer economy into a war economy. President Johnson even undertook expensive Great Society programs during the war.

Excessive dollars were floating in Europe in the form of aid, and as payments for purchases for the Vietnam War. The French were especially suspicious of the dollar's true worth and began redemption of excess dollars for gold at the Federal Reserve.

France also withdrew from the **London Pool**, a regulatory apparatus that maintained gold at $35 per ounce by getting central banks to sell gold to counter the depreciation of the excessively printed dollars.

Across the Atlantic, Britain devalued the pound in November 1967, and triggered a gold run. Gold outflow from central banks increased 40 times by March 1968, when 200 tons of gold was leaving the vaults each day, compared to the average amount of 5 tons, which had been the norm for many years. Over 50% of the gold left the U.S. Treasury vaults from 1959 to 1971.

On August 15, 1971, President Nixon shut down the exchangeability between the dollar and gold. The U.S. currency became completely fiat. Since all other currencies were connected to gold through the dollar, the entire currency on the planet became fiat. This was equivalent to the U.S. declaring bankruptcy, as dollar devaluation hurt those who maintained dollar reserves.

Because the dollar was the currency used for international trade instead of gold, there was always a demand for it. Global traders had just got used to dollars. This and the need to convert currencies into dollars for investment in the strong American economy somewhat maintained the dollar's value. This is why the U.S. can continue to run huge deficits.

I. Post 1971

The raging inflation of the 1970s was a consequence of excessive money supply. Nixon repeated the folly of wage and price controls committed by Diocletian in the Roman era. Inflation coupled with caps on commodity prices ensured that farmers could not even recover their cost of production. Wholesale dumping of peaches, milk, and chickens by farmers in protest fueled further inflation through shortages.

Oil prices rose during the 1973 Yom Kippur War – the Fourth Arab Israel War – when the Organization of the Petroleum Exporting Countries (OPEC) placed an oil embargo against the U.S. as punishment for its support to Israel. This rise was more because of excessive dollar supply; the increased price was only compensation to recover the lost purchasing power of the dollar. Interestingly, oil price actually declined in terms of gold.

James Ulysses Blanchard III led a movement to legalize private ownership of gold and succeeded in 1974, when President Gerald Ford finally legalized gold ownership. However, gold was traded as a commodity, not as a currency, as people had gotten used to paper dollars.

All this changed in the mid- and late 1970s, as the dollar's purchasing power declined – starting in 1971 – and became more pronounced in the latter half of the decade. Naturally, gold rose to $200 per ounce and gold started to act as currency again. Heavy investment caused further appreciation, and it crossed the $300 mark in 1979.

Mainstream media and professionals warned that gold had reached its peak, only to be proved wrong by further continuing appreciation of gold. The dollar was not improving, and people were doing what has always been done in times of economic uncertainty: investing in gold. The situation became a 20th century gold rush with lengthy lines in front of coin and jewelry shops.

Many people bought gold, but this was the manifestation of the herd mentality of investing when gold was already priced high. The golden opportunity that occurred between 1975 and 1978 when gold was priced $100 to $200 an ounce was missed by general investors. Clever investors, however, profited through their *early purchase, buy low, sell high* strategy.

Just like in 1934, the will of the people on which market sentiment is based asserted itself over the autocratic attitude of the government and bankers. Despite a loss of 50% of the gold reserves between 1959 and 1971, the period between 1980 and 1981 saw the total value of gold reserves increase steadily and outperform:

· Base currency (dollars in circulation plus cash reserves at the Federal Reserve and at other banks) at $135 billion.

· Base currency plus revolving credit outstanding (unpaid credit card balances) at $195 billion.

Gold went on to top out at $225 billion, even though over half of gold reserves with the U.S. flowed out between 1959-71.

Another opportunity was available for the U.S. to go back to the gold standard, but not doing so allowed gold investors to profit. Unpaid credit card balance is an unpaid loan that increases money supply until the seller of the good or service is paid by the bank and the loan is extinguished. The credit card debt factor has to be considered when calculating money supplies.

J. Hide and Seek of the 1980s

Among the stock market crashes in history, the one on Black Monday – October 19, 1987 – is probably the largest one-day crash. The genuine reasons for this crash can be traced in the 1970s, when runaway inflation was the norm rather than the exception, and monetary policy had to be increasingly used in the next decade.

The decade of the 1980s is said to be a 'Great Moderation' period, where cyclical fluctuations in the economy were controlled by proper application of monetary policy through the federal funds rate. What cannot be ignored, however, is that the cyclic nature of booms and busts makes such control very tricky, and controlling one phase leads to another. This cycle repeated itself throughout the 1980s.

When the dollar was delinked from gold in 1971, gold prices took off in the late 1970s. Despite the Treasury possessing a depleted quantity of gold reserves, the value of these reserves equaled and even exceeded the total money and credit in circulation between 1980 and 1981.

Real interest rates – interest rates minus inflation – were increased to control the raging inflation and runaway rise of gold prices in the late 1970s by Paul Volcker. Volcker took over as chairman of the Federal Reserve (Fed) in 1979.

As explained earlier, this move worsened the slowdown of the economy. In March 1983, the Fed eliminated the reserve requirement on time deposits of thirty months or more, and extended this exception to time deposits of eighteen months or more beginning in September. As a result, currency supply increased by 21% between January 1983 and January 1985.

Time deposits are those deposits with banks that can be withdrawn only after a certain duration, when they mature. Premature withdrawal is financially penalized. The other types of deposits include savings accounts and current accounts from which funds can be withdrawn any time, subject to certain pre-declared conditions.

Following Volcker's actions, the Fed was able to reduce rates from over 11% in late 1984 to around 6.25% by late 1986. A boom resulted, and the S&P 500 jumped from 100 points to 338 in a short period, going from severely undervalued to severely overvalued as the boom turned into a bubble that, inevitably, had to burst.

The sell-off began on October 14, 1987, when the DOW lost 10%. On October 19 – three days later – a massive sell-off began when everyone tried to sell simultaneously, but there was no one left to buy. The

DOW depreciated by 22.6% and more than $500 billion of wealth was *transferred* in one day. As if to emphasize global connectivity, markets in the U.K. fell by 26.4%, Australia by 41.8%, Canada by 22.5%, and Hong Kong by 45.8%.

With the specter of a worldwide depression and a banking crisis looming large, the Fed increased the money supply, which converted embryonic real estate booms in various parts of the country into new menacing bubbles. Housing prices rocketed by more than 200% between 1986 and 1989 and caused yet another speculation frenzy.

Once again, the Fed shifted to the other end of the spectrum by increasing rates from just over 6.5% to almost 10% in order to halt the speculative investment. The result was the shifting of the country into another, slower economic gear that started from the East Coast and made its presence felt in the entire country.

They say that when it rains, it pours. To aggravate matters, the U.S. entered into another war that it could not afford – the First Gulf War – on January 17, 1991. This was in retaliation to the Iraqi invasion of Kuwait on August 2, 1990. Inflationary deficit spending to finance the war became inevitable.

Between 1991 and 1992, the Fed cut interest rates from 8% to 3%, cut the reserve requirement on time deposits from 3% to 0%, and reduced transaction deposits from 12% to 10%. This time, however, slashing of rates had little effect because the war was on.

During wars, money is printed to finance the purchase of war supplies. The newly-produced money is used for production of war goods, not consumer goods, as before. The second factor may not be very significant for the U.S., which has a huge military production industry in place. The first factor, however, is important.

War inflation is fueled from two sides: excessive printing causes currency to depreciate, and diversion of production causes an acute shortage of goods. Because the production of goods and services does not expand to absorb the increase in money supply, inflation continues to gallop.

Housing prices bottomed in 1992 as the rate cut failed to stimulate the economy, though the increase in currency supplies did produce a delayed response from 1995 onwards. Availability of excessive liquidity is bound to show effects, sooner or later. Between 1995 and 2005 the currency supply increased by around 120%. More money was created in that 10-year period than in the 83 years before.

All of the new currency had to go somewhere, and it went into housing, fueling the largest real estate bubble in the economic history of the U.S. Similar bubbles were also observed in bonds, debt, stocks, derivatives, consumption, and, of course, internet companies that created the famous dot-com bubble.

K. Dot-com bubble of the late 1990s

In 1995, an enormous increase was observed in the number of internet users, creating immense business opportunities for online companies. Market sentiment was in favor of internet companies, as their star was seen to be on the rise. Investment and speculation in such companies was, therefore, inevitable in view of the huge liquidity in the market.

Riding on the back of a strong performance by a few genuine internet technology companies adhering to sound business practices, many internet companies started to employ daring, unsound business practices such as increasing market share even if it meant operating at a loss – in the hopes that later profits from an increased market share and rising investments would more than compensate the present risk.

Hundreds of such companies were being formed every week, and some only wanted to profit from the bubble without doing any real business. Freebooters always profit from such situations and much like those pirates of the past, these sophisticated robber barons were even worse than those following unsound business practices. Many such internet companies could not be valued properly, and this only served to increase the confusion.

When the fraud and unsound business culture became apparent through lawsuits and government investigations, the inevitable followed: people lost confidence, the stocks of internet companies fell, and the bubble burst on March 10, 2000. The crisis was named "the dot-com crisis" after the *.com* in the web addresses of many such companies.

Profits of authentic companies declined along with those of the rabble companies. Companies such as Global Crossing, WorldCom, and Enron collapsed. The crisis was compounded by outsourcing that drove many computer developers out of employment. By the 9/11 terrorist attacks, the stock markets took a nose dive.

Better internet companies soon acquired those with shoddy work cultures as the latter went into bankruptcy. If you think we are past this crisis, hold your breath – the explosion in the number of broadband users at present creates conditions for another dot-com-like crisis.

As is always the case with booms and busts, the herd mentality of investors was again observed – during the boom as well as during the bust. The moral of the story is simple: if you invest in the market on the basis of advice from brokers, analysts, TV programs, or large investment firms, like everyone else is, you are late and have missed the bus. You are purchasing the stock or the commodity that is already on the rise.

Early bird prices – and fortunes – go to those who have strong fundamental market knowledge, who are ready to take the time to investigate the practical workings of the market, and who are confident enough to act on the basis of these two preceding measures.

Identification of an undervalued asset class is of paramount importance. Such classes are the ones you should be investing in, for these will appreciate in the near future and add value to investments. Such identification, in turn, requires education, investigation, and application.

Financial upheavals do not destroy wealth; they transfer it. They also create opportunities for those financially shrewd investors who can sense the difference between price and value. Price keeps on changing. Value doesn't.

Since 2000, in General

Inflation of the 1970s was controlled in the 1980s. The new decade saw the 'Great Moderation' – or decline of cyclical fluctuations – in the entire economy through appropriate application of policy interest rates and the federal funds rate set through open market operations like trading of government bonds and securities. This was believed to be a potent monetary instrument.

Two financial crises in 1991 and 2001 – prior to the 2007 to 2008 subprime mortgage crisis that exploded into the current global economic slowdown – were shallow and short-lived. The macroeconomic picture in 2005 was perceived to be stable largely due to low consumer inflation.

Problems were, however, simmering underneath. The housing bubble inflated housing prices by 128% between January 1997 and January 2006. Household leverage – the ratio of household debt to household disposable income – was rising and was considered positive because:

· Rising house prices would cover any possible defaults.

· Securitization of mortgages was lowering risk for lenders and cost for borrowers.

· All bubbles attract investment.

Leverage is the use of debt / loans for finance against issuing equity securities.

Bubble is the excessive and speculative investment in an asset or an economic sector that is expected to rise in value.

Securitization is the conversion of assets into securities that can be traded in financial markets.

· Between 1997 and 2006, the U.S. current account deficit grew from 0.5% to 1.9% of the world's output, sparking fears of the U.S. being increasingly funded by foreigners who could withdraw their funds at any time, leading to the fall of the dollar and of economic activity. This potential crisis could then travel to the rest of the world.

Current Account Deficit is the excess of the value of imports over the value of exports – this deficit contracts in a recession as imports decline naturally.

Low consumer inflation and economic growth before the crisis was not sufficient to ensure stable macroeconomic conditions. Excessive leverage with households and financial intermediaries was due to low lending interest rates before the crisis. When the crisis hit, traditional monetary policy was not enough to address the falling demand.

The subprime housing crisis of 2007 was a result of:

· Structural **Changes in Banking,** such as the originate-to-distribute model and increased loan securitization, lowered lending standards and precautions and prevented re-pricing of complex financial products during liquidity crunches.

This lowered trust between financial intermediaries slowed, or even stopped, interbank financial transactions. That, in turn, stopped the flow of interbank credit.

In the **originate-to-distribute model**, loans are not held until maturity by the lending institution, but sold to other institutions or investors.

· Excessive **Reliance on Short Term Financing** by banks exposed them to funding risks.

· Financial **globalization** spread the toxin of securities based on non-performing subprime mortgages to global financial markets. Europeans are always interested in investing in American assets.

Causes for the current crisis include the great global demand and limited supply of safe liquid debt instruments, the U.S. monetary policy, and global external factors, especially increasing external deficits of the U.S. (also referred to as global imbalances).

In 2006, housing prices were on the rise. Banks issued mortgages to borrowers with risky credit history in the form of subprime mortgages. Even if the borrowers defaulted, confiscation of rising-price houses would more than compensate any losses.

As expected, there were defaults. Then came another catalyst: foreclosures/ confiscation of the defaulted houses led to a decline in housing prices, and banks were left with confiscated homes worth a fraction of the value of the money owed on the home. With assistance from certain investment banks, bad mortgages were converted into tradable securities by these banks.

Investment banks ensured great ratings for such rotten securities through their influence with credit rating agencies and advised investors to actually purchase them. In globally connected financial markets, the subprime virus spread like wildfire and gobbled up many businesses, banks, and livelihoods.

Base money – the sum of cash in circulation and deposits left at the Federal Reserve by large banks – increased from $825 billion in 2008 to $2.4 trillion in 2010. The money supply is deliberately increased by central banks in such times and leads to inflation.

We have already noted the deflation just before the Great Depression, during which the contraction in the money supply was observed. A similar contraction was observed in the U.S. economy in 2010 when the M3 – widely regarded as a good measure of money in the economy – declined by $1.7 trillion, falling from above $15 trillion to just below $14 trillion.

Is the present slowdown set to worsen? Most probably, yes.

Markets always try to seek the best price by striking equilibrium. As real estate and stock prices bubbles crash, markets will show what economic analysts call the **dead cat bounce** – a low after the highest point followed by a slight rise and then continued fall. This slight rise is the reason for deflation followed by runaway inflation, and can be seen in the DOW in 1928-34, the NASDAQ between 1998-2004, and is expected again in the DOW between 2007 and 2014.

Moral of the Story

We can take away several points from the historic study of the economic issues involved in our monetary development. There are some broad lessons we can learn, looking back at the outcomes of our recent economic history:

- Monetary Systems change every thirty to forty years. The last time it was changed was in 1971. That was more than forty years ago. It is widely known in financial circles that the G20 is trying to forge a new monetary system after the decline of the dollar assumes dangerous proportions in the near future.

  Some connection of money with gold and silver is bound to be established in the new monetary system. When this happens, gold and silver prices will rise and rise and rise.

- Prices of gold and silver rise when there is an expansion in money supply. This happened in 1933 when President Roosevelt banned the private ownership of gold and again in 1971 when President Nixon delinked the dollar from gold reserves.

- Until 2008, we witnessed the longest lasting bubble or speculative rise in price in stock markets. A good measure of the undervaluation or overvaluation of a stock is its Price to Earnings or P/E Ratio. It has a fair value of 12 that also means investors can expect to recover their investment in 12 years.

  If this ratio is greater than 12, the stock is overvalued and a value greater than 18 means a bubble. From a high of 45 in 2000, the P/E ratio for DOW collapsed and then rose to between 23 and 26 in 2008. This bubble is bound to crash as real estate and stock markets take a downward plunge, money deteriorates and gold and silver appreciates.

  Since 2003 and especially from 2008, stock markets across the world have demonstrated remarkable similarities in rises and falls – probably a manifestation of increasing globalization. This means a crash is imminent across all global markets.

The moral of the story is that gold and silver prices are about to witness a galloping rise. As an individual, you can profit from this by investment in gold and silver right now. Until some years ago, an undeclared sale of gold stocks by European central banks has kept the prices of gold in check. Now they can no longer continue to do so.

Smart investors invest in an asset when it is priced low and expected to go up. What goes up must come down. Therefore, those smart investors sell the asset when it is at or near its peak and invest in another asset whose price is low but starts to rise as it receives investment. Then, when the second asset is near its peak, they sell it and invest in the first one that has already fallen due to the earlier sale. This is the **economic cycle,** and it continues.

With the price of gold and silver currently going up, now is the time to invest. Latecomers usually have to be satisfied with returns of a second order. Gold and silver prices have already appreciated considerably in the last decade. Therefore, the time to invest is NOW. There are just a couple of things you need to watch out for:

- **Dead Cat Bounce** will create an impression that markets are recovering and gold and silver prices will not rise and may even decline.

- **Deliberate Price Dampening** by large banks such as JP Morgan that sell the gold and silver so they do not have to bring down the prices. This can be done through futures trading when the purchase is to be completed at some future date, but the still unpurchased commodity can be sold to someone else.

  When prices decline, they purchase gold and silver again. Their profit is the difference in the selling and the buying price. Knowing the fundamentals, you can also avoid the sale of gold and silver during such organized charades.

The fiat money system allows the concentration of monetary decision making power and is, therefore, liked by governments. Understanding the economic cycle and the fundamentals of the price mechanism, you can actually benefit from the falling value of money. Such an understanding is precisely the reason some families become dynasties and maintain their position at the top of the socio-economic hierarchy.

Chapter 3 – Quantitative Easing, Bubbleconomics, and Fiscal Cliff

"I think when you spread the wealth around, it's good for everybody."

- Barack Obama

When considering the financial status of individuals, governments, and corporations, assets are an important component in addition to debt and savings. All assets and liabilities of a government belong to its people in the final analysis. Similarly, assets of a private company belong to its shareholders and bondholders.

This is because the GDP of an economy-country is the total value of all goods and services produced by people in the geographical limits of that country. Similarly, all governmental liabilities can be settled through the proceeds of taxes imposed on the economically productive activities of people in that economy.

In economic terms, an asset is any belonging that can be sold for cash. Assets also include entities that can improve or provide access to flow of cash because these can be pledged as collateral in order to obtain a loan. Four entities – cash or deposits, stocks, bonds, and other possessions such as real estate – make up almost all the assets owned by a person, corporation, or a government.

As of the third quarter of 2012 (Q3 2012), total assets of households and non-profit organizations in the U.S. are $78.2 trillion. Wealth in the U.S. is $62 trillion, according to the Global Wealth Report by Credit Suisse. In the previous chapter, we have seen that our debt is hovering around $16 trillion, while our unfunded liabilities are to the tune of $87 trillion.

Total debt and liabilities combined become $103 trillion. If we add the obligations of local and state governments, corporations, households, and the financial sector, this figure would go up even more. With a population of around 315 million, the per capita debt comes to about

$50,793. For a family of four, their portion of the debt would be more than $200,000. That is not a small amount, and we have not even considered unfunded liabilities and other obligations.

Rewind to 2008 when the authorities were painting a rosy picture of the American economy despite the subprime bug corroding the global financial markets. Then, the total net household worth in the U.S. was around $57 trillion. Since 2003, there has been a $19.8 trillion increase in this statistic, and we were told that the debt level was not a concern as we had enough assets to bridge the shortfall.

As always, official figures do not tell more than half of the truth. There were two slightly beyond-the-obvious, related aspects not discussed, as these would have placed the entire question in a broader context and stolen the sheen out of the apparently bright economic landscape:

- **Debt is largely unrelated to economic conditions**. It either remains constant or gets worse. On the other hand, the value of assets varies with economic cycles.

- **Asset-debt mismatch widens during economic downturns** when the price of assets falls in tune with the fall in demand, as people do not have enough money to purchase assets. Such a mismatch is also due to confiscation of assets bound as collateral.

Between 2000 and 2003, the American economy was battling the effects of the crash of the dot-com bubble. This was when the net worth of households actually declined. The growth period between 2003 and 2008 was a direct consequence of the Fed's move to bring down the interest rates to as low as 1%. This launched the greatest credit and housing bubbles in history.

Around 80% of the $19.8 trillion rise in total value of assets came from a growth in financial assets, while 20% was contributed by appreciation in real estate and other tangible assets. Of the $57 trillion of total assets in 2008, 72% or $41 trillion was comprised of financial assets, while the remaining 28% was made up of tangible assets.

That $41 trillion included most of the four elements of assets we have described – cash and deposits, stocks, bonds, and other belongings *except* real estate and consumer durables. The exceptions made up $16 trillion, or the remaining 28%. Real estate constituted three-fourths – $12 trillion of this $16 trillion – a development that can be attributed to the real estate bubble fostered by low interest rates after 2003.

A marked decline in the total net assets owned by Americans was witnessed between 2000 and 2003. As mentioned, debt remains constant or increases, while the values of assets fall. Foreclosure and attachment of assets obligated as collateral also leaves people with fewer assets than before. While falling prices somewhat compensate falling wages during slowdowns, constant or increasing debt is the genuine source of misery.

Again, the assets represented by the $16 billion is comprised of real estate and consumer durables – asset classes that cannot make money unless sold. And once people start selling these types of assets, their values drop – meaning the market value of these assets will be much less than what is reported.

An example will illustrate the point. Suppose a person purchases a house for $500,000 and over a period of five years, the value of that house goes up to $1,000,000. The Fed will record this as an appreciation of $500,000. But the person does not get the surplus of $500,000 unless he sells the house.

Again if he wants to move to a similarly sized home, he will have to shell out the same $500,000 or even more, since the prices of all houses have increased. What the person can also do is borrow using his home as collateral. However, that will not free up his wealth; it only exchanges a certain fraction of that wealth for debt.

If he sells his house and moves into a smaller house, he will be able to liberate some of his wealth. This cannot be done en masse because then large homes will lose value due to lack of demand and small homes will gain value due to increased demand. The point: *statistics do not present the complete contextual picture.*

Now, let us do a bit more exploration. The household net wealth calculation **does not include** liabilities of the government. As mentioned earlier, liabilities of the government are finally repaid by the people through taxes. If this factor is taken into consideration, net household wealth would in fact become negative – remember total obligations of the government are more than $103 trillion.

So far we have considered the overall picture. **Unequal distribution of wealth** adds another problematic dimension. Those at the top own a disproportionately large amount of wealth: the top 1% owns 35% of all net household wealth and 56% of the value of all stock and the top 20% owns 85% of the total net household wealth, as well as 80% of all stock by value.

Only 15% of the wealth of this nation is owned by 80% of the populace and here, too, the distribution favors those at the top. An imbalance between the rich and the poor is the oldest and the most lethal social disorder in republics across history. Such an imbalance fosters social tension that can lead to popular and somewhat chauvinistic movements which can explode into *revolutions based on radical demands.*

Economic recovery is premised on the concept of increasing the purchasing power of people who can spend and create demand for the production of goods and services. If most of the people are at the bottom end of the economic ladder, they will save more money before they start to spend and, therefore, the economic recovery will be slower and more painful.

Another aspect of demographics is the equation related to the **baby boomers**. The term 'baby boomers' was forged in 1974 when advertisers realized the unique demands and spending power of this generation – people born between the end of the Second World War in 1945 and the late 1960s, when the economies and populations of certain countries such as the U.S. took rapid forward strides.

Most of these baby boomers are nearing retirement, and will start to withdraw from their social security accounts. When they do this, the Social Security Trust Fund will be under tremendous pressure for two reasons:

- The number of workers per retiree has dropped significantly, from 42 workers per retiree in 1935 when social security was created to a low of 2.9 at the end of 2012. This number is further expected to decline to 2.0 by the year 2030 as more and more baby boomers retire. The fund, therefore, will see fewer deposits and more withdrawals.

Entitlement programs such as these operate on the transfer of wealth from current workers to retirees. Note that the term *worker* is used in the economic sense; it refers to anyone who participates in the production, distribution, and exchange of goods and services.

- Our government has not saved much into these entitlement programs, and this will aggravate the problem. The aforementioned $87 trillion of unfunded liabilities include expenses on Social Security, Medicare, and Medicaid. Unfunded liabilities are those for which the government does not make any long standing financial arrangement.

Demographic profiles with younger populations and lesser retirees can fund entitlement programs. Beginning with the 1960s, Americans started to live longer, have fewer children, and earn salaries at lower rates than the rate at which the number of retirees increased. This has made the current demographic profile highly unsuited for entitlement programs.

Such entitlement programs invest into stocks and bonds where they can make between 8% to 10% returns per annum. With fewer and fewer funds available for investment, these programs will make lesser returns. Stock markets will suffer collateral damage as they lose an assured source of investment funds necessary for maintenance of an upbeat performance. This will further erode the returns of these entitlement programs and spark a downward spiral.

As the baby boomers find their retirement dreams slashed by shortfalls in entitlement programs, they will probably go on a selling spree. This generation is fairly wealthy and owns a lot of assets. But such sale overdrives bring down the value of assets being sold. More importantly, to whom will they sell their assets?

Debt is based on the assumption that the future should be economically better than the present. However, the future actually worsens progressively under the current financial system. This means the future generation will be in greater debt. Already, they have to pay back very high levels of college loans. Such a generation certainly cannot afford to purchase assets from the retiring baby boomers. Therefore, the next two decades will be different from the preceding ones.

Family Incomes

In June 2012, the Fed released its ***Survey of Consumer Finances.*** This report is compiled every three years and is among the most authoritative sources for exhaustive data, as well as insightful analysis on the financial status of American families.

Before we get to the specifics, it will we worthwhile to understand the difference between *average* and *mean* and *median* – all used as measures of the central tendency of data. The *mean* is determined by adding up values and dividing the sum by the number of values. The *median* is the middle value in data, with frequency distribution arranged in ascending order. In case the number of values is even, the median is the average of the middle two values.

The *average* is useful only if the values are symmetrical. For example, during the calculation of average income of a group of people, if some individuals earn too much or too little, the mean will not correctly define the central tendency. With incomes arranged in ascending order, the income at the middle position will better denote the central tendency of the group's income.

With all figures adjusted for inflation, the following trends came to light in the report for the period between 2007 and 2010:

- **Wealth and Income** findings include:
    - The median wealth of American households declined from $126,400 to $77,300, something that can be directly attributed to the decline in house prices.
    - The median income of American families declined from $49,600 to $45,800.

  Households with income in the middle 60% of the population suffered the most because they had most of their wealth in housing, whose equity dropped from $110,000 to $75,000.

Those in the middle income category were also hit the hardest by the decline in income, compared to the wealthiest and the poorest. The wealthiest hedge their fortunes in investments, while government aid cushioned the fall for the poorer sections.

- **Savings** presented a mixed picture:
  - The percentage of families that reported to have saved over the previous year declined from 56.4% to 52%.
  - The amount of savings increased, meaning a small number of families saved more.
  - Most families reported savings as a *precaution* against the economically precarious times we are living in at present, while lesser numbers of households said they were saving for retirement, down payments on mortgages, or for education.

  This partially confirms that unless most of the population has saved a sum they regard as "enough," they do not spend despite money floodgates being opened. The resultant inflation makes people save more, and the enormous income and wealth disparities ensure that most of the people always feel short of funds.

- **Debt** remains constant or even increases if not repaid *irrespective of the economic conditions* while incomes and prices fall during economic crises. Debt findings include:
  - A 2.1% decline in the number of families under debt, while 74.9% families were still under some kind of debt.
  - The percentage of families with educational loans increased from 15.25% to 19.2%, and for the first time exceeded the total debt obligations of automobile loans.
  - The number of families reporting that they did not carry credit cards increased from 27% to 32%, while the share of credit card debt declined from 46.1% to 39.4% and the median credit card balance dropped to $2,600 – a fall of

16.1%.

While falling incomes might have prevented any major decline in overall debt obligations, some people have profited from the low interest rates by refinancing mortgages with longer terms and deferring payment on education loans.

Refinancing of loans is the replacement of an older loan with a new one that charges a lower interest and offers other related benefits.

Most of the conclusions based on the findings of the Federal Reserve's report confirm suspicions voiced by the sober sections in the financial world who were not quite satisfied with the rhetoric of the authorities, remembering that it was all within control in 2008.

Monetary Explosion: The Necessary Evil

If we have to understand the current situation, we need to understand the fundamentals of the present financial structure, which has made inflation-deflation or boom-bust a part of our economic, social, and political life. Bubbles are a part of the boom time of the present economic structure based on continuous expansion of the money supply and, therefore, debt.

Charging of **interest** on a loan makes it impossible for a debtor to make a complete repayment unless the money supply expands. Suppose a person contracts a debt of $100 with 10% rate of interest per annum – he will have to pay back $110 after one year. Where will the additional $10 come from? *It comes from an expansion of money supply*. Nevertheless, the debtor has to work in order to catch hold of that $10, at least.

This brings us to the second link in the chain, a **fiat money system** in which there is no restriction on the authority of the government to print money through the central bank. Every time the government is short of funds, it orders the purchase of its bonds by the central bank, which makes that purchase with freshly printed money.

Major economies of the world were on the classical gold standard until 1913, when the amount of money in circulation in an economy was equal to the value of gold held as reserves with the central bank of that economy. Quite naturally, the government could not print money arbitrarily.

Wars are expensive and governments need to spend prodigiously in order to finance them. A pure gold standard prevents such a financing mechanism. With war clouds gathering over Europe in the early part of the last century, major European economies abandoned the classical gold standard for a more pliable gold exchange standard where the amount of money in circulation could be 2.5 times the value of gold reserves.

By doing so, the mechanism of **Fractional Reserve Banking (FRB)** was unleashed, and nearly a century later the entire world is still reeling under its effects. FRB is a system in which the reserves held at a bank are only a certain percentage of the amount of money it lends out. With a 10% reserve requirement, the total money *consisting of the deposit plus circulating money* multiplies to ten times the reserve, creating an unstable, inverted pyramid of expanding money.

When central banks adopt the same FRB model, other commercial banks that are required to maintain reserves with them create another inverted pyramid on top of the *already inverted* pyramid of the central bank money supply. An ever-expanding money supply is the result of this system.

Governments expand the amount of money in circulation for any or all of the following reasons:

- **Fighting Economic Slowdowns,** as more money with the general populace causes them to spend, thereby creating a demand for goods and services that stimulates production and brings the economy back on track.
- **Funding Social Welfare Programs** that may or may not include freebies promised during election campaigns.
- **War Finance.**
- **Increased Borrowing**, an outright cover for fiscal indiscipline on its part.

- **Maintenance** of **Bubble Economies.**

Methods adopted by governments to increase money supply include:

- **Quantitative Easing (QE)**, the direct printing of money wherein the central bank prints fresh money and purchases government bonds with it.

- **Monetary Policy** that:

  - Reduces lending interest rates and makes cheap credit easily available.

  - Decreases the reserves that commercial banks are required to maintain with the central bank, thereby releasing extra money into circulation.

- **Tax Reduction** and **Tax Holidays.**

- **Increasing Expenditures**, especially on public infrastructure projects such as roads, railroads, bridges, and dams, so extra money is available for people to stimulate production.

Inflation, however, is the trillion dollar dilemma in this money expansion process. According to the rules of supply and demand, increased supply of an entity brings down its price. An increase in the supply of money, therefore, reduces its purchasing power. Honest, naïve folks who save for their retirement or for their small dreams suddenly find themselves desperately short of cash as their savings lose value. This monetary increase is stealing, plain and simple!

Benefiting the most from money printing are those who print it – the central bank. Such printing doesn't cost much, while the banks make a fortune by lending the printed money and charging interest. *Hold on.* If you and I did this, wouldn't that be a crime, a grave crime? Isn't this money printing press, therefore, a fraud of gigantic proportions?

Those who immediately borrow this fresh money derive benefits of the second order, for they use the money before the money enters circulation, and it loses value as people realize there is too much cash floating about. It takes time for expansion and contraction of money supply to respectively cause inflation and deflation as the market slowly feels the increase or decrease and acts upon this realization.

Not to make this sound like blame shifting, but *we the people* are also a part of the problem. We ignore the common sense rule that democracies work on the pressure mechanism – as voters we can exert the right kind of pressure – informed pressure – to get our government and administrators to design and operate vibrant systems.

Instead, we demand free lunches. Politicians oblige through welfare programs that are sponsored with printed money. Yes, a portion of society does get something free, but inflation reduces the worth of the free stuff and makes that portion of society demand more freebies. Because we do not understand the issue completely, we repeat our blundering errors, and this trap is sustained forever.

In respect to FRB, money is created every time a debt is contracted and is extinguished every time the debt is repaid or when there is a foreclosure following default. This also means that every time money is created, someone goes into debt. Our government contracts debt every time its orders the Fed to purchase U.S. Treasury bonds with freshly printed money.

Debt is based on the assumption that the future will be better than the present. But such continuous printing of money, necessary for the continued functioning of the present economic system, actually ensures a continuous expansion of debt, making the future much bleaker.

Bubblenomics

As we learned from the Austrian Theory of Business Cycle, any expansion in credit loaned out by banks creates conditions for a boom-bust, an inflation-deflation supply. Credit expansion increases the money supply, and some of this money inevitably travels as excessive and speculative investments into an asset class, creating a bubble where the expectations of returns are based more on perception than on the performance of the asset class.

A bubble is when a certain asset class witnesses excessive and speculative investment to the extent that the inflation in that particular asset class rises beyond what can be sustained by incomes. Bubbles can actually be spotted; don't be taken in by the Fed's rhetoric that bubbles are impossible to detect *until they pop*, and then it is too late.

Prudence is abandoned and people flock to the bubbling asset class without verification of the credentials of companies that deal in such asset classes. Another reason people invest blindly in bubbles is that increased money supply causes inflation, eroding value from their savings. Naturally, people look toward more lucrative avenues for investment.

Needless to say, this frenzy creates an **opportunity for fraudulent companies**. Some honest companies will also find it difficult to return dividends to their shareholders to match the hyper expectations created by the bubble frenzy. And some honest companies will go bankrupt, as well.

When scandals and genuine failures come to light, or even when the returns do not match the amplified expectations of the shareholders, investors start to have second thoughts. Also, authorities may reduce monetary supply to rein in inflation. This is when the bubble starts to pop. Funds to the inflated asset class dry up and bona-fide companies go bankrupt with the cheaters.

Jobless Growth is another toxin released by bursting economic bubbles. Speculative investment creates an *impression of growth* without any real increase in the production and productivity of goods and services that create jobs. Bubbles, therefore, also mean an unfair distribution of returns because the returns from the meager growth are appropriated by speculators, not genuine workers or investors.

Next, bubbles **divert capital** from where it is more needed into asset classes that are on the rise, mainly on account of speculative investments. For example, investment into manufacturing will suffer as the real estate bubble offers apparently more lucrative returns in the short term.

Also, bubbles create conditions wherein they cannot be done away with – once a bubble gets formed, printing more money to feed it further is the only way forward, especially if the economic growth is driven by bubbles alone and not by any fundamental driver. Even minor cuts in money printing either pop the bubble or, if the bubble has already burst, take the economy on a downward, vicious spiral.

Sustained economic growth over a fairly long duration can be achieved only through increase in productivity, not through bubbles. It also enables economic recovery when things go wrong, and is more effective in a non-bubble economy. Argentina recovered from the debt crisis by improving productivity, which allowed it to increase its exports to the U.S. and China.

It is imperative to mention here that increased money supply is not inflationary if the production of goods and services grows faster than the growth of money in circulation. This happens in free capitalism conditions, as in the 1880s in the U.S. Despite monetary expansion, if people save (i.e. do not spend) as a precaution against financial uncertainty, there is no inflation, as happened during the First World War in Germany.

Money Flood and Bubbles on the Global Landscape

Six bubbles – stocks, real estate, private debt, consumer spending, dollar, and government debt – thrive in the American economy. In turn, these have pumped up the dollar and the government debt bubble. The global economy is made of multiple bubbles that are maintained by money printing by major central banks. Central banks of Japan, Taiwan, China, and Korea created $5 trillion in money between 2000 and 2008 in order to purchase dollars. This depressed their currencies in relation to the dollar and helped their exports. The dollar returns from exports were reinvested in U.S. Treasury bonds, equities, and corporate bonds, as well as mortgage financers such as Fannie Mae and Freddie Mac.

Each year the U.S. imports more than it exports, and this trade deficit made repetitive purchases of such dollar denominated assets necessary for foreign central banks. Availability of such overseas funds drove down interest rates, raised asset prices and caused misallocation of capital in the U.S. Coupled with the Fed's low interest rate, these conditions led to the buildup and bust of the *global* economic bubble in 2008.

This printed money also found its way to trade deficit economies in places like the U.K., Spain, and Greece, where it similarly promoted housing bubbles. When these popped, the Fed – along with Bank of England, European Central Bank, and the International Monetary Fund (IMF) – printed more money. With that money they purchased the depreciated assets, like real estate, from large banks in order to prevent collapse of the global financial system.

Somewhere in mid-2010, real deflation and a mini-collapse of the currency supply were observed as M3 decreased from around $14.7 trillion to just under $14 trillion. The decrease for the aggregate of M3 minus the base money was $1.7 trillion. M3 minus base money represents the money that we borrow into existence. Such a colossal collapse occurred only once in U.S. monetary history: at the very beginning of the Great Depression.

As a countermeasure, the Fed announced another round of money printing in November 2010: $600 billion to maintain the upbeat stock market. When the Fed prints money and purchases Treasury bonds with it, private investors have money available, but cannot invest it into Treasury bonds. These investors, therefore, find equities and the resultant demand provides the upward fillip to stock markets.

Americans now had more money to spend, and this stimulated imports into the U.S. with positive effects for the entire global economy. However, this was short lived, for nothing was done to increase the productivity of the American economy. Americans continued to outsource manufacturing to other economies, where cheap labor was readily available.

Starting in December 2012, the U.S. government will print $85 billion per month. Already, $40 billion per month is being printed for the purchase of mortgage backed securities. Another $45 billion will be printed every month for the purchase of Treasury securities. The Fed will also be keeping the federal funds rate – its benchmark lending rate – to near 0% to keep money flowing.

The Fed's balance sheet will be extended to $4 trillion by the end of 2014 from the present $2.9 trillion, and this policy will continue until unemployment levels fall below 6.5%, provided inflation stays below 2%. Shortly afterward, similar announcements were made by the central banks of Europe, Australia, and Japan, confirming the necessities of a global bubble economy.

One of the stated aims of this latest round of QE is to stimulate growth and employment in housing. However, the opening of the money floodgates will only further inflate the housing bubble. Extremely low interest rates in the aftermath of the crash of the dot-com bubble in 2000 were aimed at stimulation of the economy, but ended up fostering another bubble – the housing bubble – that crashed between 2007 and 2008.

We know than an economic crisis usually follows low real interest rates, such as the Latin American debt crisis of early 1980s, the 1997 Asian debt and bubble Crisis, and the housing boom and bust in Ireland, Spain, Portugal, and Greece.

It is widely whispered that once every two months, chiefs of the world's top central banks meet in Basel, Switzerland, to discuss plans of pumping billions into the global economy to fight the slowdown. This elite section represents a total GDP of $51 trillion. Since 2007, these banks have created over $11 trillion and plan to continue this injection into mortgages, government bonds, and business loans.

Such a move by central bankers to bypass their political masters, who have failed to address the situation through fiscal policy – like how to balance tax revenues and spending during economic slowdowns – is outrageous. These bankers form an informal network with links forged during their university days. They are heavily influenced by academic works produced at the Massachusetts Institute of Technology in the 1970s and 1980s.

Or worse – have our governments outsourced their responsibility and abandoned our fate to bankers who, with respect, are bureaucrats or technocrats who do not fully comprehend the human element involved with all this?

As participants in this economy, we can only hope they get it right and pull the global economy out of stagnation, preventing a repeat of the central banking errors of the 1930s. Otherwise, it will produce unprecedentedly high inflation and trigger another financial crisis as the mother of all bubbles explodes violently. And with every round of inflationary money printing, the possibility of a golden medium path recedes.

Because the disease is left unaddressed and only the symptoms are treated, such printing has to be repeatedly undertaken.

Compulsions of a bubble economy ensure the Fed and other central banks cannot stop monetary expansion, for the bubble will collapse immediately. However, all bubbles burst and more violently so if artificially prolonged. Shaky foundations create 'symptom-treatment mechanisms' that can offer piecemeal solutions, at best.

Historic Bubble Follies

One thing common across all eras in history is human folly inspired by hope, greed, or simply by the lust for quick and easy money. And because we refuse to learn from history, we are perpetually condemned to repeat it. A glimpse at the economic history of bubbles in the world doesn't reveal anything different.

In the 1600s, a tulip bubble started in Holland after stunningly attractive tulip coloration varieties were developed and were in great demand. Semper Augustus was the most sought after tulip, and at the height of the speculative madness, a single bulb of this breed fetched the same price as a plush house would cost in the finest neighborhood.

By 1637, it had slowly sunk in that tulips were flowers that could be grown anywhere with some determined effort. The tulip bubble popped on the first day of the selling season in February 1637, when prices crashed.

Another example comes from England from around 1720. The South Sea Company was a fairly ordinary company that made normal profits. It was granted a monopoly for trade with South America, in accordance with a pact with Spain. Stock markets operate more on sentiment than on anything else. The grant of monopoly caused its stock to surge and there developed the 'South Sea Bubble.'

No one bothered to check the monopoly charter that described the company as '*a company for carrying out an undertaking of great advantage, but nobody to know that it is.*' And, hold your breath, the great Sir Isaac Newton lost over 20,000 pounds when that bubble collapsed. One of the greatest brains in history was beaten by a speculative madness.

Intellectual capacity does not guarantee returns from bubble investments, for they are driven by primal instincts of hope, fear, and the greed for the quick and easy buck; logic, wisdom, and even a modicum of caution are thrown to the wind.

Certain common characteristics of bubbles are apparent from a detailed study of multiple bubbles:

- Bubbles reinforce themselves on the way up, when the high price commanded by them becomes a justification for a still higher price, thereby creating upwardly spiraling prices.
- On their way down, the reverse is true, and low prices become a justification for even lower prices; this produces the downward spiral.
- Bubbles exhibit *time symmetry*, when the duration required by them to reach the highest point during appreciation is roughly the same as it takes for them to reach the lowest point after the burst.
- Price symmetry is maintained by bubbles – their price before the ascent is around the lowest price after the collapse, with a slight tendency to overshoot during decline, when their lowest price in the aftermath of the collapse usually goes below the price before the ascent of the bubble began.

These features of bubbles can also be observed across an entire cross section of financial systems, asset classes, and eras. The commonality simply means that at the fundamental animalistic level, humans think similarly in all ages. They get swept away by ideas of making easy money at the drop of the hat, and when things don't go as expected, they lose faith all too easily.

Repetitive bubbles mean that humans do not usually learn from their own errors, let alone develop wisdom from other people's follies. Maybe because they want their investment to succeed so much, and maybe because they are too proud to acknowledge their prior blunders, they form a mental illusion of, "*Well, this time it's different.*"

Because these features are identical in almost all bubbles, such price fluctuations can be used as a starting guideline for detection of an emerging bubble. The early stages of a bubble, when suspected unsustainable appreciation is witnessed, are critical, for this is when bubbles can be nipped in the bud through targeted reduction of credit towards that asset class. Agreed, bubble detection is difficult, but it certainly is not impossible.

Another bubble is under construction in the housing sector. And the 'this time it's different' syndrome has taken so much control of investors that they have forgiven and forgotten the housing bubble collapse of 2007, which is not even ten years old. Most importantly, the fact that this collapse triggered the current global economic crisis seems to have been wiped out of their minds.

It's all quite strange. It looks like Darwin's Theory of Evolution is taking its toll on the educated, tech-savvy investors who seem to have outsourced their thinking and memory processes to computers and, in the process, have forgotten to do so themselves (all puns intended).

During the previous housing crisis, investors and consumers behaved in an insane manner. Homeowners sought to profit from their rising priced homes by borrowing with those homes as collateral. The proceeds of such loans were used by many to purchase unnecessary items that depreciate in cost over time, such as TVs and other consumer goods.

It was the availability of cheap credit, a result of the Fed slashing interest rates to stimulate the economy in the aftermath of the dot-com bubble crash that created the housing bubbles of the last decade. The present QE is specifically directed towards housing and will cause history to repeat itself, sooner or later.

In the long term, housing prices always depend on the cost of the material required for building and construction, and housing prices have roughly proceeded along the cost of construction after neutralization of the effects of inflation. Between 1890 and 1998, housing prices averaged 101.2, with 100 being the inflation-adjusted line for construction cost.

Of special interest are the bursting bubbles in the 1970s and 1980s. One, they are a recent example that will rekindle some memories. Two, they give us a rough idea of the time and price symmetry of bubbles and allows us to guesstimate the timing of the collapse of the present bubble and the approximate price of housing at that time.

If we can make such an analysis, why can't the Fed do the same? After all, it has an entire army of financial experts. The warning signs were there way before 2007, when the previous housing bubble popped. Again, we arrive at the inevitability of money printing in a bubble economy. The Fed ignored the symptoms because that was the only course available to it.

As considerate individuals, we can understand the Fed's dilemma. What cannot be ignored, however, is that the Fed published reports that justified the bubble. A 2004 Fed study titled '*Are Home Prices the Next Bubble?*' attributed the rising home prices since mid-1990s to strong economic fundamentals, an increase in family incomes, and low mortgage rates.

Now, it is widely known that the real growth in the average income of Americans is merely income appreciation after negating the rise due to inflation, which has been almost nil between 2000 and 2008. This has been a principal failure of our economic policy. So much for the perception manipulation exercises by the authorities.

Time and price symmetry suggest that housing prices will hit bottom around the year 2015, while prices will decline to approximately 34% of the prices in 2008. Considering the tendency of falling prices to overshoot and fall below the price of the asset class before the bubble started to rise, this fall in price may go down to between 40% and 50% of 2008 housing prices.

It should be remembered that we as a people and as a nation have become reckless spenders. Since 1985, it seems that we have strayed from the conservative habit of saving. This places all the bubbles since 1985 in the proper context, in the debt bubble. Easy credit coupled with the disappearance of the saving habit and the tendency for making a quick buck, has resulted in the creation of bubbles and taken our debt to unprecedentedly high levels.

During the 1979 and 1989 housing boom-bust cycle, the median incomes of people did not deviate much from the price of houses before the bubble ascent began. This prevented the aftermath of the collapse from being too painful. This time the deviation is more. The only way the 'this time it's different' syndrome will apply to the present housing bubble is that the collapse will be more painful than ever before.

Bubbles divert funds from those sectors or asset classes where they are more needed to those that already possess surplus finance. This creates a glut, and in this case more-than-necessary-constructions that cannot be completed or do not find buyers once the bubble collapses.

Funds invested in such construction projects even by honest construction companies will be locked in, and these companies will face foreclosure and bankruptcy. People employed by them will face wage cuts, or even worse, unemployment. Everything else financed by cheap credit – like stocks and low quality bonds – will also similarly collapse. As incomes drop and debt does not, foreclosures begin and these are the causes of the real human tragedy during slowdowns.

Considering the stated objectives of the latest round of QE and lowered interest rates – coupled with the imitation of this measure across the globe – one doesn't have to be Einstein to figure out that we are in the midst of the greatest bubble age. In a world where globalization has established two-way links between different regions of the world, a collapse of one bubble will produce a chain reaction and deflate the other bubbles.

Deflation-Inflation Cyclical Combination Scenario is the most likely outcome, as the current threat of deflation is being countered with a monetary flood that will cause larger inflation. Interest rates will be increased to control inflation, but such depressants are useless in a bubble economy. Another round of money printing will follow and lead to hyperinflation.

Whenever there is an expansion of money supply, values of gold and silver rise. This enhances the value of gold reserves with the Fed that becomes equal to the amount of money in circulation, as happened in 1934 and 1981. Such a balancing has always taken place, since 407 BC when the first grade inflation in Athens was recorded.

Naturally, the same will be repeated. This is how free markets and the will of the public impose themselves over manipulations by the authorities. You can benefit by moving your wealth into gold and silver, starting now.

Previously, a bubble was witnessed once in a generation, as the painful experience of one burst took some time to evaporate from public memory. In a space of seven to eight years we have witnessed the crash of two bubbles – in both the dot-com industry and the real estate market. The latter is still being fattened through QE and lowered interest rates.

This is where the inevitability of printing money for bubble maintenance in a bubble economy comes into play. The toxic effects of a bubble collapse are known to all. Yet the Fed and major central banks continue to feed the global, multi-bubble economy, for there is no other way to deal with the situation.

Bubblenomics

We live in a world where the foundations of the global economy are unstable. Such a shaky state of affairs makes us prone to recurring economy-wide problems that the authorities deal with through half measures, the only course of action available to them under the current financial system.

Chief culprits of this system are fiat money, FRB, and interest charged on loans. These ensure that the money supply expands continuously and erodes the purchasing power of the existing stock of money. Under FRB, debt and money are twins that are born together, and such monetary expansion also expands debt on a perpetual basis.

Debt is contracted on the assumption of an economically brighter future, but monetary expansion ensures just the opposite. Debt, therefore, can never be completely repaid under our present financial system – a system that has to progressively expand debt or face the horrendous effects of a collapse.

Again, while incomes and prices fall during economic slowdowns, debt retains its independence from the general economic condition – it either appreciates or remains constant unless repaid. This feature of debt results in foreclosures and is the real human face of economic disasters when people lose the things that make up their world.

As global citizens, we dig a hole for ourselves through excessive spending and sparse saving. The materialist-consumerist lifestyles adopted by us make us embark on a path of consumption that robs us of the financial buffer in hard times, prevents an accumulation of capital that can be put to productive use, and degrades the environment.

Assets are a reasonable way to hedge against economic downturns, but assets are subject to price fluctuations. During slowdowns there are not enough buyers and sellers in the market, and the result is a collapse in asset prices. What this also means is unless sold, assets are not very useful. Yes, they can be used as collateral, but that makes only limited funds available. Again, falling asset prices will facilitate only smaller loan amounts.

Demographic realities will further add to the woes of the situation in the near future. The baby boomers are retiring and there are not enough workers in the economy to replace them. Withdrawals from the Social Security Trust Fund are much greater than deposits, and a time will come when the fund goes bankrupt as it is unable to invest and make returns simply because there are *no funds available* to invest.

Continuously burgeoning the money supply makes money available not only for productive purposes, but also for speculative investments. This creates bubbles – unsustainably rising prices in certain asset classes.

A *financial tumor* would be a more appropriate description for a bubble, since it corrodes the economy from within. Among its cancerous effects is an illusion of growth bereft of growth in employment and parasitic in appropriation of investment funds from other asset classes that have a greater need for such capital.

Worst of all, once a bubble is formed, it cannot be done away with, especially if the economy is not based on a fundamental driver of growth such as productivity augmentation. Money supply has to be continuously increased to feed the bubble, otherwise the economy goes into a slowdown. But such money printing only postpones the inevitable bubble pop and makes the eventual explosion more painful. The bubble and debt trap is complete.

Judgment Day of the global financial system is not far away. When it does arrive, common people will be the greatest losers. We deserve a part of the blame for living in a fool's paradise and allowing the authorities to hoodwink us into believing the merits of the financial mechanism and the benevolence of our governments.

Across all ages, precious metals such as gold and silver always surge upward when the swelling money streams erode value out of existing cash and savings. Bursting bubbles make investors lose confidence in most other asset classes, turning to precious metals that again witness a northward revision in their prices. On Judgment Day, you will be better off with wealth comprised of gold and silver. Nothing else will have the same value.

Ever since humans developed a sense of ownership that matured into the concept of private property, man has wanted to own more and more. Today, wealth can be in various forms – cash, deposits, land, gold, stocks, silver, and other miscellaneous possessions. Cash, at present, seems to be floating everywhere. Yet, as a society and as individuals, we don't seem to have enough for our needs.

Why? Have money supplies increased to such an extent that they no longer have the value they once had? Why is it that we always want to own more? Why is it necessary for central banks to print money around the clock? How do they precisely increase money supply? Is all of this sustainable? And, most importantly, what does the future hold for us?

Booms that expand into bubbles and then bust into economic slowdowns are integral parts of the present day fiat money regime of the economic world. Today's global economy is a multi-bubble economy being fed and fattened by the inflationary printing of money, with the latest instance (as of December 2012) being the $85 billion a month printed by the Federal Reserve.

Realities of a globalized world cannot be wished away, and the announcement by the Fed that more money was to be printed was followed by similar announcements by other important central banks around the world. In a world increasingly connected through trade links, the explosion of bubbles in one economy will bust similar and somewhat related bubbles in connected economies.

Economies of developing countries that depend on exports to the U.S., Europe, and Japan will suffer the most as the demand for their products and raw materials fall. Depreciating currencies of the developed world will make it increasingly difficult for them to import from the developing economies.

Gold, however, will appreciate as currencies fall in comparison to it and also because it has been the 'investment of last resort' for mankind for ages. During financial crises, wealth is not destroyed, but transferred. All that needs to be done is to find the undervalued asset classes and invest in them. As of now, gold *is* that undervalued asset class.

The Inevitable Boom-Bust Cycles in a Fiat Money Regime

In the economic context, a *bubble* exists when the market price of a freely exchanged asset class rises and falls rapidly at a rate that is not related to the expected rate of growth of income that can be realized from ownership or holding of the said asset. To put it simply, the said asset class is overvalued.

Prices of an asset class rise for numerous reasons. The most important cause is the expectation of increased income from holding the asset. For example, stock prices of companies engaged in the software business can go up if most of these companies make profits and announce increased dividends.

A similar appreciation can be expected if technological breakthroughs promise to make the functioning of such companies more efficient or if the government is set to make favorable policy interventions. These are only some instances, since stock prices can also raise due to an infinite number of reasons.

Expectation is the keyword here. All increases in asset prices are not based on concrete factors. Asset prices can also rise if the market sentiment expects such appreciation. Such sentiment may not be based on concrete facts, and perception based on intuition can also play a role.

When the role of perception is greater than that of concrete factors, asset prices rise and fall for largely abstract reasons. People who invest money based more on perception than fact are usually known as speculators. Excessive and speculative investment into an asset class or asset classes contributes to causing bubbles.

However, perception is only one factor encouraging bubbles. Availability of money makes it possible for speculators to act on the basis of such perceptions. When the economy is doing well, money is available for genuine as well as speculative investment.

Conversely, when the economy is not doing well, central banks loosen money supplies to facilitate investment. This also increases disposable money for people who can make purchases that stimulate production of goods and services and bring the economy back on track.

Under a fiat money regime, where money supply is elastic – where it can be increased or decreased – economic booms and busts form a cyclic process. Central banks can increase money supply by decreasing the rates at which they lend to commercial banks. These banks then decrease their lending rates, and credit becomes freely available. The reverse is done to decrease money supply.

The sale and purchase of government securities in the open market respectively decreases and increases the money in circulation. When the government wants money, it simply issues bonds that are purchased by large banks from freshly printed money by the Treasury.

As any increase in the supply of an entity decreases its value, the increase in money supply decreases the purchasing power of money. In simple terms, this is called inflation or price rise. Availability of money makes it possible for people to invest as well as to speculate, and can create bubbles in certain asset classes that are expected to fetch returns.

Bubbles encourage fraudulent activities by fake companies and fake investment managers. Banks have to cut down the money supplies in order to rein in the raging bubbles. Some honest businesses will also slow down due to various professional reasons, causing drops in profits and dividends.

When people do not get their expected returns or when fraudulent activity is exposed, people lose their confidence in that asset class, and the market sentiment turns negative – the bubble turns into a bust and the asset class moves from being overvalued to being undervalued.

Bankruptcies, defaults, unemployment, and falling prices result from the bursting bubble. During booms, manufacturers produce more goods in expectation of higher sales as people have money to make purchases. Economic slowdown converts this foresight into a nightmare as excessive production decreases its price.

Apart from banks cutting down money supplies, a contraction in money supply results from defaults and foreclosures. Under a fractional reserve banking system, money is created when a loan is issued and money is extinguished when the loan is repaid. Foreclosures are loosely equivalent to a repayment, although less productive.

In order to bring the economy back on track and stimulate the production of goods and services, central banks pump money into the economy. Again, the availability of money encourages bubbles, and the whole cycle repeats.

Quantitative Easing Unlimited

Quantitative Easing (QE) is the introduction of freshly printed money in an economy by the central bank of that economy. Presently (as of December 2012), freshly printed money in the U.S. will be used by banks for the purchase of Treasury bonds and of securities backed by mortgages.

The U.S. economy is showing signs of a slowdown in the last months of 2012 as observed from the following indicators:

- **Confidence Index** of the University of Michigan fell from 82.7 to 74.5.
- **Index of Manufacturing Activity** of the Institute for Supply Management (ISM) fell to 49.5, the lowest since July 2009.

On Wednesday, December 14, 2012, the Fed announced a major expansion in its bond buying program that has been on since

September – it's planning to purchase $45 billion treasury securities per month in addition to the $40 billion in mortgage-backed securities that it is already purchasing every month.

By the end of 2014, this move will expand the Fed's balance sheet to $4 trillion from the present $2.9 trillion. This announcement of the Fed was followed by announcements toward similar ends by central banks of Europe, Japan, and Australia.

Apart from this, the federal funds rate – a benchmark lending rate for the Fed – will be at or near the zero level just as long as unemployment hovers around 6.5% and inflation does not cross the threshold of 2.5%. Effectively, this means a linkage between unemployment and the primary lending rate for the first time. Problems inherent with this approach include:

- It is widely believed that U.S. corporations are sitting on top of hoards of cash – $5 trillion of it. Banks and corporations are not putting the extra cash available from quantitative easing and near-zero interest rates into productive investment that could eventually create jobs, and are instead hoarding it or using it for speculation, which creates bubbles.

- Unemployment is expected to continue at the 6.5% level for about three years, meaning that the extra money printed for the purchase of these bonds and mortgage-backed securities can create another bubble, the bursting of which will prove disastrous in present conditions.

- **Participation Rate Contradiction**: Participation rate is that percentage of eligible workers who actually participate in the labor force. An error is introduced in the calculation of the unemployment rate because of this contradiction.

  Participation rate decreases as economies slow down and increases when economies are expected to do well. It also increases and decreases respectively with the increase and decrease in the unemployment rate.

  With economic slowdowns, some people simply give up looking for work, thereby decreasing the participation rate.

The reverse happens when the economy starts to do well. Since unemployment rates increase and decrease respectively with economic slowdowns and upswings, participation rate has a direct relation with the unemployment rate. This means that if and when the monetary policy does increase employment opportunities, the unemployment rate will still remain high as participation rate increases in view of the cynics rejoining the workforce. Therefore, the addition of $85 billion per month to the current economy – through quantitative easing – will continue for quite some time.

Before the crisis, the participation rate was 66.5%. After the crisis, it was 63.6% – a drop of 2.9% – roughly around four million people. To accommodate these four million, 150,000 jobs will have to be created every month. The minimum required time for this is between three to four years, assuming a rapid economic recovery.

In the meantime, the Fed will have to create an extra $3 to $4 trillion. In 2013 itself, the money created will be three to four times the money created since the Declaration of Independence.

- One of the stated aims of these monetary expansions is to reduce the interest rate on mortgages, thereby encouraging purchase and investment in the housing sector that will stimulate residential home building and create jobs.

- Growth, on numerous occasions, can be jobless. Furthermore, excessive availability of money can encourage another housing bubble of the type that exploded in 2007 and the effects of which are still being felt.

Results produced by these measures did not match the expectations. Stocks climbed initially, but then stopped rising and even declined. During this brief period, gold, silver and other commodities did not appreciate because the dollar did not fall. And the dollar did not fall because someone mysteriously sold off tons and tons of gold, something that cannot go on forever.

What is disturbing is that the entities responsible for the present crisis – banks and corporations – are being given special privileges to rectify the situation. This is similar to appointing former poachers as game keepers.

These financial poachers continue to be predators and yet are being appeased through favorable monetary policy, fiscal stimulus, and direct bail outs – something that has maintained corporate profits and partially maintained the stock market bubble.

While everything is being made available for the upper classes – extra cash is even being printed to pamper them – the masses are being deprived of welfare benefits under the pretext of lack of funds. Budget for social programs, government health care, and retirement benefits are being slashed relentlessly.

How Will Bursting Bubbles Impact the World?

Economic hardships on a global scale are inevitable as the dollar rate of debasement increases and the dollar eventually collapses. Some regions will, however, perform better than others due to the inherent realities of international trade and the strength or the weaknesses of economies. Those economies that rely on exports of manufactured goods and raw materials will be most affected as demand from the U.S. falls.

The U.S. economy will be least affected by the busting of multiple bubbles and by the aftershock. The U.S. will cut down on imports in view of the galloping hike in the price of imports as the dollar depreciates. This is the international market's mechanism of balancing the trade imbalance, and car and oil imports will fall drastically.

Europe and Japan will be the second least affected regions as they are second least reliant on exports after the U.S. These countries will impose protective tariffs and provide protective subsidies for their manufacturers. This will decrease imports from other countries and add to the downward spiral of international trade. Food and energy imports will continue into Europe and Japan more than in the U.S.

Unemployment, stocks and real estate will do badly. Welfare schemes and generous benefits and paychecks for labor will come down. However, unlike the U.S., Japan and Europe will not default heavily on their debt for three reasons:

- The euro and yen will not decline dramatically because their value is not being maintained by excessive foreign investments, as is the case with the dollar. Lesser decline means lesser deficits and, therefore, lower defaults.

- Decline of the dollar will cause investments to shift from the U.S. to Europe, thereby making capital available to European economies for productive investment.

- Investors in European bonds will lobby hard with European governments for restraining debt, as it can lead to bankruptcy that will render their investments unproductive.

China has made rapid strides through ever-increasing exports of manufactured products and raw materials to the U.S. This is a consequence of the increased demand for such goods on account of the multiple bubbles in the American economy. As the American bubbles explode, exports by China will be hit and its manufacturers will face a hefty slowdown.

China has also been preventing the fall of the dollar by purchasing the American currency with its yen in the foreign exchange market. This has resulted in vast reserves of dollars. As the dollar loses value, these reserves will move towards the value of simple paper.

China has pumped huge amounts of money into its economy. In the first quarter of 2009, her banks loaned $640 billion, compared to a maximum of $30 billion a month the U.S. is spending on its stimulus package for the construction industry in the second quarter of 2009 for QE 1. All this money has created multiple bubbles in the economy.

Chinese bubbles in real estate, banking, and stocks will bust, and construction and affiliated industries will witness rapid reversals. Printing inflationary money to rectify the situation won't prove very useful because Chinese citizens, unlike Americans, are not used to prosperity and will cut down to a low demand lifestyle when their economy goes into the doldrums.

When these bubbles burst in a chain reaction, the economic instability will, as has always been observed, create political instability and demands for political reforms and changes. Tiananmen Square II – when it happens – will enlist greater popular support and the authorities will be hard pressed to control it this time around.

The Middle East will end up in a situation similar to the Chinese, except Israel will deal with the situation like Europe and Japan. Slowdown of global economies will reduce demand for oil. Cutting production will take years as the oil production apparatus has its own inertia and associated economics and politics.

Apart from supplies being greater than demand, the falling dollar will make oil more expensive to import for the U.S., the chief oil guzzler in the international market. Oil prices will, therefore, fall to around $20 per barrel. Falling income will be devastating, as these countries are already poor in relation to the U.S., Europe, or Japan.

Political turmoil is already a reality on the Arab streets. Similar to the buildup in China, political turbulence – especially under the monarchical rule of Saudi Arabia – is already simmering with discontent. Syria and Egypt won't be too far behind.

Energy drives our economies. Most of our current energy needs are derived from polluting fossil fuels. Despite the urgency regarding global warming, **green technology** will suffer a setback as investments dry up; when markets decline, good and bad investments suffer alike.

Adding to the woes of the environment will be a reduction in government subsidies for green technology, which is essential for its development. As governments struggle to find funds to address their short term priorities that can be politically important, such subsidies will be put on the back burner.

Newer, largely unproven technologies require subsidies because any research and development process is full of trials and errors – funds are required to take care of the errors. Also, practical deployment of the technology is a costly process that again requires funds in the form of subsidies and aid assistance.

However, the world will slowly climb up this slippery and treacherous financial slope and witness huge investments in green technology as the devastating economic and human cost of using fossil fuels makes its presence felt. It would be much more economical to use greener technologies that nip pollution in the bud.

By this time, the efficiency and cost viability of clean technologies will also be demonstrated. Initially there will be a strong thrust towards coal power plants with carbon sequestration, where carbon emissions from these plants are captured. This is the best green technology option in the middle term, considering the economics of new technologies. Eventually, solar power plants are expected to become the largest source of clean energy.

Busted Bubbles and the Dollar

Contrary to popular misconceptions, the fact that the U.S. economy will be the least hit by the **busting of the world's bubble economies will not be good for the dollar.** The exchange rate between currencies is not entirely a reflection of the relative performance of the economies – it primarily depends on the simple rule of supply and demand.

Demand for the dollar comes from:

- **Liquidity Supply**: The U.S. has been supplying liquidity to global markets since at least 1952. It sells safe liquid debt assets such as Treasury bonds, and invests into risky assets that have longer maturity periods, such as equity and direct investment.

  This explains why the dollar is the reserve currency of the world and why U.S. debt instruments are regarded as safe. During the panic that followed the collapse of leading investment banks in early 2008, the demand for U.S. Treasury bonds increased because they were the only investment avenue regarded as safe enough.

- **Investments into American Assets** requiring conversion of currencies into dollars, which creates a demand for dollars.

Busting bubbles in the American economy will hurt investor sentiments as they stop getting the huge returns on their investments they have become accustomed to receiving. They will then start to sell their dollar denominated assets and seek safer and more productive investment avenues, mostly in Europe. Initially, investors will merely stop buying dollar denominated assets, followed by sustained sale and finally followed by panic sale.

But because the U.S. provides liquidity to the global markets, because it is the largest economy in the world that is also much diversified, and because of the sheer volume of its imports and exports, the dollar will continue to be among the most widely traded currencies in the world.

Gold Appreciates as Bubbles Bust and Currencies Collapse

Collapsing multi-bubbles in the global economy will be good for gold as it appreciates in comparison to falling values of global currencies. Apart from economic reasons, gold is a much favored item in many cultures around the world, especially in Asia and the Middle East. India purchases about 20% of the world's gold, compared to the U.S., which purchases only 10% of the total – the same as is done by an economic minnow, such as the country of Turkey.

A *gold bubble*, therefore, will be a natural consequence of these developments. This bubble, too, will eventually bust. However, before that happens, it will present huge wealth creation opportunities for the intellectual, proactive, decisive investor. This is precisely the undervalued asset class that was referred to in the earlier part of the chapter.

The decline of the dollar and the rise of gold is inevitable as mountains of dollars are printed. The covert sales of gold to maintain the value of the dollar cannot go on forever because the gold reserves in the world are finite. Right now, gold is the undervalued class. The billion dollar question is: *Are you ready to take the informed plunge*?

Chapter 4 – Inflation and Debasement

"A system of capitalism presumes sound money, not fiat money manipulated by a central bank. Capitalism cherishes voluntary contracts and interest rates that are determined by savings, not credit creation by a central bank."

- Dr. Ron Paul, U.S. Congressman and Former Presidential Candidate

Economic bubbles are a dead giveaway of an upcoming long term financial disaster. If an economy lacks the fundamental driver of growth – productivity augmentation – a bubble becomes the only option for economic growth. Once a bubble is created in such an economy, it has to be fed and fattened through continuous expansion of money supply. Any measures to the contrary slide the economy along a vicious downward spiral.

Fiat money regimes come with inherent boom and burst cycles. This is the same as the inflation-deflation cycle, during which bubbles are formed and burst. Unfortunately, major central banks across the world are pumping trillions into the global economy to maintain the present bubble economy on a global scale. *Make no mistake, we are living in the ultimate "bubble" age.*

All blame cannot be placed with the authorities, though. Collective ineptitude of the people and their excessive dependence on government allowed the latter to spread its tentacles into the economic sphere and, thereby, insert its control over our very livelihoods. It seems we have yet to get over the medieval habit that every miniscule collective question was placed for adjudication with feudal lords.

Financial storms do not destroy wealth, they merely transfer it. Prices are temporary; value is permanent. Inhabitants on snowcapped, windy mountains dwell on the non-windy side of the mountain. Similarly, savvy investors peg their fortunes with those asset classes that not only weather the financial storm, but actually appreciate. When the going gets tough, the tough get going.

Such asset classes are undervalued before the turbulence hits the economy and then later grow during tumultuous times. As of now, these tough asset classes are physical gold and silver. Instead of blindly believing in the authorities and expecting the government to rescue us when the financial bubble pops, we can make our own destiny through informed investment decisions.

Approaching Global Economic Storm

Great events do not arrive unannounced – they can be sensed months, if not years, before they actually take place. Doomsday prophets would have the world believe of the apparent connection between one destructive event and another, although the two are a result of separate agents at work.

Will it, therefore, be worth investigating if the world is headed for chaos? And, is there some rationale in the Mayan prophecy even if they have missed the timing of our planet's appointment with doom (*no pun intended*)?

When Hurricane Sandy hit the Caribbean, Mid Atlantic, and Northeastern United States in late October 2012, it left behind at least 253 dead and losses worth $65.6 billion across several countries. Economically, it was the second-most devastating storm after the infamous Hurricane Katrina. Over $63 billion in losses were suffered by the U.S. alone.

Heavy rains, turbulent winds, and furious floods killed people, destroyed homes, snapped water and power supplies, drowned standing crops, fell trees, and caused shortages of essential commodities. The Appalachian Mountains saw the rain turn to snow, adding to the woes of the relief efforts.

Increased strength of hurricanes in recent years is being attributed to global warming. Temperature of the sea surface has to be a minimum 26^0C for a tropical storm to form over it. While it may be that global warming is not causing them directly, the environmental issues are certainly catalyzing the process of their formation.

It's a pity that investments into green technologies will most likely decline in the immediate aftermath of the dollar collapse, as funds available for investment decline drastically and good investments suffer with the not-so-good and the outright bad.

But if we think the worst is behind us, we are wrong. Agreed, global warming is a potent threat that can drown half the world and dry out the remaining half. Lurking behind the present financial crisis is an economic storm of epic proportions that, when it strikes, will make Hurricane Sandy look like a pleasant sea breeze.

A Honey Trap Named *Bubble*

In the simplest of terms, a bubble is the appreciation of the price of an asset class that is based more on the *perception of growth* of that asset class rather than its *actual performance*. When authorities increase the money supply, banks make credit easily available. This results in excessive borrowing, spending, and investment.

Not all investments are directed towards safe avenues. Declining purchasing power of money is one of the important reasons why people seek high-returns, risky investments – people's savings lose value with inflation. Such excessive and speculative investment is a bubble that further fuels inflation.

Once a bubble has been created in an economy, printing more money to help it continue becomes inevitable. If the economic growth is driven by bubbles alone, and not by any fundamental driver, any cut in money supply either pops the bubble or, if the bubble has already burst, slides the economy in a vicious downward path.

All bubbles pop – painfully. The catalyst to such a bursting comes when money supply into the bubble dries up. This can be the result of deliberate monetary contraction by government through monetary policy. Bubbles encourage fake companies and when those companies are unearthed the scams cause investors to lose confidence – a contraction follows.

It must also be remembered that increased money supply cannot be inflationary if the production of goods and services grows faster than the growth of money in circulation. This happens in free capitalism conditions, and did happen in the U.S. in the 1880s. The same can happen if uncertainty prevents people from spending, as happened in Germany during the First World War.

Bubbles are also harmful because they cause **jobless growth**. Speculation creates an impression of growth without any substantial increase in the production of goods and services. It is this increase in production and productivity that creates jobs. Bubbles, therefore, also mean an unfair distribution of returns.

Ultimately, **productivity increase is the only long term solution for real economic growth**. It enables economic recovery and is more effective in a non-bubble economy. Argentina recovered from their debt crisis by increasing exports to the U.S. and China – two countries that were doing well. Argentina's export augmentation was based on productivity improvement.

At present, there are four main bubbles in the American economy: stocks, real estate, private debt, and discretionary spending. When these burst, the dollar bubble and the government debt bubbles will explode in an uncontrolled chain reaction and create an economic storm that will destroy livelihoods and cause calamitous hardships.

In a globalized world where economies are increasingly connected, this would mean similar consequences for other economies. And because the world today is a multi-bubble economy, the popping of one distant bubble will pop all the other connected bubbles.

Global Money Printers

Declining productivity and a multi-bubble economy is the source of mounting debt that is being increasingly financed by printing money that, in turn, is fostering these bubbles. Price rise is only a symptom of inflation. Actually, inflation is the depreciation in the purchasing power of the currency due to the presence of too much money, as compared to the amount of goods and services in the market. When the demand for goods and services exceeds the supply, a rise in prices occurs.

Inflation can cause political consequences as people find it more and more difficult to go about their lives. Central banks, therefore, raise lending rates to dry up the money supplies. With less funds available for investment, and especially for speculation, the bubbles will burst.

Foreign investors will lose interest in American investments and Treasury bonds, causing the dollar and government debt bubbles to collapse.

Inflation is a more potent culprit than it appears. What makes it most lethal is that it is not regarded as an evil, but has been accepted as a part of our lives. Many cheerleader economists even promote inflation as a necessary driver for the economy. It isn't true: even without continuous inflation, we saw economic development between 1665 and 1940.

Continuous depreciation of the purchasing power of money makes people work harder; now both parents have to work, when one breadwinner used to be more than enough. Worse still, it makes people invest in risky ventures that may, in turn, be used to feed bubbles that cause further inflation. Such effects change the very ethos of society and are at the root of many socio-economic ills.

Since 2008, central banks around the world have been pumping hordes of money into circulation because this is the easiest way to solve all financial problems except inflation. These include the Federal Reserve (Fed), the European Central Bank, the Bank of England, and central banks in Japan and China.

Printing money enables governments to:

- Borrow more.
- Boost economic activity as increased availability of money causes people to spend which creates demand for production of goods and services.
- Bring about a semblance of order in disturbed stock and bond markets.

Although the boosting effects of printing are not very conspicuous because the present global economic growth is very slow, this expansion of money supply is calming down financial markets around the world, as money is available for investments. Meltdown of financial markets adversely affects that economy and, in an economically connected world, the entire global economy.

It seems the Fed has completely forgotten its 'exit strategy' for mopping up excess liquidity, something that was much talked about in mid-2011. The Fed, however, is in good company, and this frenzied printing of money is fostering the global bubble economy. Increased money supplies in Europe usually find their way into dollar denominated American assets and ease the printing pressure on the Fed.

Because money printing presses keep the stock markets afloat and attract investment, they generate demands for dollars and maintain the dollar bubble. It also has been encouraging dependence on foreign funds that inflates the government debt bubble and makes us neglect soaring deficits.

Lag factors are the reason inflation does not immediately follow money expansion. It takes time for the extra money in circulation to lose its value as people start spending, and they only do so when they are certain they have enough money. It also takes time for the buyers and sellers to realize that there is money floating around, something that causes further inflation.

This lag and the temporary respite offered by printing money are the reasons people feel that such money expansion is beneficial, and this perception creates a climate of opinion in favor of further expansion of money. Of course, the perception management mills work overtime through the media and hired 'intellectuals' create such an opinion.

Academic support for this money-printing frenzy is provided by the **New Monetarist Theory**. Such an approach is essential in order to provide what is needed for bubble economics to succeed in the short term – creating a groundwork where problems are simply ignored.

New Monetarist economists believe printing money is a long term solution, not merely a short term one. They argue that because such money is used by central banks to purchase government debt bonds, it does not cause inflation, but makes such fresh money a mere 'balance sheet adjustment.'

If the argument of the New Monetarists were to be accepted for the sake of the discussion, the government could borrow all the money it needed by selling Treasury bonds to the Fed, which will purchase these with freshly printed money. The government could also eliminate taxes, which, along with increased money, would incentivize and boost economic activity. With zero inflation, this would be a perfect solution to all economic problems.

Printing money does provide short term relief as it finances government debt. However, to boost economic activity through increased demand for goods and services, this money has to find its way into the hands of the general public. And when that happens, inflation follows.

What is most disturbing is that such theories have come from outside the economic mainstream. *Genuine* reformist economic thought is expected to come from outside this mainstream in the next few decades. The present quagmire, in no small measure, is a manifestation of the failure of the economics profession. In the long term, theories such as these will further defame this profession in the popular perception.

Shocking Globalization

Political dangers to the U.S. economy are likely to come from **Greece, China, Iran,** and the ***passage of time***. The first three are related to globalization, while the last one is related to a term that our present administrators and politicians absolutely detest – the long term.

A. Greece: Recovery in Greece has created a bullish feeling in U.S. stock markets. A default has been avoided through the bailout and loan package. Greek economy was propped up in the last decade by a debt bubble that has burst.

With no other domestic economic stimulant and an absence of demand from Europe – and the rest of the world – the Greek recovery is temporary, and when Greece slides back into economic chaos, the U.S. markets will feel the punch.

Unemployment in Greece soared from 7% in 2007 to 22% in June 2012. Eight years down the line, even optimistic projections place the debt to gross domestic product ratio at 120%. Greece does not have the ability to increase two specific bubbles – those of government debt and the dollar – since the Greeks cannot borrow any more.

The U.S. will be in a similar position when the government debt bubble and the dollar bubble explode. Increasing more bubbles only postpones the eventual demise by addressing the symptoms. The long term solution involves swallowing the bitter pill – allowing the bubbles to pop and concentrating on a productivity increase. It is a pill that does not have even an iota of sugar coating.

Greece's economic woes can be better understood if we place them in the context of the **European Sovereign Debt Crisis** or the **Eurozone Crisis**. The Eurozone comprises 17 out of the 27 member nations of the European Union (EU) that have adopted the euro (€) as their common currency and sole legal tender. With a GDP of €9.2 trillion ($12.2 trillion), the Eurozone is the economic and financial core of the EU.

Monetary policy for this zone is controlled by the European Central Bank, which unfortunately does not have mechanisms to understand the views of the countries represented by the Eurozone. This divorce between a monetary union and a political union is at the root of the Eurozone crisis.

Sovereign debt is the money or credit owed by a government. It is also called public debt or national debt. Such debt can be raised by issuing bonds in local-currency government bonds or in foreign-currency sovereign bonds. Theoretically, sovereign debt is considered risk-free, as the borrower nation can raise taxes or print money to repay this debt.

However, sovereign debt default can result when:

- Economic development in the borrower country is very slow.
- Unfavorable change in currency exchange rates increases the liabilities of the borrower.
- The returns from the projects financed by such debt are over-valued.

Since the lender nation or investor cannot seize the assets of the borrower country, a re-negotiation of the terms of the debt becomes inevitable in the case of sovereign default. The defaulting country, however, will find it difficult to further raise such debt if it defaults because its credit rating will be downgraded.

This crisis started with governments borrowing beyond their means. Economic lightweights such as Greece and Italy could borrow like robust countries such as Germany, because banks were assured of returns on Greek and Italian Treasury bonds. As the bonds migrated to the Eurozone, it was expected that the change could not devalue the currency and would simplify repayment.

Investors did not make an early distinction between bonds of troubled economies and those of the healthy economies because of the false sense of security inspired by the use of the euro. This made investors ignore high debt in Italy and Greece, as well as real estate bubbles in Ireland and Spain.

Regulators permitted banks to treat sovereign bonds as *risk free*. Large banks were asked to assess the risk of sovereign bonds of some countries by themselves and hold some capital as a security against possible sovereign default by such nations. This rule was never enforced. On the contrary, banks were permitted to regard sovereign bonds as safe and hold *them* as reserves.

European and American banks have loaned heavily to Italy, Spain, and Greece. Investment banks – such as Goldman Sachs – made billions by finding buyers for the Treasury bonds of these troubled nations. This is the same Goldman Sachs that converted non-performing subprime mortgages in the U.S. into securities and found buyers by first getting them top-class credit ratings.

After joining the euro, cheap credit was available, and this also fueled the real estate and debt bubble in Southern European countries, such as Greece, Spain, and Italy. In this boom time, wages in these countries rose in leaps and bounds and reduced the competitiveness of their exports. Plus, the boom encouraged imports.

Germany made laws to put caps on wages that improved the competitiveness of its exports to the booming economies in Southern Europe. The returns were used by Germany to provide loans – again, to Southern Europe.

Greece, Spain, and Italy now face recessions because no one wants to spend in the aftermath of the popped bubbles – they are too busy paying their earlier debts. Their exports are uncompetitive; in other words, a source of income is unavailable. Also, governments are planning to cut expenditures, an approach that doesn't work in bubble economies.

B. China is the second-largest economy in the world and has been the main driver of international economic growth since the financial crisis. A collapse of its bubble economy will spell doom for the entire global bubble economy, including the U.S.

As much as 50% of China's economy is driven by the massive construction boom, spurring the government's obsession to continue with it. Now, with 50% of the second-largest global economy, China becomes a colossal economic figure. At their peak, housing bubbles in the U.S., Spain, and Dubai were not more than 17%, 23%, and 30% of their respective economies.

Riding on the back of robust export-based growth in the past two decades, the Chinese began to divert money into construction over the past few years. They acquired wealth by introducing market competition, but are diverting this wealth into sectors not favored by the market.

Credit was made available for the construction industry through state-directed banking that in turn received wads of freshly printed money from the government. State intervention is the reason many believe the bursting of the bubble will be controlled.

However, government cannot create demand for housing out of thin air the way it can create money. The construction industry will not expand building projects in the absence of demand – cheap credit means little if it cannot be repaid in the absence of demand for housing. As exports decline with the global slowdown, the main source of funds for the construction bubble will dry up and make its bursting inevitable.

The export- and construction-driven Japanese economy of the 1970s and 1980s popped with a hard landing, even though it was managed in a more sophisticated way than the Chinese economy. Housing bubbles in Spain and the U.S. burst hard, too.

The Chinese construction bubble won't merely pop, it will explode into a meltdown. Its psychological effect on global financial markets will be devastating – remember, financial markets function largely on sentiment. Sometime in the next few years, this catastrophe will hit China and the rest of the world. The typical knee jerk corrective reaction of printing money will be of little consequence.

C. Iran: As the Organization of Petroleum Exporting Countries' (OPEC) second-largest exporter of oil, Iran is an energy superpower. The country also ranks third in the list of global oil reserves and second in the list of global reserves of natural gas. Oil, coal, and natural gas are the main energy sources of the world.

Israel now ponders the timing of a possible intervention in Iran's quest for nuclear warhead capability, and an Israeli attack over Iran's nuclear facility could disturb the West Asian balance of power that favors Israel at present; oil prices could rise alarmingly. If and when the attack is actually executed, oil prices will soar and shock the already fragile health of global economies, especially those of Japan and Europe.

Iran has acquired missile capability, and the ability to endanger the oil transports through the Gulf of Hormuz. The Gulf provides passage to around 20% of the world's petroleum. Trouble in the Gulf of Hormuz can prolong the oil shock and send the global financial markets in a downward spiral, plus make already slowed-down economies crawl at a snail's pace.

D. Time is probably the greatest leveler, and what goes up must eventually come down. The events that trigger the explosion of the bubble may or may not occur, but all bubbles will pop. In a globalized world, where bubbles economies are connected, the bursting of one bubble will pop all related bubbles, resulting in a global financial meltdown.

Recovery: Myth or Reality?

Because of the illusion created by the bubbles in the U.S. economy, it is very difficult to judge whether there has been a genuine recovery.

Recovery in the stock market is there for all to see. But, there is more: in a bubble economy, the market recovers at the first sight of positive signals, while comfortably ignoring the negative ones. Negative signs include:

- **Corporate Earnings** in the first quarter of 2012 (Q1 2012) have not been very good, and the companies have not given any strong growth indicators for the near future.

- **Insider Trading on Wall Street** in Q1 2012 has been the greatest in a decade. Coupled with the fact that numerous company managements are selling hard, it means the belief in the long term stability of markets has eroded substantially.

- **Stock Market Volume** has been very weak, indicating the low strength of the price movements in stock markets. The average monthly volume has been down by 32% since October 2011. About half of the present volume is due to trading by high frequency investors, not by long term investors – meaning many still doubt the longevity of this recovery.

- **Slowdown in:**

    - **Job Growth**, compared to the eleven consecutive months up to April 2012, when more than 100,000 jobs were created.

    - **Manufacturing** since late spring 2012, likely to drop further in view of declining demand from Europe and China.

  These slowdowns have caused many to make a downward revision of the expected economic growth for 2012.

- **Government Borrowing** has been increasing. The recovery is a result of printing of money as well as from borrowing that continues to feed the six bubbles in the American economy. The increase in borrowing has far exceeded the increase in GDP since 2008. The paradox of this situation, as already explained, is that decreased borrowing will burst the bubbles.

Stock markets hit a low in October 2011, but recovered by up to 10%

by mid-June 2012. This tempted many to think that the worst was over and things were looking up again. Investors comfortably forgot that a similar optimistic start in 2011 ended in the low of October that same year, as shocks from the Japanese tsunami, European market turmoil, and Libyan political issues hit the stock market. The same can repeat in 2013. More such shocks can be delivered by China, Europe, and Iran.

Continued borrowing and unprecedented printing of money means that the Fed is worried and wants the economy to do better. Considering the dynamics of a bubble economy, the recovery is apparent and temporary – maintained by borrowing and printing money.

What almost stamps a seal of authority on the possibility of another recession is a prediction by the **Economic Cycle Research Institute (ECRI)**, which has accurately forecast every recession since 1996, when it was formed. ECRI strongly believes that another recession will hit the American economy very soon.

Employment will continue to grow after this point, as changes on the employment front always lag behind economic growth or slowdown. Employers do not hire unless they are sure that the growth will be sustained and they do not downsize unless economic stagnation or decline persists. This is the *employment lag factor*.

Federal Response

As expected, the Fed announced another round of money printing, technically known as Quantitative Easing (QE), in December 2012. The freshly printed money will be used by banks to purchase $45 billion of Treasury securities per month. This is in addition to the $40 billion per month of mortgage-backed securities that are already being purchased. Additionally, the Fed will be keeping the federal funds rate to near 0% to keep the money flowing.

Therefore, $85 billion of fresh money will be printed every month, a move that will extend the Fed's balance sheet to $4 trillion by the end of 2014 from the present $2.9 trillion. Shortly afterward, similar announcements were made by central banks of Europe, Australia, and Japan. Hurricane Sandy's $63 billion loss is only a fraction of this monthly printing volume.

One of the stated aims of the latest round of QE is to stimulate growth and employment in housing. The loose relation between bubbles and jobless growth has already been noted and, therefore, employment generation remains only a stated aim to be used as bait to lure the naïve.

It is now an almost established fact that very low interest rates between 2001 and 2004 – maintained to fight the slowdown due to the bursting of the dot-com bubble – were responsible for the housing bubble that burst in 2007 and triggered the current crisis.

Does this mean that the authorities have not learned anything from the mistakes committed a decade ago? The simple answer is, even if they have, the inevitability of money expansion in a bubble economy makes them repeat the folly. Many in financial circles believe that the Fed can also intervene directly to keep the stock markets from floating high.

The fact that the Federal Reserve is printing money at an unprecedentedly high rate means that the Fed is worried. Apparent recovery is due to excessive borrowing and massive printing. We are presently borrowing about $1.2 trillion per year, 10% of our annual GDP. Even minor cuts in borrowing can reduce GDP growth by 1% to 2%. Considering that our economy is growing only at 1.5%, almost the entire growth is due to borrowing.

Popular Fallacy about Democratic Setups

Unfortunately, we the people are a part of the problem of bubble trap, not a part of the solution. Our herd mentality, blame-it-on-the government tendency, excessive dependence on government, and our love for quick fix solutions that ignore the fundamentals makes us demand freebies and symptom-treatment measures that perpetuate the problem.

These days, the only way a politician can win an election is by promising more free stuff than the other guy. This free stuff is financed by printing money and borrowing, which fuels inflation and takes the vitality out of the freebies. The free lunches cannot be sponsored by tax hikes because we are so opposed to them.

Another method to right-track the economy is to cut down expenditures. Suggest defense expenditure cuts and you will be accused of being in league with terrorists. Propose cuts in the social security budget and there will be a wave of protests by the American Association of Retired Persons (AARP). Advocating decreases in Medicaid and Medicare will get the proponent politically lynched. Also, such austerity does not work in bubble economies.

In a democracy, people deserve the government and the governance they get. Beneath the façade of free market capitalism, we have acquired a pseudo-socialist mindset that wants the government to do everything for us and fix all problems that we create for ourselves, in full or in part.

We seem to have forgotten that we are a part of the democratic government. The government is not an isolated, benevolent magician with hoards of treasures and a magic stick. Democracies work well only when the people participate and apply informed pressure along the right lines with due respect for ethics and for limitations of administrative processes.

Because of this, we have elected the wrong kind of people to decide on economic issues on our behalf. And they do what they are elected to do – provide freebies by printing inflationary money and take credit for their largesse to prepare ground for the next election.

If we try to explain this to protesting groups who may have gone from herd psychology to an enraged mob mentality, we can be in serious physical danger. Instead, do what intellectuals do: as bubbles explode, investments will be diverted towards physical gold, and then towards physical silver, which will move northwards. This is precisely the time to invest in these precious metals – before their prices go sky high.

A direct consequence of the popular expectation from the government to play savior of last resort is **big government** and **big banking**. And once the state apparatus takes over those responsibilities that, ideally, we should shoulder, the state acquires greater control over the lives of its subjects. If even well-meaning politicians and bureaucrats can commit errors in judgment, what can we expect from the crooked, insensitive, unmotivated, and the corrupt?

Eminent economist Milton Friedman outlined this phenomenon, stating that governments must be limited to defense of national frontiers, enforcement of contracts between individuals, and the protection of citizens from crimes against themselves and from crimes against their property.

Even with positive intent, if the government tries to rearrange the economy, legislate on morality, or help special interests, the people at large pay the price through loss of freedom, inefficiency, and loss of innovation. Friedman sums this up as, "Governments should be a referee, not an active player."

Some parallels are clearly visible between the views expressed by Friedman and those of the Jacksonian Movement of early 19th century, which was against the then start-up concept of central banks. They were also against fractional reserve banking, big government control over banking, and special treatment to any business group.

Once the government is allowed to assume greater control over the lives of its citizens, it establishes an institutional mechanism – a system – to administer and even expand this control. And once this system is put in place, the possibility of systemic failure becomes more and more real.

Of course, governments and banks became bullies over a period of centuries due to the collective ineptitude of the people. Acceptance of fractional reserve banking and allowing central banks and other commercial banks to operate on this principle allowed these government controlled entities to print tons of money. With President Nixon terminating the link between gold and dollars in 1971, even the mild restriction on money printing was eliminated.

Sector Specific Prospects

This is how developments are likely to unfold in the following areas:

- **Stocks** found a great godfather in QE and did well throughout 2012 despite being occasionally volatile. Stocks usually fall when quantitative easing is discontinued. This time, however, QE is expected to be continued for quite some time and the approximate time when this bubble pops cannot be estimated.

- **Bonds** go into temporary decline with each round of QE, as stocks become a more profitable option. Financial uncertainty in Europe will maintain demand for Treasury bonds.

  Although interest rates on bonds in the U.S. are at a minimum, shorter-duration, high-quality bonds such as two-year, three-year, and five-year Treasury bonds, mortgage-backed bonds, and treasury inflation-protected securities (TIPS) will show good performance.

- **International Equities** are often said to be viable alternatives to investment in the American stock market. However, European, Chinese, and Indian markets declined by between 10% and 20% while the money printing press in the U.S. kept up its stock markets. As of now, these equities are worse than American stocks.

- **Gold** will appreciate in the long term because it will be among the few investment options available. Interest rates will rise to rein in inflation and this will knock out stocks, bonds, and real estate investments. Because gold comprises only 0.14% of the global investible assets, any diversion of demand in favor of gold will cause its price to soar.

  Demand from China and purchases by central banks of Turkey and Korea will further raise its price. In the last decade, gold rose five times while the S&P 500 was flat and the NASDAQ lost 50%.

  A slight dip in gold prices has been observed since 2011. This can be attributed to manipulation sales of gold by central banks and the sale of gold for dollars by a financially-unstable Europe. During the 2008 liquidity crisis, gold dropped by 30% as panic-struck Europe sold gold for dollars.

  Manipulation sales by mysterious entities were observed in December 2012, when the latest round of QE was announced.

Considering the limited stocks of gold available, such manipulation and resultant price drops will be a short term phenomenon.

In the very long term, this will create a gold bubble that will eventually pop. In the meantime, proactive investors can make heaps of golden dollars before the gold and silver bubble starts inflating.

- **Silver** is a monetary as well as an industrial metal. While financial instability will divert investment towards silver and drive up its price, declining industrial production due to the economic slowdown, particularly of electronics production in China, will cause a drop in its demand. Because physical silver is more affordable than gold to the general public, as gold prices increase and become more unaffordable to the general public, the investment demand of physical silver will dramatically increase.

- **Other Commodities,** such as oil, cement, and steel, will see a drop in prices as demand from China, Brazil, Australia, Canada, and Hong Kong falls with the global economic slowdown.

  China gobbles commodities, consuming almost half of the global cement production, and uses more steel than the combined demand by the U.S., Europe, and Japan. However, a war between Iran and the West or Iran and Israel will send oil prices through the ceiling.

  Balancing this decline will be the printing of money that maintains the investments in stocks represented by these commodities and thereby raises their prices. QE can also cause inflation, which may propel commodity prices despite decline in demand.

Economy Wide Prospects: An Unholy Alliance for Economic Destruction

Inflation and deflation are opposites, but both are a part of the cycle in a fiat money regime. Most probably, these two apparent enemies will join forces in an unholy alliance to pull down the economy as one thing leads to another, and another leads to the first. With every new round in the cycle, there will be a marked increase in the intensity of both of these players.

Economists cannot agree on whether this approaching economic storm will hit the U.S. and the global economy in the form of inflation or deflation. Coherent arguments are, as usual, being put forward by both sides, which only adds to the complexity. Let us examine both of these possibilities and then arrive at the prospect of the combination.

Deflation Scenario: Deflations cause a drop in money supply, prices, wages, and the GDP. The problem is that **debt remains constant**. Even though falling prices take the sting out of falling income, the value of debt payments, such as mortgages, car loans and the like, remain constant. *This causes defaults.*

Even if banks and other creditors confiscate the collateral, debt is left outstanding because the price of the collateral has gone down. Creditors then seize other assets of declining value from the debtor. The creditors know that once the economy recovers, the price of the assets will rise again. They profit later while honest earners lose everything they toiled for.

This is precisely what happened during the Great Depression, when debt as a percentage of GDP grew from 180% to 280%. One of the reasons for this depression was the enormous accumulated debt of the 1920s that exploded during the crisis. The current level of debt is more than 350% of our GDP. It seems history is just waiting to repeat itself.

Aggravating the problem is the IOU – an abbreviation for the informal document *'I Owe You,'* which admits that debt is owed. Our present monetary system is heavily dependent on IOUs, which have value only if the borrower has the ability to repay.

Foreign investors purchase IOUs in the form of U.S. Treasury bonds, real estate, mortgage-backed securities, and corporate bonds and stock. Such purchases maintain the government debt bubble. America then invests money into foreign lands in the form of risky equity and direct investments that have longer maturity periods. This way,

America supplies liquidity to most of the remaining world.

With the current level of debt and deficit, foreign investors will lose trust in American IOUs because they know the U.S. cannot honor them with a promised rate of return. Also, the world knows that the Fed will try to print its way out of deflation, causing a downgrade in the credit rating of the government. Normally, bonds work well during deflations. But the depreciated credit ratings will render them ineffective and burst the government debt bubble.

However, when bubbles pop, deflation results. With prospects of returns from investments into dollar denominated assets declining, foreign investors will sell these investments and convert dollars into their own currency. This will reduce demand for dollars and cause it to decline; the dollar bubble will pop. Naturally, gold and silver will appreciate in relation to the dollar.

In order to fight the depression, the Fed will expand and diversify the purchase of assets such as foreign and domestic government debt, mortgages and mortgage backed securities, and corporate bonds. It can also cut taxes. These measures will inject liquidity into the economy, but will further depreciate the dollar.

Another reason for appreciation of precious metals is that investors will seek safe asset classes into which they can channel their investment, as all the other bubbles start to burst. Despite huge technological advances, man still cannot print genuine gold and silver, and this will prevent them from losing their value.

During the Great Depression, numerous central banks maintained gold reserves that limited the availability of gold-for-investment. That is not the case now. Increased globalization and the communication technology revolution ensure that price related information travels fast and cross border investments can be made at the click of a mouse. Savvy investors can make this click.

Inflation Scenario: Printing money to fight a depression can attain only limited success. The resultant inflation eats up real growth, thereby stunting employment generation and productivity increase. Such inflation can be mild, large, or hyper.

Mild inflation and continuance of the present scenario is a sweet dream, for rising debt and deficits cast aspersions on the ability of the government to pay returns to bond holders. This makes them lose confidence in the American economy and a sale of dollar denominated assets becomes inevitable. Then, the purchasing power of the dollar will depreciate rapidly.

Large inflation and even hyperinflation are genuine possibilities, considering the fact that $85 billion will be printed every month from December 2012 onward. This will last until inflation does not exceed 2.5% and until unemployment does not fall below 6.5%. By the end of 2014, such QE will inflate the Fed's balance sheet to $4 trillion from the present $2.9 trillion.

Hyperinflation is the scenario in which the faith in currency falls at a rate faster than the rate at which currency can be printed. With $85 billion being printed every month, this possibility is indeed very real, and collapse of the dollar will be the natural consequence of this printing frenzy.

Reading between the lines of Ben Bernanke's expressed opinions, it appears the authorities are planning a soft landing for the real estate bubble. This can be achieved by creating more inflation in other asset classes than is created in real estate. However, the fact that the Fed has been purchasing $40 billion in mortgage backed securities per month to stimulate home building and to create jobs might negate this possibility.

If the real estate bubble does land softly, it adds another investment option for the smart investor in addition to gold and silver. This option is real estate purchased with availing loans. Because real estate prices will either stay flat or increase very slowly, it becomes an undervalued asset class that appreciates in the future. By the way, debtors always benefit from inflation.

Real estate purchased through a low-rate interest loan before hyperinflation sets in can be a treasure hoard. Profits come from both ends – loan payback is easier because money depreciates during inflation and the price of real estate will soar as it moves from undervalued to overvalued.

An even more aggressive approach is to use the rising real estate prices to refinance loans and use the savings to purchase even more real estate. This, however, requires an expert player who can sense when the hyperinflation will end, and sell off the land before the tipping point.

In the interest of your financial health, manipulative real estate investment is best left for those who have the instinct to grasp economic situations and the stomach to digest uncertainties. The real estate bubble can explode at any time. Outside of such real estate maneuvers, gold and silver investments will fetch stellar returns as their astronomical rise is certain.

Deflation-Inflation Cyclical Combination Scenario: The current threat of deflation will be countered by printing money, which will cause large inflation. Interest rates will be increased to mop up liquidity, but such depressants are useless in a bubble economy, as they slide the economy into a depression – it's either a bubble or nothing. Again, printing money to deal with this burst will lead to hyperinflation.

The federal funds rate, the benchmark lending rate by the Fed, is near zero. When the rate of inflation exceeds interest rates, people borrow heavily. This is because even if the amount paid to repay the loan is as per the agreement, the purchasing power of that amount has declined with inflation, making the repayment easier.

Ever-increasing inflation can also make the savings rate negative as the rate of returns from savings falls below the inflation rate. Such conditions can encourage speculative investments, creating a bubble. The U.S. has a negative savings rate at present and her citizens have successfully followed her in this regard. The last time the personal savings rate was this negative for so long was during the Great Depression.

Printing money and decreasing interest rates makes money available, and banks have been issuing mortgages at zero down payment to encourage borrowing. With real estate prices on the rise, people are encouraged to borrow with their home as collateral. Reckless use of credit cards is further fueling the private debt bubble.

History bears testimony that big spending leads to depressions and big savings lead to inflation. More savings make funds available for borrowing, and lending rates come down to incentivize lending. Availability of money encourages borrowing, spending, and speculative investments or bubbles. Prices rise, and when interest rates are raised to contain inflation, a depression follows.

This time around, the collapse of the discretionary spending and the real estate bubble will probably trigger the crisis. When the retiring baby boomer generation finds out that their retirement investments have lost value due to inflation, they will go into a saving and selling overdrive and burst the spending bubble.

Panic sales decrease the value of the assets being sold and make them nothing more than a distressed sale. Excessive savings contract money supply because that money does not circulate through the economy, something needed for growth. With spending cuts bursting the spending bubble, funds for speculative investment into real estate will dry up and burst this bubble. Stocks of real estate will take a hit and pop the stock market bubbles, marking the onset of depression.

Debt remains constant during a deflation, and this causes bankruptcies, defaults, and foreclosures. Under a fractional reserve banking system, money is created when a loan is issued and is extinguished when the loan is repaid or when the collateral is confiscated.

Federal authorities will then pump in trillions of dollars, buy mortgages, mortgage backed securities, and other debt instruments that investors want to sell. They will introduce tax cuts. They will negotiate purchases of each other's debts with other central banks, but the global economy will continue to decline. Even if the Fed purchases stocks to keep the markets afloat, decline in retail sales will neutralize the Fed's buying spree.

Spending has to increase when the money supply expands. There will be a diversion from the script because when people have lost faith in the economy, they save for the rainy day – or when it rains cats and dogs, as it is already raining. During World War I, despite a fourfold increase in the German currency supply, there was no inflation as people's anxiety about the future caused them to save, not spend.

Every income class has a certain sum in mind that it believes will take care of its future needs. When their savings reach this stage, they spend – provided inflation is not continuously eating up their savings. With deflation around, the inflation factor can be ruled out. To get the whole economy to an average threshold, the Fed is likely to open all the flood gates of the money supply. Then, *all hell will break loose.*

Hyperinflation with loss of confidence in money occurs faster than the printing of money that follows. The stock market will crash invisibly as inflation steals all value from any rise. With all investment avenues sending out bleak signals, investments will be diverted into gold and silver.

International confidence in the dollar will be eroded, and the dollars sitting with other countries will either be exchanged for their own currencies or used for purchase of goods and services to do away with dollars. This will burst the dollar bubble, and hyperinflation is not far away. Even at present, there are enough dollars floating around to cause it.

Beware of Liars

Before every financial crisis in history, the authorities and their hired economists promised they had the situation under control. Later, people realized the blunder in placing trust in such perpetual liars. This time, they will do the same. We can choose to believe in them, or we can choose to make our own destiny by investing in undervalued asset classes – gold and silver.

With due respect to President Obama, if his reelection has rekindled hopes, forget it. Bubble traps make money printing and borrowing necessary. Any viable alternative for managing the deficits such as a tax raise will be blocked by Republicans, despite their minority in Congress. Deep cuts in defense, social security, or Medicare are, as always, out of the question.

Foreclosures are the real economic storm, as people see their world and everything that gave meaning to their life collapse around them. This is the **human face of an economic crisis**. Behind all the statistics, accusations, denials, and perception manipulations through hired intellectuals and the media, it is the human suffering, material and spiritual, that defines the crux of such meltdowns.

Under such an onslaught, traditional rationale manifested in Warren Buffet's buy-and-hold-value investment approach will not work well. In a changing scenario, those who stick to soon-to-be-outdated practices will find their investments lose heavily even before they can sell their holdings through the quickest channel, online trading accounts.

Forget about appreciation, stock market investors will be lucky if they can make a dime for an invested thousand. And this brings us to the focal point of our discussion. The way out of this predicament is an early investment in asset classes that are undervalued at present: physical gold and silver.

Chapter 5 – Global Debt Crisis

"Never spend your money before you have earned it."

- Thomas Jefferson, Early U.S. President

Debt is the money owed by one entity to another. Since 1985, the U.S. debt has ballooned to unmanageable levels. 1985 was also the year when the personal savings rate started to fall. The debt bubble in the American economy and its links with other bubbles in the American and global economy makes the entire global financial edifice shaky.

Size, strength, and diversity of the American economy make it a tremendous attraction for global investors. Such inflow makes funds readily available, and our authorities ignore all financial shortfalls such as debts and deficits. The spendthrift work culture permeated downward, and we as a nation forgot the age old wisdom behind living within our means.

Exporters to the U.S. benefit from a strong dollar in relation to their currency. If they sell the huge stocks of dollars obtained from exports and buy their national currencies – as they should, according to foreign exchange (forex) rules – the dollar will crash. They, therefore, buy U.S. Treasury bonds with these dollars.

Such purchases mean that the U.S. debt bonds have a ready market and make debt easily available, keeping the dollar strong. However, this also inflates the debt and the dollar bubble. Furthermore, our trading partners have to print their national currency in order to balance such bond purchases. This chain of events inflates the global currency supply.

Aggravating the problem are unfunded liabilities like the expenditure on Social Security, Medicare, and Medicaid. Demographic realities like aging populations will make fewer people contribute to the Social Security Trust Fund, while more retirees will be withdrawing from it. If we add the debts of local and state level governments, households, businesses, and the financial sector, the amount becomes mind boggling.

Derivatives are a threat not only to the U.S., but also for the entire financial health of the world. The fluctuation in their value is based more on speculation than on the value of the underlying asset. A very relevant example of derivatives is the result of the infamous mortgage backed securities (MBS) that spread the subprime mortgage crisis to the global financial markets.

Excessive and speculative investments into certain asset classes form a bubble, and it is encouraged by derivatives. Bubbles create an illusion of economic growth that is also jobless growth. Sadly, today's globalized economy is composed of multiple linked bubbles that have to maintain each other or burst in a chain reaction.

Once a bubble is formed, the only way ahead is to feed it continuously or face the painful consequences of its burst. But such feeding frenzy not only prolongs the explosion, but also makes the eventual burst more problematic. All bubbles pop, today or tomorrow. Genuine and sustained economic growth is possible only with real increase in productivity. Such growth also creates considerable employment.

Availability of surplus money provides the means for bubble investment. Under a fiat money regime, there is absolutely no restriction on the power of the government to print money through central banks. Governments do so in order to fight economic slowdowns and to finance wars and seemingly-beneficial welfare programs. Such monetary expansion brings down the purchasing power of money, causing prices to rise.

Under FRB, money is created every time a loan is provided, and money is extinguished every time the loan is repaid or when there is a foreclosure. Such a system multiplies money supplies. Because interest is charged on loans, a total repayment of the principal amount, plus the interest payment, makes it necessary for the money supply to expand continuously.

Settlement of debt, therefore, takes two broad forms: repayment with money that has lost value or default, which means the creditor has money but is unable to obtain it. Effectively, this means debts can never really be settled under the present system.

At the governmental level, tax increases and expenditure reduction can boost finances for repayment. Such measures decrease the money supply that, in a bubble economy, can catalyze the crash. Governments, therefore, settle debt by printing money that further feeds the bubble economy and postpones the biting of the bitter pill to someone else.

Debt, therefore, is a part of the trap laid by the current financial system. The trap is aggravated by our spendthrift mentality, a product of the materialist-consumerist culture so actively promoted by corporations. Debt is contracted on the assumption that the future will be better. But all debt settlement options make the future bleaker.

A spendthrift mentality also causes consumption of more environmental resources and generates more waste. Any environment can maintain life only if the rate of assimilation of waste is less than the rate at which it is created. Excessive or affluent consumption hampers this vital environmental function and causes ecological destruction.

With central banks around the world continuing their money printing spree to fight the current economic slowdown, all bubbles in the global economy will expand. The consumption bubble will continue to degrade the environment. When these bubbles explode, the entire environmental, economical, and socio-political-cultural landscapes will tremble violently.

As an individual, you can transfer your wealth to assets that rise during such ground shaking events, namely to investments like gold and silver. The collapse is inevitable, as all bubbles pop and people lose faith in depreciating values asset classes. Considering the current multi-bubble global economy, most asset classes will fail and investments will be diverted into precious metals, which are bound to appreciate.

Live within your means is something that used to be taught to children by their parents. It still is, but not as much as before. The culture of materialism measures people's worth by what they own, not by what they do. Consumerism follows as people try to own as much as possible – more for prestige than out of necessity.

Work cultures and lifestyles always percolate from top to bottom simply because those at the top are regarded successful and are therefore idolized by most of those in the lower rungs. Extravagance at the top echelons of governments, corporations, and banks create a collective spendthrift psychology that spells disaster for all spheres of life.

While people haven't been living within their means for some time, it seems that governments and corporations have never done so – at least since the fiat money regime with the fractional reserve banking model was adopted. Because these two prime movers have enormous authority, and because the people have outsourced their welfare to these entities, these giants can shift the consequences of their failure to the people.

The Debt Trap

There are different ways to look at and define debt. In the simplest of terms, it is the money owed by one party to another. Note the inclusion of the term *money* in the definition of debt. In our present economic-financial structure, this is a fundamental weakness with vastly negative implications.

Money is anything that can be considered a socially acceptable medium of exchange. A more inclusive definition of money is a claim on human labor. The word *claim* implies that the human labor in question might have been provided in the past or is expected to be provided in the future.

By including the more representative definition of money, it creates a more comprehensive definition of debt because it is a **claim on future human labor**. Such a description of debt sheds light on all the facets and implications of what debt is. Most importantly, it points to the grave problems debt will cause in the near future.

Financial debt is a contractual obligation to repay a specified amount of money at a specified point in the future. Since we have mentioned contracts, debt can also be described as a legally binding contract of providing money today in exchange for repayment of the amount *plus interest* in the future.

Debts, therefore, allow us to borrow money which we do not have. We can use it for different purposes and it has to be repaid through money earned later by utilization of the proceeds of the debt and through application of efforts or labor. This is why description of debt as a claim on future human labor is more depictive.

Secured debts are those when an asset is pledged as collateral. Such an asset is confiscated in case of default or non-repayment of debt. Unsecured debts do not involve such collateral. In small or large measure, defaults are inevitable and lead to foreclosure, creating an attachment or confiscation of the collateral.

Again a 'good' debt – loosely referred to as *investment debt* or *productive debt* – is debt that enables the debtor to augment his future income and enables him to repay the loan. In banking jargon, this is referred to as *self-liquidating debt*. Examples of such debt include educational and business loans.

Non-self-liquidating debt does not increase the earning capacity of the borrower. Such unproductive loans are purely for consumption purposes – such as those for a vacation, a fancier car, or even for discretionary wars. These loans are largely unnecessary and the borrower can do without them. The point is, not all debt is bad – only excessive and unproductive borrowing is unhealthy for the economy.

There are two ways to settle a debt for common people – pay it back, or default and face foreclosure. Governments have a third option, that of printing money. In a fiat money regime, there is no limitation on the government's authority to print money. When the U.S. government wants money and they don't have it, they simply ask the Treasury to issue its bonds, which are purchased by the Federal Reserve with freshly printed money.

If the truth, the whole truth, and nothing but the truth is told, these printing presses are a huge scam. And, they are perfectly legal. It is fraud because it increases the supply of money and thereby decreases its purchasing power, so the same amount of money can now purchase lesser amount of goods and services than before.

Such price rises are also known as inflation, and it is also a kind of regressive tax; it **steals** value from existing money. People save as a financial arrangement for the future, as well as for emergencies. When the government prints money to finance the effects of its policy failures, people can actually feel the sinking of the financial ground beneath them.

Those most affected by such inflation are least equipped to deal with it, and are largely those who can least afford it – the poor and the middle classes. It will be imperative to mention here that freebies demanded by the people from their democratic governments are also a major component of this problem, for free packages are sponsored by *Federal Printers*.

Consider this: the total debt of the government in December 2012 is around $16 trillion, but this is only the tip of the iceberg. The total of all of the unfunded liabilities – such as Social Security, Medicare, Medicaid, and federal pensions – increases that amount to $87 trillion. Unfunded liabilities are those obligations for which the government has not made any long standing funding arrangements.

Adding these liabilities to the debt, we arrive at a staggering $103 trillion. If we add the shortfalls of local and state governments, corporations, households, and the financial sector, this figure would go up further and further. With a population of around 315 million, the per capita debt comes to about $50,793. If we add all other liabilities, this will skyrocket. *'God bless the United States of America'* won't be a mere slogan – we will really need His blessings.

For a family of four, the debt would be more than $200,000. That's a lot of money. The reference to the family is important, because no matter who owes the debt – individuals, governments, or corporations – it is finally repaid by the taxes levied on the returns made by people from economically productive activities. Another source of funds for the government is borrowing, *but that creates more debt.*

As long as the borrower repays the loan, there is no problem. Excessive debt that is also non-self-liquidating is the real problem. Debt that remains unpaid has to be paid by future generations. Remember, debt is the claim on future human labor. This gets us to the issues related to the sustainability and ethics of debt.

Debt is based on the implicit assumption that the economic future will be better than the present, and that the borrower will possess more money in the future. For the entire economy, this means that the current level of debt can be repaid only if we grow faster than the rate at which debt grows. But that is not happening.

As mentioned earlier, debt can be settled in two broad ways:

- Repayment with printed money means that although the creditor is repaid, inflation erodes the purchasing power of the repaid amount.

- Default means that the money is still worth something, but the creditor does not get it back.

Both ways, this makes the future worse than the present, but debt comes with the assumption of the future being brighter. This would effectively mean that under the present financial structure, debt has to continuously expand, making the future poorer. The next quarter century will be completely different from the preceding twenty-five years because all the accumulated debt will explode. This will make the economic future bleaker, not brighter.

Welcome to the debt trap, a direct consequence of fiat money, fractional reserve banking, and the charging of interest on loans. The entire economy and financial structure is critically dependent on continuous monetary expansion, and we make the problem worse through reckless spending.

Interest is one of the fundamental flaws in the current financial system. If a person obtains a $100 loan and agrees to repay it with, say, 10% interest per annum in one year, he will have to pay back $110 at the end of the year. Where will he get the $10 from? He has to put the borrowed $100 to productive use and make at least $110 in one year to repay the loan.

Effectively, this means the money supply in the economy has to expand – euphemistically referred to as *economic growth*. But such monetary expansion brings down the purchasing power of money. And under a fiat money regime, the government's power to print money is virtually infinite.

Retirement and pension funds are an avenue for governments to save the funds that they collect from taxes. These funds should not be looked upon only as a source of investment, but as a trust, because the post retirement life of many depends on these. Here, too, we see a remarkable decline since 1985.

The Net Present Value (NPV) method is used to calculate the financial position of municipal and state pension funds. It is equal to the present value of the returns from an investment that will be received in the future, minus the initial investment, after accounting for inflation and returns.

A positive NPV indicates a profitable investment, while a negative NPV indicates a loss-making investment. The NPV technique is also used to determine the profitability of a project, and to compare the returns from two separate investments.

At present, all state and municipal pension funds are under-funded, to the tune of more than $1 trillion. This means more than $1 trillion will have to be invested in those fund pools for them to have zero value. Similarly, corporations have under-funded their pensions by more than $1.5 trillion. This includes even profit-making corporations. These amounts will increase with each passing year.

Usually, pension funds invest in the stock and bond markets and expect 8% to 10% returns. These markets are not doing very well. This partially explains the current shortfall. Also, these figures of under-funding do not include the effects of inflation. When included, the amounts will increase further.

Low savings also means low investments. A 2005 assessment by the American Society of Civil Engineers concluded that an investment of $1.6 trillion would be needed from 2005 through 2010 in twelve infrastructure categories if the U.S. was to be at *first world* infrastructure standards. The categories included roadways, bridges, drinking water systems, and waste-water treatment plants. At present, this amount can be estimated roughly around $2.5 trillion.

When the bigger debt-liability picture at the federal level is considered, the $2.5 trillion ($1 trillion plus $1.5 trillion) NPV shortfall pales in insignificance. The total debt plus liabilities of the federal government are $103 trillion. That is almost seven times the $15.1 trillion GDP for 2012.

This means our government is *insolvent*: total liabilities have exceeded total assets. Insolvency is the first step on the dangerously higher and shakier ground of bankruptcy, when cash flows are not sufficient to meet the current obligations.

Demographic realities exacerbate the problem. Like most other industrial nations, the U.S. will be an aging society with an increasing number of people out of the workforce. What this effectively means is while lesser numbers of people will contribute to Social Security, Medicare, Medicaid, and federal pensions, more and more people will withdraw funds from these accounts.

In 1935, when Social Security was created, there were 42 workers for every retiree. Contributions into the Social Security Trust Fund were more than what was required to be withdrawn from it. Today, this number has dropped to 2.9 per retiree. This number will further drop to 2.0 by 2030.

Starting with the 1960s, Americans began to live longer, have fewer children, and earn wages at a slower rate than the rate at which the number of retirees increased. Even as we speak, the fund depletes faster than it can be replenished. With fewer funds available for investment into stocks and bonds, the demand will come down and bring down the stock market, as well.

In 1981 President Reagan signed the Kemp-Roth Tax Cut, which increased the deficit by almost three times. The act also made Social Security benefits taxable. But people have already paid the Social Security Tax, the proceeds of which have been deposited into the Social Security Trust Fund, from which the contributors derive benefits after retirement. Such a tax, therefore, is an example of *double taxation*.

Then some financial wizard predicted that the Social Security Trust Funds would suffer losses in 1982. It is another matter that the year ended with the fund being in $598 million surplus. This was probably a step in the creation of a climate of opinion for increasing the Social Security Tax, a measure finally implemented a few years later.

What was also done was a decrease in income tax. Surplus funds from the Social Security Trust Fund were diverted to the general funds and spent. In lieu, government bonds were deposited with the Trust Fund. Because both these funds are under the executive authority of the government, it says this debt does not count. Bush era tax cuts do remind us of this story from a not-so-rosy past.

A similar attitude is adopted by the government, with its debt held by other government agencies. The 'Intragovernmental Debt Holdings' page in the U.S. Financial Statement (Budget) starts by saying 'these intragovernmental debt holdings are eliminated in the consolidation of these financial statements.'

Nice way to settle debts – the Social Security Trust Fund is not the only federal agency fund being legally plundered. The point is that the real financial shortfall of the government – money owed by governments at all levels in all forms – is much, much greater than what is revealed. What is published is a half-truth, at best.

Our government is in good company. Across Europe, a similar explosion of debt and unfunded liabilities can be witnessed.

Trade Imbalance: A popular fallacy is that current U.S. borrowing and debt is being funded by excessive global *savings. The reality is this: our borrowing is funded by currency creation of our trading partners.* China is the best contextual example.

When the Chinese export goods to the U.S., they get paid in dollars. They convert these dollars to Yuan, the Chinese national currency, and the accumulated dollars finally make their way from Chinese commercial banks to the People's Bank of China (PBC), the Chinese central bank. So long as the goods and services exchanged between the U.S. and China are of an equivalent value, a crisis is averted.

Because China does not import much from the U.S., it does not have any use of these surplus dollars. International Trade and Currency Exchange rules mandate the sale of such surplus dollars in the foreign exchange (forex) market for the purchase of Yuan. Sales of dollars and purchases of Yuan increase the price of Yuan in relation to dollars. This will make Chinese exports to the U.S. expensive and, therefore, uncompetitive.

To bypass such a possibility, China invests the surplus dollars into U.S. assets denominated in dollars, such as U.S. Treasury bonds. Such a course of action maintains the value of the dollar, thereby keeping Chinese exports to the U.S. competitive. This bypass mechanism is referred to as 'neutralization' or 'sterilization' of excess currency inflows, something that the U.S. did in the 1920s regarding gold inflows.

But then, where will the PBC get the Yuan to pay for the dollars deposited with it by other banks? The answer is simple: it prints them. Central banks for Asia have consistently demonstrated their pliability in this regard. The U.S. current account deficit is thus financed by money printed by our trading partners. Such printing is, however, inflating the global money supply.

During the 1920s, Europe paid us in gold for the goods we exported. Being on the gold exchange standard, an increase in gold reserves should have increased the money supply. The resultant inflation would have made exports expensive, as the cost of production increased. It would also have increased imports since money was available for imports. These imports would have to be paid in gold and the gold reserves would have depleted.

To get around this obstacle, the U.S. did not inflate money supplies. The deflation ensured continuity of cheap exports, and gold disappeared into the dark rooms of the Federal Reserve. As a result, the global money supply contracted, causing the Great Depression.

Chinese sterilization of excess dollar inflows, however, is inflationary, as it has to print mountains and mountains of Yuan to balance such neutralization. The will of the free market has slowly started to impose itself on such manipulations as inflation and in return it is making Chinese exports to the U.S. increasingly expensive.

Inflation increases the cost of living, leading to demands for wage and salary hikes. Such hikes increase the cost of production. The very action that was meant to maintain cheap exports – printing Yuan – is causing prices to gallop. Until the trade imbalance is corrected, the second part of this story – that of Chinese exports becoming costlier – will continue.

If our trading partners decide to dump U.S. Treasury bonds in the global markets, the entire global bubble economy will go into deflation as the dollar loses value. Also, most reserves with central banks across the world are comprised of U.S. treasury bonds. That is the last thing anyone wants, so they continue with this dangerous dollar bubble game. The more they prolong it, the more intense the final fall will be. This also means that our debt can never really be repaid.

Japan was in the grip of an economic slowdown for most of the 1990s, after its stock market crash of 1989. It took the advice of our Fed Chairman Ben Bernanke of 'dropping money from helicopters to prevent or cure a recession.' This advice was part of the now infamous speech made by Bernanke when he was an economics professor at Princeton University.

Over a period of fifteen months beginning from January 2003, the Japanese created 35 trillion yen and purchased U.S. dollars and U.S. Treasury bonds with them. The printing and purchases kept the yen down in comparison to the dollar and stimulated Japanese exports. This was also the period when the Fed had kept interest very low to stimulate the economy in the aftermath of the dot-com crash.

We have seen how money is created every time a loan is issued under an FRB system. Surplus funds available from the sale of bonds and those released due to low interest rates went into the housing bubble as banks issued mortgages even to borrowers with poor credit histories. Even if some borrowers defaulted, the foreclosure of rising-price homes was expected to more than compensate the possible loss.

Cheap credit fueled the purchase of homes and caused housing prices to skyrocket. This invited speculative investment into housing that further appreciated the prices: the housing bubble had begun. People began to treat their homes as ATMs and spent the money obtained on the security of their homes on depreciating items such as cars and televisions.

Such indulgences meant that defaults were only a matter of time, and when homes foreclosed, they suddenly lost value and banks were left with bad mortgages of little value. This was the twist in the mortgage tale that caused the best laid plans to go awry.

Investment banks had already been securitizing mortgages. Now, they stepped up this activity. Charging heavy fees on banks, they packaged non performing subprime mortgages into securities and sold them in the financial market after manipulations that gave such weak securities top-class ratings. Such a shifting of debt is in keeping with the originate-to-distribute model in banking, wherein the original creditor does not keep the debt, but sells it to another entity.

It has to be remembered, the U.S. provides liquidity to most of the other capital markets. Treasury bonds of the U.S. and other securities are a highly sought after investment from numerous investors across the globe. Since at least 1952, international investors have been purchasing such securities while the U.S. uses the proceeds for equity and direct investment in rest of the world – these investments are a bit risky and have long maturity periods.

Such demand allowed the packaging of bad securities, such as the mortgage backed securities (MBS) with the better and good ones. Once purchased, the subprime virus became globally contagious and brought the global economy to its knees. Quite naturally, U.S. Treasury bonds do not enjoy the undisputed investment preference they once did.

But nothing can be worse than this, for most of the currency reserves with the central banks across the world are in the form of U.S. Treasury bonds (U.S. IOUs). IOU stands for 'I Owe You.' A bond seller tells the purchaser, '*I Owe You X amount with Y% interest*.' We have already noted the purchase of U.S. IOUs by the Chinese.

Such IOUs are also issued by the government when it needs money. It simply asks the Treasury or Finance Ministry to sell these bonds to the central bank, which prints fresh money to purchase them. Later, the bond can be redeemed for currency, so a bond is an IOU for currency. However, currency can be exchanged for a bond, so currency is also an IOU for a bond.

A derivative is a financial instrument whose price and value are derived from the price and value of the asset that underlies it, such as stocks, bonds, commodities, currencies, market indexes, and interest rates. Common types of derivatives include options, swaps, futures, and forward contracts.

An MBS is a derivative backed by real estate that serves as the underlying asset. In a way, derivatives are securities based on another security; the mortgage is backed by the asset, and the MBS, as its name suggests, is backed by the mortgage. Fluctuations in the price and value of the underlying asset cause similar fluctuation in the price and value of the derivative.

Derivatives are the single largest threat to the financial stability of the world. Their value is based more on speculation than on any other concrete criterion – an MBS can appreciate even if the price of the real estate underlying it is only remotely expected to increase. To keep up such prices, continued reckless lending and more speculative investment become necessary.

To put is simply, ***derivatives foster bubbles,*** and once bubbles are formed, they encourage the further inflation of bubbles. Bubbles create an illusion of economic growth, but such growth is based more on inflation, and employment does not grow with it. Real economic growth for the long term can only be achieved with a real increase in productivity.

All bubbles pop, and do so with catastrophic consequences for the economy that goes into deflation. The fear of deflation causes authorities to increase monetary supplies to maintain the bubble. Through such actions, the eventual demise of the bubble is postponed, but the explosion is more violent and more painful.

Speaking about the speculative connection of the value of derivatives, the **present value of all derivatives in the world is more than fifteen times the total global GDP**. Derivatives themselves make up the largest financial market in the world. Coupled with the two way links between the global markets, derivatives encourage a multi-bubble economy on the global scale.

What makes derivatives even more lethal is they are created through private agreements and traded over the counter. This keeps them away from the ambit of regulatory agencies such as the Securities and Exchange Commission (SEC) and allows them to wreak havoc with the financial markets of the world.

Derivatives have a fixed life span and before one expires, a new derivative contract based on the *about-to-expire* one is signed between two new parties. This forms a **daisy chain** of derivatives and no one knows the final buyer at the end of the chain. If this final buyer is a bankrupt entity, the entire chain is left unpaid.

Such chains are often a deliberate creation of a small group of traders who purchase the derivatives from one another to create an impression that the security has an active market. Frequent selling and purchase also increases its price; the rise is based on speculation, not on the performance of the asset on which the derivative is based.

Inflation increases with the increase in quantity and velocity of money. The latter is a measure of how frequently money changes hands. Similarly, frequent buying-selling of the derivative causes its price to appreciate without any improvement in the performance of the asset class that underlies the derivative.

Money that moves around at high velocity indicates that people expect the economy to do well. If people are fearful of the fate of the economy, they hoard money – decreasing its velocity. Similarly, a high velocity derivative would mean that it is highly sought after. On the other side, however, such high velocity for the derivative can also mean that people want to get rid of it as quickly as possible.

At some point, when sufficient numbers of outsiders have been lured inside the chain and the manipulative trader group has made considerable returns through the sale of the rising price derivatives, this group sells all its positions, causing a sharp drop in price; the naïve investors are left with falling price derivatives.

In 1998, Long Term Capital Management (LTCM) – a highly leveraged hedge fund –suffered depreciation resulting from international events going against their bets. Currency crises in Thailand and Russia during 1997 and 1998 caused the fund's assets to shrink from $4 billion to $600 million. LTCM, however, had $1.25 trillion in derivative bets.

A silent bailout was the only alternative for LTCM, because its collapse would have spelled doom for the global financial world. This was arranged by the Federal Reserve Bank of New York. This happened despite LTCM's board, which included some of the best known Wall Street wizards and two Nobel laureates who had worked out a formula for minimizing risk. Imagine the plight of derivatives handled by lesser intellectuals or by the outright fraudulent ones.

Derivatives such as the MBS have already demonstrated their catastrophic potential on the global economic canvas. This time, central banks across the world are bailing out the subprime mortgage sector by pumping trillions into the global economy. It is only a matter of time before destructive derivatives hit the global bubble economy again. Even Warren Buffet, the world's most successful investor, regards derivatives as "financial weapons of mass destruction."

From early 2007 onward, when the toxin of MBS could no longer be concealed, the Federal Reserve cut interest rates while the European Central Bank (ECB) made cheap credit available to European banks in order to expand the monetary supplies. Our Congress complemented the efforts of the Fed through repeated upward revisions of the debt ceiling of the government.

Despite these frantic efforts, panic runs were witnessed at the Countrywide Bank of California and Northern Rock, the eighth-largest bank in England at the time. Both these banks were involved with subprime mortgages and MBS. An $80 billion bailout was arranged for Northern Rock by the Bank of England (England's central bank). ECB and the Fed continued to inject liquidity in one form or the other.

Then, Carlyle Capital Fund discovered the MBS it had purchased from Fannie Mae and Freddie Mac was worthless. Carlyle had, however, borrowed almost 97% of its funds for investment into MBS. A large part of these borrowings had come from Bear Sterns that, incidentally, was a major participant in the creation and sale of MBS. When Carlyle announced its bankruptcy, Bear Stearns collapsed, as well.

A takeover was arranged by the Federal Reserve, and JP Morgan Chase agreed to acquire Bear Sterns only if the Fed purchased the worst MBS from Bear Stearns. This purchase for the Fed caused a $30 billion loss to the American taxpayer. Interestingly, JP Morgan Chase is the largest stockholder in the Federal Reserve.

Such bailouts will only get bigger as derivatives continue their onslaught. There will come a time when even uncontrolled printing of money will not be of any use. And then, *may God be with us all.*

Currency creation is probably the greatest white collar crime. Money printers steal value from the savings of honest folks because inflated currency supplies erode the purchasing power of savings. It does not cost the printers anything to print extra money, but they make a lot of money by loaning out these freshly printed mountains of currency.

Immediate borrowers of freshly printed money are the second line beneficiaries of this process. They use the money before it enters circulation and degrade the value of existing money. Such borrowers, therefore, are able to utilize the full purchasing power of the fresh money while honest breadwinners are left with depreciated money.

Bubbles are another consequence of currency creation or any currency expansion. Wise investors move their money out of overvalued asset classes, such as those in which bubbles are being inflated, and invest it into undervalued classes, whose value will go up as the bubble explodes.

Apart from this mess in the financial sector, global warming and ecological destruction is being fueled by excessive consumption across the globe. The more they consume, the more natural resources are extracted; waste is generated faster than can be broken down by the environment. This hinders the environment from maintaining life on the planet.

Furthermore, terrorism is just round the corner, oil supplies are evaporating, and U.S. foreign policy is being increasingly detested by most other people in the world. Political developments deeply influence the economic scenario and vice versa. The sum total of all these developments will add to the overall uncertainty. When the future is increasingly unclear, the governments usually abdicate their responsibility towards their citizens. Even in normal times, they don't show much responsibility.

In such precarious times, it is best to think for oneself. Smart people can even turn adversities to their advantage. To be smart, start investments into gold and silver now – at present they are the undervalued class. Their price will go up as every other asset class looks like a dangerous investment. And no one can print gold and silver to bring down their value, like can be done with currency notes.

We have already noted how international investors will slowly lose confidence in U.S. Treasury IOUs. Just like in the 1970s and 1980s, when government bonds were named 'certificates of wealth confiscation,' they will find themselves another degrading sobriquet. Bond investors beware.

Ten-time Congressman Ron Paul, who has been on every banking and monetary committee since 1976 and speaks very candidly, says the government will continue to send the Social Security check to retirees, but inflation, the most lethal result of all this mismanagement, will render the check nearly worthless.

David Walker, a former comptroller with the U.S. government who worked hard to raise awareness about the perilous financial shortfalls of the government, aptly summed up the situation as our government operating on a broken business model that is not revealing the truly abysmal condition of its finances.

Walker attributed this to massive leadership deficit at the very top. This fueled the deficits in budget, in savings, and in balance of payments. He was so disgusted by the fiscal imprudence of the federal government that he preferred to resign in 2008 and is now aggressively spreading financial literacy.

Through all this, we are leaving a debtor legacy for our future generations. "*We*" includes all of us who have been lured into the consumerist trap. This trap ensures that its victims are shopaholics who are never satisfied with their possessions and always want to own more. Therefore, they spend more on the assumption that they can make more in the future to pay off their debts. *Such a sunny future never arrives.*

As a savvy investor and as a shrewd individual, you can be your own leader in the absence of leadership from the top. You can stop being extravagant and you can invest in gold and silver, starting today.

From the point of view of ethics and idealism, the suggested course of investment may not be entirely correct. But if the authorities refuse to deal with the situation, and people refuse to understand the subtleties of it, what is an individual who understands the system supposed to do? Wait for the whole world to be enlightened by some divine light?

Chapter 6 – Impending Global Market Collapse

"We need to understand the more government spends, the more freedom is lost."

- Dr. Ron Paul, U.S. Congressman and Former Presidential Candidate

Incentive is what drives humans toward excellence. Since the 1980s, easy money brought in by the bubble economy has made us progressively lazy, and we seem to have erased the importance of diligence from our lives. The same is the case on the global platform, where bubble billionaires make headlines and regardless of merit, they are increasingly glorified as role models.

Bubbles are parasitic and once formed cannot be eliminated without pain to the host economy. This pain is intensified if the economy is devoid of the essential device for veritable growth over a longer duration: productivity improvement. All economies need this instrument for *bona fide growth,* and bubbles only provide illusory growth.

Because amplification of productivity is a protracted process, its subjugation in favor of bubbles brings the economy to the point where it can only slide down further into the vicious bubble trap. This is precisely where the U.S. and most of the global economy is at present – on the verge of a plunge like the world has never seen before.

It seems the world is about to pay for a mammoth sin – the price of easy prosperity for more than a generation. The more we try to get out of this quicksand, the deeper we go into it. Dilution of the incentive has stripped us of our survival instinct, and we seem to be painfully short of any innovative ideas to deal with the situation.

For shrewd investors who like to drive their own destiny, the difficulty presents an opportunity in the form of calculated investment into gold and silver. These precious metals have been saviors since time immemorial, and humans have always flocked to these in times of economic distress. The road ahead is not easy, but isn't it high time we really *earned our wealth*?

At the cost of sounding repetitive, the defective foundations of the present global financial system have to be elaborated. This places all of the broader financial economic developments in the proper context for thorough understanding. It can make a person cynical, for most official financial doses only treat the symptoms. The system does not permit more.

Three entities are the Critical Flaw in this trial: the fiat money system, fractional reserve banking (FRB), and charging of interest on loans. Such a system serves the interests of the heavyweight players in this plot – governments, central banks, and big businesses. These big-shots use weapons such as bubbles and employ perception management through a pliable media.

The accomplice of those accused is the naiveté of *'we the people.'* We have been tricked by the vested interests into placing trust in the present system. This short-sightedness makes us live in a fool's paradise, deriving happiness from shopaholic-ism, something that accentuates our dilemma and strengthens the inconspicuous grip of the big players over our lives.

Because this grasp is cleverly designed to be invisible, we are perpetually condemned to the clutches of the heavyweights. We demand freebies and trinkets, but there are *never any free lunches.* These giveaways are granted with an ulterior motive – the concealed control over our lives.

Lest we forget, the prosecution team is comprised of only a few good men who understand the critical flaws, and they try to spread awareness on the issue. Needless to say, they are ignored and laughed at, even by the accomplices against whom they prepare the case meticulously. Justice, then, makes the accomplices pay through eternal subjugation to the accused.

As the markets around the world start to collapse under the weight of their own follies, the investor is left confused, and unprecedentedly so. What is he or she supposed to do? Wait for a rebound as traditional rationale would dictate, or try sailing into uncharted waters as the old world starts to collapse? After all, *fortune favors the brave.*

The Charge Sheet

Under a fiat money system, there is no restriction on the authority of the government to expand the supply of money. Every time the government needs money, it asks the Fed to purchase its bonds using freshly printed money. Creation of new money is called Quantitative Easing (QE). Therefore, money is borrowed into existence and a debt is contracted and has to be repaid in the future.

The Fed expands the monetary base that is further expanded when debt is issued with these funds by other commercial banks that operate on the principle of fractional reserve banking (FRB). Money is created when a debt is issued. A deposit of one dollar 'creates' another nine dollars in circulation if the banks are required to maintain a reserve of 10%. Conversely, money is withdrawn when debt is settled through repayment or through foreclosure.

Because of interest charged on debt, total repayment requires a continuous expansion of the money supply. Otherwise, the borrower will never be able to return the principal plus interest. Persistent increases in the money supply cause prices to rise as surplus availability of money wears away its purchasing power.

Debt is based on the assumption of the financial *tomorrow* being better than the *present*. How else can debt be repaid? Debt increases every time money is created, and expanding money becomes a fundamental necessity of the present system. Therefore, money printing makes the future bleaker by increasing debt and postpones the redressal of this dilemma to the future. This conflict of interest is at the root of financial perils under the current financial structure.

Governments, through central banks, can increase money supply in order to:

- Fight economic slowdowns.
- Fund social welfare programs.
- Finance wars.

- Increase consumer borrowing.
- Maintain bubbles in a bubble economy.

In a financial system based on fiat money, where interest is charged on loans and banks are allowed to maintain fractional reserves, *debt and money go hand in hand* and printing money to address economic woes only treats the symptoms. Such money creation is counterproductive in that it increases debt and negates its stated purpose of improving the financial situation – something that is impossible without settlement of debt.

Bubbles are excessive and speculative investments into a certain asset class where expectations of returns are based more on *perception* than on the *genuine economic performance* of that asset class. Bubbles are cancerous, for once created they cannot be done away with. They have to be maintained through monetary expansion or the economy faces deflationary collapse.

Through augmentation of money supplies, a debt bubble gets created. It has to be perpetually fed and fattened, otherwise the entire financial system collapses. In a way, this is the root bubble that is inherently linked with the very groundwork of our financial system. The only strategy for sustained economic growth is productivity enhancement.

With every round of monetary augmentation, the debt is increased and the future is made grimmer. Essentially, we are borrowing prosperity out of the future. The cash that we have today is owed to the future. Bonds have an average rollover of four-and-a-half years, and then the bond can be renewed. Therefore, today's prosperity has to be repaid after four and half years, on average.

Money printers benefit most from this system because it does not cost much to print money, but they make trillions by lending this free-of-cost production. The borrowers of such money – like governments, large banks, and big businesses – are the second rung beneficiaries, as they get to use this money before it enters circulation and loses value. Naturally, they have a huge stake in the continuation of the system.

Monetary expansion pushes up the prices of assets like stocks, bonds, commodities, and real estate. This benefits the wealthier sections that possess them. Food prices also increase and impart a body blow to the poor, who have to spend most of their income on food.

While the authorities and the big fish certainly deserve the blame, we the people are not very far away. We have allowed ourselves to be taken in by the false promises and illusions created by these powerful entities. Furthermore, we dig our own financial grave through heavy spending and low savings, indicating our callous disregard for our own future.

We did not resist in 1913 when the classical gold standard was diluted, the Fed was created, and income tax was imposed. And, we have become shopaholics because we measure our status by what we own, *not by what we do*. This materialist-consumerist outlook is a systematic creation of rogue capitalists who benefit through the high demand lifestyles of people. Of course, our naiveté makes this strategy successful.

Cyclic Inflation and Deflation

Expansion and contraction of money supplies best define inflation and deflation. Both these phenomena are an integral part of the present financial system; one thing leads to another, the other leads to the first, and the cycle continues. The elasticity of money supply with its contraction and expansion – possible under the present system – is the cause for such a cycle.

When the economy does well, production of goods and services that comprise the GDP increases. People make money and like to spend it on essentials, as well as luxuries. This creates demand for goods and services. Entrepreneurs have to borrow for expansion and even diversification of business activities. When they borrow, *debt and money are created.*

In conditions of free capitalism, such an economic expansion is not inflationary, as goods and services are created faster than the rate of monetary-debt expansion, and those activities absorb the augmented money supply. Again, if people hoard money instead of spending – as a precaution against economic uncertainty – there is no price rise, as happened in Germany during the First World War.

However, we do not live in an ideal capitalist economy. Inflation occurs when the money is put to unproductive use and many times even honest businesses default. Rising prices increase the production cost and make repayment difficult as the load of interest in each debt creeps up. And there are the freeloading borrowers who never intended to repay their obligations in the first place.

Slowly, the contribution of inflation in GDP growth increases at the cost of real increases in production. Now, banks are left with fewer and fewer funds to lend. When debt contracts, so does money. That contraction also marks the start of economic slowdown.

Central banks are lenders of last resort and help banks fight default by printing money that they use to purchase government securities. The government then releases this money into the market in the form of bailout and stimulus packages to banks and industry. At this stage, the money has not entered circulation and has yet to lose its value. Therefore, even in a half-decent economy, the boom-bust cycle is unavoidable.

Bubble economies are those that witness excessive and speculative investments into a particular asset class. The availability of cheap credit is the main reason people have the resources to invest in such unsustainably rising juggernauts. Another reason is that inflation during such times makes people seek more lucrative investment avenues, for their savings lose value rapidly.

Because people invest money blindly, many fake companies and fraudulent investment managers make hay while the money flows. The rising stock creates an illusion of economic growth that does not create any employment. The eventual defaults and unearthing of scams dent investor confidence, and they withdraw from most companies of that asset class, *honest* as well as *fake*.

A burst in the bubble is harmful, as it slows down the economy and people lose jobs. In order to maintain the bubble and the economy, central banks print more money. However, all bubbles pop and do so more violently if their demise is prolonged through such artificial money expansion.

Considering this cycle, the following is how the financial tragedy of the global economy thriving in bubbles is likely to unfold, starting from the crash of the real estate bubble in late 2007:

- **Deflation Threat** was created after the catastrophic events of late 2007 – early 2008.

- **Big Inflation** as central banks around the world gave a green signal to their currency's printing presses to fight the 'threat' of deflation.

- **Real Deflation** or the collapse of the currency supply, as occurred in mid-2010 as exploding money supplies failed to trigger the markets and the broader economy.

- **Hyperinflation** is only a matter of time as central banks around the world have started to print like crazy since the developments in mid-2010. Unsurprisingly, the lead in this regard was assumed by the Fed with a $600 billion printing venture.

  Hyperinflation is a phenomenon when people lose faith in the currency faster than the rate at which new currency is printed. Falling value of currencies, especially dollars, will cause a massive appreciation in prices of gold and silver.

Real deflation and hyperinflation stages have to be seen from the prism of the *Dead Cat Bounce* that we will discuss later.

Recent History of Debt in the U.S.

In the U.S., debt as a percentage of GDP exceeded the 50% line only from the Second World War onward. Debt can be traced from 1792, when the Coinage Act was created. Then, the debt was due to the Revolutionary War and later due to the Civil War and the First World War.

Debt really shot up during the Great Depression because while incomes and prices drop during deflation, debt remains constant or even increases, unless repaid. Deficit spending for the Second World War caused debt to exceed the 50% mark for the first time because the new fiat currency system was in operation.

Wars are a huge expense and create mammoth problems for the economy. Every war in American history has been a source of economic misery. Inflation is a result of the increased printing of money. This new money is essential to purchase war supplies that are needed in immense amounts, as the rate of destruction of war machinery is high.

When the rate of production of goods and services exceeds the rate of money expansion, there is no inflation because the extra money is '*absorbed*' by the increased production. The problem during wars is the extra money is not '*absorbed*' by expanded production, simply because the produced war goods cannot be purchased by people.

That extra cash is instead left with people who can use it to make purchases. This increases demand, but there is no supply, for the war goods are used for destruction at some other place. Cash is left behind, while production disappears in the war. Inflation therefore gets fueled from both sides: *rising demand and reduced supply.*

Another phenomenon closely related to war is diversion of the production apparatus. Machinery used for making *consumer goods* is diverted for production of *war goods*. Then again, production capacity itself is reduced through targeted attacks on production facilities by the enemy. All this creates an acute shortage of consumer goods. Hoarders and black marketers accentuate the inflationary situation.

Governments also increase money supply during economic slowdowns by increasing expenditures, especially on infrastructure development projects such as roads, railroads, ports, dams, bridges, houses and the like. Employment is created and people have money to spend. This creates a demand for goods and services and facilitates economic recovery.

Taking a cue from all this, the economy grew faster than deficits in the post-Second World War era. Such growth was based on productivity amplification for debt, as a percentage of the GDP went down despite the Korean and Vietnam Wars being in progress.

Along came President Reagan with his famous words, "D*eficits don't matter*." Unsurprisingly, debt went up. A slight dip in debt as a percentage of GDP was observed during the Clinton administration.

However, there were no real surpluses, even during the Clinton era, as absolute national debt never went down.

Since the turn of the century, our economic woes have proliferated. First came the dot-com bubble and its crash in 2000. In order to fight this slowdown, the Fed progressively brought down the lending rates to as low as 1% by June 2003. Such cheap credit created another boom and bust, this time in the housing sector, which eventually spread its venom throughout the world.

On the global platform, central banks of Japan, Taiwan, China, and Korea created $5 trillion in money between 2000 and 2008 to purchase dollars. This depressed their currencies in relation to the dollar and helped their exports. The dollar returns from exports were reinvested in U.S. Treasury bonds, equities, corporate bonds and with mortgage financiers such as Fannie Mae and Freddie Mac. Availability of these hefty sums from overseas helped us to ignore our trade deficits.

Considering the excess of American imports over its exports, repetitive purchases of such dollar denominated assets became necessary for foreign central banks. This fund inflow depressed interest rates, raised asset prices and diverted capital towards housing in the U.S. Along with the Fed's low interest rates, these conditions led to the buildup and bust of the global economic bubble in 2008.

As is always the case, there were some defaults on mortgages. Subprime mortgages resulting from home loans to less-than-decent borrowers were regarded as safe investments, since the exploding prices of real estate were expected to more than compensate for any possible defaults. Here, there was a twist in the mortgage tale. *Defaults caused the prices to go down.* Remember, markets operate largely on sentiment, and defaults meant housing was no longer perceived to be a safe investment.

Meanwhile, two more related developments were under progress in the banking and financial world. One was the *originate-to-distribute model* in banking, where a lender does not hold the loan until maturity, but sells it to some other entity. The other was the securitization of loans, wherein loans were converted into securities that could be traded in the open securities market.

Securitization of mortgages was touted to lower the risk for lenders, as well as the cost for borrowers. The originate-to-distribute model was expected to increase mobility of a loan. In combination, these developments lowered the standards of lending – creating facilitated subprime mortgages – and prevented the re-design and re-pricing of complex financial products during a liquidity crunch.

Financial intermediaries lost confidence in each other, resulting in a financial tragedy: slowdown or even cessation of interbank financial transactions that brought interbank credit to a grinding halt. Such a loss of confidence was a significant impediment to the path of quick resolution of the subprime crisis because *no one trusted the other party*.

In the meantime, investment banks had packaged bad mortgages as securities and found buyers for these inferior securities, using their influence with credit rating agencies to garner top ratings for such securities. Of course, they did this first for a heavy fee, and then they allowed rogue banks to free their hands of these noxious mortgages.

Under the originate-to-distribute model, the process of securitization had begun even before the housing bubble had burst, and was a cause as well as an effect of the crisis. Once the busting of the bubble became common knowledge, however, this process slowed down and, later, stopped altogether.

Now, investment banks played the classic 'run with the hare and hunt with the hounds' game. While they attractively packaged septic securities and found buyers, they also bet against these very securities in the synthetic security market. Synthetic securities are derivative instruments, formed to bet on whether the underlying security will rise or fall. It served them well when the bubble collapsed, and many of the gamblers were left with these polluted securities.

Some of the money printed by central banks in Asia between 2000 and 2008 ended up with trade deficit economies, such as those in the U.K., Spain, and Greece, where it similarly promoted housing bubbles. When these popped, the Fed, Bank of England, European Central Bank, and the International Monetary Fund (IMF) printed more money to purchase the depreciated real estate from large banks in order to prevent collapse of the global financial system.

In order to deal with this collapse, the Fed has been furiously printing money. In a globally connected economy rife with several bubbles where the pop of one bubble will produce a domino effect and burst all the other ones, the Fed's response is being passionately copied by other central banks around the world. Again, this confirms the bubble trap; once formed, it has to be continued with, and such money creation will explode our debt in the near future.

Then, in mid-2010, there was a minor collapse of the currency supply when M3, also known as *broad money* and is a good indicator of the liquidity in the economy, decreased from about $14.7 trillion to slightly below $14 trillion. M3 minus base money – which represents the money we borrow into existence – decreased by $1.7 trillion. Such an immense collapse has occurred only once before in the U.S. – just before the Great Depression. Ominous signs for all of us.

Inflation-deflation always occurs in a cycle under the present financial system. To counter this deflation, the Fed printed $600 billion in November 2010 to maintain the upbeat stock market. When the Fed purchases Treasury bonds with fresh money, the money is released in the market, but private investors cannot invest them into the already purchased Treasury bonds. Equities are the second preference, and the resultant demand drives the stock markets upward.

However, nothing was done to increase productivity of the American economy, the real long term driver of growth. Yes, there was more money to spend, and that stimulated imports into the U.S. with positive effects for the entire global economy. Manufacturing was still outsourced to other economies with cheap labor, and to this day this folly is still being repeated.

In September 2012, the Fed announced it would print $40 billion a month to purchase agency mortgage backed securities to stimulate growth in the housing sector, facilitate improvement in employment, and drive down interest rates on government bonds. Low interest rates on government bonds indicate buyers' confidence in that economy.

Unlike the earlier two rounds of QE, this time the Fed did not announce a limit on how long these exercises will be continued. In August, economists expected the Fed to print money if a deflation occurred, the stock markets crashed, unemployment increased, or the yields on government bonds spiked.

Despite none of these developments, the Fed still announced this step. Also, the U.S. drought has sent food prices upward, and such money expansion would only further inflate food prices. The reason for this was the Fed was afraid of the global economy being on the verge of collapse due to:

- **Low Economic Growth**. The U.S. clocked only 1.3% growth during Q2 of 2012. Europe was in chaos and Japan continued its 22-year downward slide due to export decline. China's export-oriented model is facing a slowdown with a paltry 1% year-on-year export growth in July because of its trading partners being under economic strain.

- **Abysmal Growth in Real Credit in the U.S.** in the mid-2011 to mid-2012 period. Credit and debt are financial twins. Credit has been the driver of global economic growth since the Second World War. Remember, total money in circulation is equal to the total credit in an economy.

  Every time the inflation adjusted credit or real credit in the U.S. grows by less than 2%, our economy records recession. This has been consistently observed from 1952 to 2007. Also, the economy does not recover until credit expands significantly.

  As of mid-2012, total credit in the U.S. is $55 trillion and has expanded by 2.3%, or $1.25 trillion, in the preceding year. When the 2% inflation over the same period is subtracted, the credit growth becomes 0.3%.

  Real credit growth has been less than 2% since 2008. Increasing credit on a total credit of $55 trillion is truly a Herculean task. A 4%, or $3.2 trillion, credit expansion is needed to achieve some economic growth.

  The overall financial mess in most sectors makes them ineligible for creating credit demand. The government cannot expand credit because it is under immense pressure to cut its spending.

- **Decline in International Trade**, as happened during the Great Depression. Low credit expansion means lower production and economic output on the global scale, which transforms into declining trade. In turn, this further dampens economic growth. Global trade expanded by an average 6% in the last two decades.

Despite slow credit growth, QE ensured some economic growth – 2.4% and 1.8% in 2010 and 2011 respectively, after the 3.1% GDP contraction in 2009. With an expansion in credit and international trade unlikely, the Fed is expecting QE to effect growth the way it did in 2011 and 2012. Again, QE will treat the symptoms, but not the disease.

Deflationary globalization is one reason QE does not work in the long run. The surge in money increases spending in the U.S. and creates a demand for imports into America, which is good for the global economy. But manufacturing from the U.S. is outsourced to economies with cheap labor. Productivity of the U.S. labor force and individual incomes do not rise. Outsourced production brings down expenses, causes deflation, and necessitates a further expansion of money.

Confirming the realities of a global bubble economy were similar moves by other central banks. The European Central Bank (ECB) is ready to open the money floodgates to maintain low interest rates on Spanish and Italian government bonds. An aggressive Bank of England purchased 30% of its government's debt with fresh money. The Japanese printed $126 billion in September 2012.

Possible Scenario

Markets always arrive at the best price by striking a balance. In the short term, stock markets may behave like voting machines, where mass hysteria can create bubbles that are destined to crash. However in the long term, markets are like weighing machines where price-related developments attain an equilibrium that represents the true worth of the asset classes represented by stocks.

Real estate and stock price bubbles will crash and markets will demonstrate the *Dead Cat Bounce* peculiar to all market crashes.

This bounce is the rise after the low point that follows the burst of the bubble. Riding on the back of this bounce, markets reach a high point that is, however, well below the peak from where the markets crashed. Thereafter, markets rapidly fall well below the low before this bounce.

Such a slight rise is the reason for inflation that follows the deflation from the peak point. History of the stock market is rich with examples of such bounces – examples are what happened at the DOW between 1928 and 1934 and the NASDAQ between 1998 and 2004. A similar development is underway currently at DOW for the period between 2007 and 2014. The deflation of mid-2010 represents the fall that caused a global printing mania that is still being continued. Eventually, this will lead to hyperinflation.

In a *Dead Cat Bounce,* if the initial crash is larger, so is the final crash that follows the upward bounce. Between 1998 and 2004, the initial and final crashes on the NASDAQ were respectively 38% and 78% from the peak. Corresponding collapses were 48% and 90% on the DOW between 1928 and 2004. Now, the DOW's initial crash in 2009 from the peak in 2008 was 59%, meaning the final crash will be more than 90%.

As an investor, you need to watch out for this *Dead Cat Bounce* that presents an illusion of recovery after the fall. Stocks rise slightly after a decline and makes market participants believe a recovery has begun. Expecting a rise, savvy investors usually purchase stocks when the price falls. In the absence of strong foundations and wider investor confidence, such a rally is short lived and is followed by an immense nosedive of stocks.

Monetary systems change once about every 30 to 40 years. 1971 was the last time it was overhauled, when the connection between gold reserves and money supplies was irrevocably severed. That was more than four decades ago, and the *time is ripe for another change.*

Financial circles are rife with anecdotes of the G20 trying to forge a new monetary system after the dollar falls into an abyss as a result of the hyperinflation stage. This means a market collapse is *a fait accompli.* Learning from the present, the future monetary system is bound to have some connection between money and gold-silver.

Then gold and silver will officially become currencies again, and their prices will rise, rise, and rise.

Monetary expansion always lends an upward thrust to gold and silver for two reasons. The first is that eroded purchasing power of money means more expensive gold. Second, precious metals are looked upon as safe investment avenues when everything else gets corroded. This has happened twice: once in 1933 and then between 1980 and 1981.

At present, we are living in the greatest bubble age of all time. We have already noted the dot-com bubble, its crash, and how measures to deal with this crash produced the real estate bubble. The same story is being repeated, but on a larger scale. In order to deal with the deflation threat of the 2008 crisis, central banks are *'manufacturing'* money – postponing the eventual blast. This will only make the outburst more devastating.

Despite the crash of the housing bubble in 2007 and 2008, real estate continues to be overvalued, supported as it is by the authorities. The **mortgage to rent ratio** compares the monthly mortgage repayment installment to the monthly rent on the same house if the house had been rented instead of being purchased. It has a fair value of 1.05.

After crashing from a high of 1.85 to 1.95 between 2007 and 2008, this ratio was around 1.25 in 2010, meaning an *overvalued* real estate market. The latest round of printing by the Fed will further inflate this bubble. Considering the fact that all bubbles collapse, this will burst, too. Now, the low of 1.25 is in fact the same as the high of 1989, and lends credence to the observation of this bubble being the largest.

A great measure of whether a stock or asset class is undervalued or overvalued is its Price to Earnings, or P/E, Ratio. It is the price of a share to the earnings of the company. This ratio also indicates the number of years that investors are ready to wait in order to recover their investment. It has a fair value of 12. A P/E ratio greater than 12 indicates an overvalued stock, and a value above 18 means a bubble.

It becomes difficult to imagine a P/E ratio of 45. Well, that was the case during the dot-com bubble in the year 2000. From this peak, the DOW *collapsed* and *recovered again* to between 23 and 26 in 2008. This means that the *Dead Cat Bounce* has put the markets into a bubble again, with a P/E ratio greater than 18.

Again, the unprecedented scale of the present bubble comes to the foreground. The same bubbles are still being fattened. This brings us to the entrapment nature of the bubble – once formed, it has to be further inflated or the economy deflates and we get caught between a rock and a hard place.

Major stock markets across the globe have demonstrated a remarkable synchronization since 2003, and even more so since 2008. They seem to rise and fall in tandem. The present day global economy is made up of multiple bubbles, and globalization has linked these together. All bubbles pop, it is only a matter of when and how loud. What this means is a market crash on a global scale is just around the corner.

To put it simply and bluntly, gold and silver prices are on the verge of a great rise. As an individual, you can profit from this by investment in physical gold and silver right now. A covert sale of gold stocks by major central banks in Europe kept prices of gold in check until some years ago. This, however, *cannot go on forever.*

This rise will be gigantic. No other asset can boom like precious metals in times of financial distress. If we define the value of the DOW in gold – by dividing the points on the DOW by the price of one ounce of gold – we arrive at the value of one share on the DOW in terms of number of ounces of gold. Since 1990, this value has averaged 4 ounces.

Compare the rising prices of gold and silver with the performance of the S&P 500. The latter is hovering around 0% growth in the last ten years. When does the price of a stock rise manifold, except when that stock is part of a bubble? With people losing trust in other investment assets, precious metals will again serve this purpose, as has always been the case throughout history.

Rabble investors chase an asset when it is on the rise. They miss the point that the bus has left without them. You can stand apart from this unruly mob by investing in an asset when it is priced low and expected to go up. That way you get to buy low and sell high.

Smart investors always buy and sell at or around the right time. Having bought an asset when it was yet to rise at a galloping pace, they sell this asset when it is at or near its peak. Then, they invest in another asset that is undervalued but is expected to go up. When the second asset is near its peak, they sell it and invest in another one that is undervalued.

Many times it happens that the asset they invest in after selling the second one is actually the first asset, which has fallen after reaching the peak and happens to be undervalued again. This is the **value cycle**, and if you can grasp its abstract subtleties even slightly, it can become *the road to genuine prosperity*.

Prices of gold and silver are going up, but haven't reached their peak yet. In the last 10 years, gold and silver prices are showing signs of appreciation. The time to invest in these precious metals is *now*. You need to be aware of a couple of things, though:

- ***Dead Cat Bounce*** will trick us into the belief that markets are on the recovery path. For some time, gold and silver prices will not rise or may even decline. Watch out for this especially if you are someone who likes to live in denial.

- **Deliberate Sale** by large banks such as JP Morgan. These banks acquire precious metals through futures trading, wherein the purchase is to be completed at some future date but the still unpurchased commodity can be sold to a third party. Large banks transact in massive quantities and such sales bring down prices.

  These banks purchase gold and silver again, and they profit from the difference between a high selling price and a low buying price. If you can see through this game, *and there will be no breaking news to alert you,* you can avoid a fall in the 'sell it while there is still some value to it' trap.

Political Compulsions: Ditching the fiscal cliff – kick it down the road.

These days, there is a lot of talk about the fiscal cliff in the form of tax hikes and reduced expenditures and how it will further slow down the economy. In a bubble economy, as we have noted before, any kind of austerity that reduces the money in circulation is counterproductive and precipitates the crisis.

While Democrats have retained the White House and the Senate, they do not have control over the House of Representatives. This fractured mandate does not enable them to push the entire fiscal cliff through Congress. They will still have to negotiate with the depleted Republicans and, instead, pass a watered-down version of the fiscal cliff – a fiscal ditch, perhaps. Interestingly, the ditch may turn out to be a blessing in disguise.

Tax increases and reductions in government comprise the planned fiscal cliff, and are expected to bring down the budget deficit of the U.S. government to $564 billion in 2013 from the present $1.17 trillion. The budget deficit is the excess of expenditures mentioned in the budget, over budget revenues.

This $607 billion reduction is 3.8% of the GDP and will contract the economy by 1.5 times $607 billion – essentially $910 billion, due to the **multiplier effect**. In this case, 1.5 is the estimated multiplier factor.

Every economy is comprised of four parts: expenditure on personal consumption, government spending, business investment, and net trade. Respectively, these make up 71%, 20%, 12%, and -4% of the U.S. economy. Government spending and tax cuts create employment and encourage greater spending and investment. Conversely, the fiscal cliff will reduce spending and investment and aggravate the economic woes.

Due to the multiplier effect, the increase or decrease in the size of the economy is greater than the actual cuts or hikes in deficit. The U.S. economy will then shrink by approximately $910 billion, by 5.7% of its present size, in 2013. The U.S. economy is already growing at a snail's pace and clocked 2% growth in 2012. On the assumption that it will grow by 2.5% in 2013, the fiscal cliff will put it in the *negative*, a 3.2% contraction (2.5% minus 5.7%).

This would be worse than the 3.1% negative growth during 2009, and will spell disaster, as unemployment worsens and corporate profits, stock markets, and real estate all take a dip. And since the global economy depends on strong import demand from the U.S., it too will take a hit. Remember what we pointed out about cancerous economic tumors called bubbles.

Then again, the Fed announced in December 2012 its intention to release $85 billion into the economy every month until unemployment continues to be around 6.5%. Rapidly growing unemployment will make the Fed continue or even increase such printing, making the entire financial edifice shakier and more perilous. No one wants that to happen, and a pact between the two parties after a hotly debated bargaining match appears imminent.

A dissection of the proposed cut will put things in a better perspective:

- Of the total cuts of $607 billion, $399 billion will be saved through tax hikes and $103 billion from reduction in government spending.
- 76% of the $399 billion tax raise will be targeted towards the wealthy, while 24% will be borne by the middle and low income groups. The latter will suffer from a 2% escalation in payroll taxes.
- Only an estimated 25% of the $103 billion cut in government spending will poke the middle and low income groups as emergency unemployment benefits are discontinued. The remaining 75% brunt will have to be endured by the well-off sections or business interests.

Wealthier sections of the populace are largely aligned with Republicans, while many of the poor and middle classes are closer to Democrats. Considering the weak bargaining position of the Republicans, their support groups will have to take the majority of the fiscal injuries.

Because nobody wants too deep of a fiscal cliff, a temporary solution was negotiated on New Year's Day 2013: government spending will be left untouched, and a diluted tax hike that reduces the deficit by about $100 billion will occur. Taxes on the middle and low income groups will be maintained or raised by small amounts. Affluent classes will be taxed more, but on a lower scale than if the deficit was reduced by $607 billion. Most, if not all, unemployment benefits will continue.

The $100 billion contraction is 0.6% of the economy – 0.9% if we are to consider the multiplier effect. This will bring down the estimated 2.5% of economic growth in 2013 to 1.6%. Stock markets, corporate profits, and real estate will continue to trudge along, and unemployment won't go down by much, but a shattering fall from the cliff will be avoided or kicked down the road.

The Flaw in Traditional Rationale

Rising bubble economies between 1980 and 2000 were a great period to make money through investment. All you had to do was to diversify your investment and *hold;* even average stocks would provide good returns as the DOW multiplied by 11 times in this period. This was the era dominated by buy-and-hold, or the traditional investment gurus.

Then came the 2000 bust of the dot-com bubble. In that year, DOW did not record any growth, and the NASDAQ dropped by 50%. Bonds did okay, but that was not enough. Traditional gurus missed the bigger economy-wide picture of collapsing bubbles, and continued with their old strategy. Between 2007 and 2008, "traditional" was left discredited.

Before the 1980s, the U.S. economy was less dependent on capital and, therefore, less vulnerable to changes in interest rates. Consumer spending and debt was limited to making the economy less dependent on spending. Up cycles far outweighed down cycles. There were very few bubbles, and even the stock bubble of the 1920s was accompanied by real growth.

All this provided a solid base for the economy and steady growth for the stock market. This steady growth is the basis for the mirage of the 'natural growth rate' – the very bedrock of traditional rationale. It assumes that the economy will always grow at this natural and average rate and, therefore, the best option is to buy stocks and hold them until the market swings upward.

There is really no such thing as a natural growth rate, because growth has to be caused by productivity improvement. Real increase in productivity is the elementary tool for long term growth. Even this is not natural, and is a result of improvements in technology, business models, and government policies for business.

The Chinese economy is an excellent example. In the 1990s, China's government encouraged entrepreneurship, free markets, and input from foreign investors that upgraded productivity and elevated their economy to the high table of rich nations.

We live in the era of bubbles that create an illusion of growth, spark inflation, do not create jobs, increase economic disparities, and perpetuate themselves. All bubbles pop and cause the markets to tank. Bubbles are, therefore, the exact opposite of this real instrument of economic growth.

Traditional rationale works well when bubbles are on the rise, not when they fall; holding stock that is rapidly losing value is worthless. Warren Buffet – arguably the best traditional investment gurus – and his firm, Berkshire Hathaway, did superbly between 1980 and 2000. After 2000, his company has slowed down and since 2008 has been in decline. Buffet still prefers stocks, but gold and silver is better right now.

More proof of the 'rising bubble limitation' of traditional rationale comes from the performance of hedge funds, most of which operate on traditional principles. Performance trends of these funds are almost replicas of the stock market ups and downs, especially since 2004. Most of these lost heavily during the 2008 market crash. However, some hedge funds genuinely hedged the investment risk through sophisticated investment techniques and continue to shine, even at present.

Warning signs in the 1970s – inflation and flat stock markets due to decline in productivity growth – were missed because the economy grew on the earlier, concrete foundation. In the 1980s, bubbles developed in the economy: private debt, real estate, the stock market, and consumer spending. These fed the dollar and the government spending bubble. Any productivity boost took a backseat and continues to do so.

Since 2000, these bubbles have stagnated or declined:

- Real Estate has shown meager recovery since the abyss between 2008 and 2009.
- The NASDAQ has fallen by 50%, while DOW and S&P have been flat.
- Consumer Spending and Private Debt are still in the doldrums.
- Gold is on the way up.

Genuine growth in productivity is a very slow process and, therefore, has to be measured or analyzed *over the long term only*. For example, the percentage of the U.S. population required to produce food for the entire nation dropped from 90% to 3% over a period of two centuries.

The U.S., Europe, and Japan – representing the major industrialized regions – have recorded declining growth in productivity since 1975, compared to the period between 1900 and 1975. Traditional rationale of the present downturn being temporary is proved wrong when we consider it to be a consequence of this productivity slump. Real economic progress will take ages, as productivity creeps upward at a snail's pace.

We have had bubbles and inflation in the late 1970s and the late 1900s, but this time there are six gigantic interdependent bubbles just in the U.S. economy and many more in the linked global economy. Pumping money created the dollar bubble. Such printing kept the interest rates on bonds low and allowed the government to borrow more; the government debt ballooned into a bubble.

Since the meltdown of 2008, the dollar and government debt bubbles have been kept afloat to prevent collapse of the *global* multi-bubble economy. But expanding money supplies lead to inflation and interest rates have to rise to rein in the rising prices. Rising interest contracts money supplies, and the bubbles start to bust.

Then again, inflation reduces the purchasing power and the value of the dollar in comparison to other currencies. Foreign investors who own over $20 trillion of U.S. assets will find dollar denominated assets less attractive and withdraw to their domestic economies. Only the naïve think foreign investors have nowhere else to go. All this will burst the dollar bubble.

With the American economy appearing weak, interest in U.S. government bonds will wane and burst the government debt bubble. Because foreigners have invested so heavily in our economy and contributed to the expansion bubbles, their withdrawal will be harmful for our bubble economy. The other four bubbles will meet a swift end once the dollar bubble and government debt bubble expires.

Even without inflation and rising interest rates, bubbles collapse for the simple reason that they are not based on a fundamental driver – they are based on speculation enabled by borrowed or printed money. Traditional believers will not agree to this. But then, they could not predict the crisis of 2008. To put it simply, traditional rationale based on rising bubbles is history.

A diversionary tactic employed by advocates of traditional rationale is the threat of deflation. They always make a hue and cry of deflation being around the corner and want more money to be printed to fight this possibility. Such printing maintains the bubbles and grants them synthetic authenticity. *Yes, deflation did occur in mid-2010.* Now we are on the brink of the aforementioned fourth stage, that of hyperinflation, where deflation is no longer a possibility.

Inflation occurs when the money supply increases at a faster rate than the speed at which the production of goods and services expands. When the money supply contracts in relation to the size of the economy, there is deflation. Price rise and price fall are only manifestations of inflation and deflation, respectively. Prices rise when demand exceeds supply, and prices fall when supply is greater than demand.

There is also a difference between the nominal price and the real price. The former is the *price paid* while the latter is the *inflation-adjusted price*. Nominal prices rise due to inflation, but the real price may fall due to increased supply or falling demand. Collapsing real prices of some assets when bubbles collapse will mean popping bubbles, not deflation. And with all the printed money, the only long term possibility is inflation.

Retiring baby boomers are expected to save more and contract money. With inflation knocking the bottom out of their savings, they are more likely to invest their retirement funds into risky, lucrative avenues, causing rapid monetary circulation that is inflationary. Even if they do save under the mattress, it won't offset the humongous sums printed by the Fed.

Money is technically extinguished when debt is settled through repayment or through foreclosures. Again, massive printing will more than compensate this tiny contraction. Also, slow expansion or contraction of credit does not diminish the existing money supply, it only slows down or stops the creation of *new money*. Existing supplies are enough to ensure inflation.

Finally, the Fed cannot rein in inflation through increasing interest rates or cessation of printing. Bubble economy ensures that monetary expansion has to be continued or the economy slows down immediately. More printing postpones and accentuates the eventual slowdown.

Living in denial just because you own a stock and do not want it to decline does not solve the problem. It only creates a mental illusion of prosperity that vaporizes when the harsh reality hits. In 2003, we denied an imminent collapse of housing prices. Today we refuse to look at the approaching hyperinflation because the cause – money printing – offers temporary respite. And this denial syndrome goes right up to the Chairman of the Federal Reserve.

Another reason for this denial psychology: we are now used to easy money brought in by bubbles for more than a generation. We did not have to work very hard for productivity improvement, and what comes easily goes away easily. The bubbles ensured a galloping rise in our asset prices, we happily cashed in, and we don't want all this to change.

Bubbles across the global economy produced easy money billionaires throughout the world. The media was quick to idolize them, and wealth management gurus said, "Don't work hard, work smart." Many did work hard, but their earnings also had a bubble return icing on the top of the hard won cake. *Even if you work smart, you still have to work.*

Such easy money changed the approach of Wall Street investment managers. They lost their survival instinct – they could not predict the crisis in 2008, and will not do so now. Without government intervention, many would have gone bankrupt. Many did go bankrupt. Contrast this with the Great Depression, when many firms survived because they were not blinded by easy money.

Proponents of traditional rationale will also say gold has not done well in the past thirty years while stocks, bonds, and real estate have. Again this amounts to denying the realities of global bubblenomics. When bubbles were rising, assets other than gold rose. Now as the bubbles slide downward, investors will slowly lose confidence and divert to age old avenues – precious metals.

Once the confidence drops below a certain threshold level, no amount of perception manipulation will work. Then, even staunch traditional gurus will go on a selling spree. In all fairness, most of the traditional advisors do not know of other strategies. Traditional rationale made them rich, and they are still living in the past; therefore, they are in denial of the present crisis.

Presently, traditional financial advisers will neglect your opinion based on this content or ask you to stop reading pessimistic books. They are paid by stock and bonds salespeople to advise customers to buy or hold and not to point out the bubbles. They are also required to own stocks or they are out of a job. Yes, there are honorable exceptions. But that is what they are – *exceptions*.

Furthermore, these managers are investing other people's money… *your money*. So long as they do as well as the other managers, they will keep their jobs, even if their own personal investment falls. Remember, investment managers work for you, so the final call is yours. Unprecedentedly confusing times like these demand you to be your own leader.

Professional economists have also let down those who look up to them. Through their expert knowledge and finer insights, they can guess the effects of economic developments with reasonable accuracy. Their status lends credence to their word. If only they had been forthright and more vocal in their suggestion of viable alternatives, a lot of trouble might have been avoided.

The Pot Holes Ahead

Investment in the present scenario requires diversification and dynamism. Movement from risky asset classes – such as stocks, bonds, and real estate – into safer asset classes – such as gold, silver, foreign currency, agricultural commodities, and short term debt – is advisable. However, even these safer assets will be volatile and would require continuous adjustment to market changes.

Gold and silver can be volatile, but each is an excellent long term option. As gold purchases spark a gold bubble, that too will eventually explode, then silver will be demand. Silver stocks are limited due to the industrial application of this metal, and this will further push up its prices once the supply limit of gold is reached.

Understanding foreign currency markets is very difficult for non-specialist investors, and it is better to refrain from this temptation. Moreover, these markets tend to be extra volatile. Agricultural commodities are similarly fickle.

Risky asset classes can be treated as short term investment avenues, but this can be a perilous game, for they will be volatile and even if you get the timing slightly wrong, the losses will be enormous. Monetary expansion will artificially boost the stock and bond markets and present such temporary opportunities.

And remember, the goal has to be *reasonable returns with limited risks.* No one times their investment's *buy and sale* perfectly. The aim has to be perfection, but practically no one can only get near the dead center. It is better to err on the side of caution. If you hold and hold and hold, as traditional rationale dictates, you will lose, and lose heavily.

Astute people never rely on the *one-size-fits-all* approach. The present precarious situation, in the face of global financial markets collapse, calls for a radically different investment strategy, one that questions long-established norms. This won't please the traditional investment advisors. But then, investors are here to profit, not to please obsolete talkers. Position yourself *wisely* for what is coming down the road.

Will the U.S. suffer the least in the present crisis?

Global economies of the present day are coupled through trade links. The decoupling myth was exposed in late 2008-early 2009 when bursting of the bubbles in the U.S. economy caused decline in other economies such as the U.K., Germany, Japan, South Korea, and Mexico. The global economy, therefore, is a connected, multi-bubble economy.

The U.S. economy will suffer least because it is not dependent on exports of manufactured goods and of raw materials. It is also the most stable economy on account of its diversity and flexibility. The rest of the world benefited from rising bubbles in the U.S. economy through investment and exports in the U.S.

It is, therefore, natural that they will be negatively affected by the bust. Also, they lack the flexibility and diversity of the U.S. economy. Other lesser affected economies will be from Western Europe, followed by Japan, Eastern Europe, India, China, Brazil, Africa, and South America.

Chapter 7 – Exposing The Lie That All is Well

"The desire of gold is not for gold. It is for the means of freedom and benefit."

- Ralph Waldo Emerson

Economic indicators published and interpreted by official sources portray a half truth, at best. In order to maintain the façade of a rosy economy, governments and officials under their command actively conspire with Wall Street heavyweights. To this end, pliant personalities among the media and economist professions are hired and the doctored opinion is reinforced.

Our government does this to retain confidence of foreign investors in the American economy. This is necessary to keep investment funds flowing in from abroad. As a people, we have forgotten the merits of saving for the rainy day. Now, savings serve as capital for economic growth. In the absence of foreign investment, we face an acute shortage of capital.

Tampered Truths and Media Machinations

Trading partners have a vested interest in accepting this grand lie. The U.S. is a humongous consumption economy, and our trading partners make trillions by exporting here. It is in their interest to have a strong dollar to keep their exports competitive. They do so by purchasing U.S. Treasury bonds and printing money in their domestic economies to balance such purchases.

Wall Street buys these arguments, and the half-truth becomes the convenient truth. Unless people expect the economy to do well, they won't purchase stocks and bonds sold by the Wall Street. Privately, however, Wall Street bets against the stock it sells, for it knows the true state of the economy. Sounds familiar to what investment banks did with mortgage-backed securities before 2007 and 2008?

We live in a free society. The fourth pillar of democracy, the media, can be seen as either lazy or downright complicit in this deceptive exercise. And so are some economists who publicly toe the official line. Yes, there are objective economic professionals. But who will risk confrontation with the authorities when the media can easily assassinate their characters?

This is not to say all Democrats are saints and all Republicans are monsters. Politicians of all feathers defer issues so the actual economic breakdown occurs when someone else is in office. In an economy with weak fundamentals, such delays only intensify the problems. We have noted the shaky foundations of the present financial structure in previous chapters.

Also, people need to do much more than just vote someone out and someone in. We have to go beyond the obvious and be incisive in our understanding of the operations of the financial machinery. Conditions change in a democracy only when people place informed, intense pressure on their representatives. The final buck stops with the people. We can start by saving more.

The Lies We're Told

In order to arrive at the whole truth, let us look into the opposite arguments in order to expose the lie. A major problem in calling the economic bluff is that all economic developments and indicators have to be put in the proper context. Needless to say, reporting out of context is the most potent tool of schemes to brainwash investors and the general public.

Argument I: Large trade deficits imply a strong and creditworthy economy growing faster than our trading partners. A growing economy creates jobs and increases disposable income, which in turn fuels a demand for imports. Trade deficits occur when an economy imports more than it exports. As of November 2012, our trade deficit is $48.7 billion.

Rebuttal: Such an argument is acceptable if the economy is based on a genuine increase in productivity, the real driver of long term economic growth, and where domestic savings provide the necessary capital for productive enterprises. Consider this:

- Our present economy is based on services, not manufacturing.
- Growth comes mostly from bubbles, not from productivity augmentation.
- We have forgotten the merits of saving and become a nation of spenders with consumption being sponsored by capital inflows from outside and deliberate currency exchange rate manipulations by our trading partners.

Adding to our woes is the fact that we are borrowing short term in order to finance this long term deficit. This keeps interests rates on our government bonds low. Sooner or later, foreign investors will understand the fundamental fault lines. Money printing keeps the economy artificially alive, but investors will pull out at the first signs of approaching trouble.

Again, our trading partners are finding it increasingly difficult to continue inflationary printing of their currency in order to maintain the high dollar. These economies make a fortune by exporting into our economy and get paid in dollars that are deposited with their central banks by exporters. This activity creates a glut of dollars held by foreigners.

If these dollars were to be exchanged for their national currencies in the foreign exchange market, the dollar would fall in relation to these currencies and make their exports expensive and, therefore, uncompetitive. To get around this, our trading partners purchase bonds issued by our Treasury.

But then, their traders who deposit dollars with commercial banks have to be paid in their national currency with dollars that have not been used for such an exchange in the forex market. Therefore, printing of money becomes necessary, and this fuels inflation in their economies.

With rising inflation, production of goods for exports becomes expensive and makes them uncompetitive. A step designed to maintain price levels of exports ends up pushing their prices higher. This is where the wheel completes a full circle; our trading partners cannot continue these manipulations forever, defeating the very objective.

Our trade deficits are a result of the excessive consumption psychology into which we have allowed ourselves to descend. We are no longer producing goods that can be exported, but outsourcing production to economies with cheaper labor. Now the full consequences of such unstable foundations are making themselves felt.

Argument II: Core inflation is well under control.

Rebuttal: Core Inflation as measured through the producer price index (PPI) and the consumer price index (CPI) excludes inflation in the food and energy sectors because these are price volatile areas that can introduce huge temporary effects. Therefore, core inflation is not an accurate measure and *actual inflation at the ground level is much more.*

Inflation erodes the purchasing power of the dollar. It also pushes up interest rates that the government has to pay foreign investors who purchase its bonds; loss of returns due to inflation has to be factored in. Our debt and deficit are huge, with savings and manufacturing at extremely low levels.

If the inflow of foreign funds dries up due to inflation denting investor confidence, we face a momentous problem. The compulsions of a bubble economy make us print inflationary money. If the Fed decides not to continue printing money, we face an almost immediate economic collapse that will spread in the connected markets across the globe.

Inflation figures are, therefore, fudged to conceal the true scale of this silent killer. This also provides a free hand to the authorities to further aggravate inflation through monetary expansion. And gloss is put over a lackluster economy by spreading the word that consumer spending that creates the deficit is an indicator of an upbeat economy.

Two examples of the period between 2001 and 2003 illustrate that point:

- Following the provision of 0% financing of new automobiles, used car sales dropped and caused a fall in their prices. Now the CPI index includes the prices of used cars, allowing officials to proudly state that inflation had decreased.

- Easy and cheap mortgages encouraged purchases of new homes so much so that no one was interested in renting properties, causing rent prices to decrease. Such mortgages were products of easy credit availability for real estate in the aftermath of the dot-com collapse.

  Back in the oil inflation decade of the 1970s, authorities replaced home prices with *equivalent rent* in the calculation of CPI index. Equivalent rent is a subjective estimate of what it would cost to rent a similar house. It came to the policymaker's rescue again during the pre-2008 housing boom, when it was used to suppress the true scale of inflation.

Both these developments were used by the authorities as evidence of low inflation and allowed them to justify the inflationary policy of monetary expansion. The more money the Fed printed, the more rents went down and played into the hands of the officials by allowing them to make tall claims on there being low inflation.

Real inflation also increased with such monetary expansion, but was not reflected in official figures. Because most things related to finance and economics are complicated and not easily understood by the layman, authorities can systematically misguide the public through active use of the media and so-called financial experts.

Exclusion of oil from core inflation presents a very deceptive picture. Yes, the percentage of GDP spent on oil has come down from the 14% level of 1980. But this can be attributed in no small measure to the import of goods that were previously produced domestically. Domestic production required power from oil, and the oil import cost was reflected in the figures.

Now that they are imported, the cost is not reflected as oil imports, but as increased prices of imported goods because these have to be shipped into the U.S. and then distributed across the country. Both these transports require oil that is much more expensive now than it was in 1980. The decrease in the percentage of the income spent on oil is, therefore, deceptive.

Again, it is argued that the financial services sector that is very strong in the U.S. economy is not oil intensive. The growing dominance of this sector, therefore, cushions our economy from possible oil price shocks. This argument is specious, too, because it ignores the effect of a possible interest rate hike on this sector. Interest rates are hiked to rein in inflation.

Rising energy costs will cause inflation and cause the Fed to raise interest rates, which is the principal factor of cost in financial services. Increased lending rates make credit expensive and cut down money supplies. This brings down the value of asset bubbles, and many such assets are used as collateral. Loss of collateral value will hit the financial sector very hard. Propaganda cannot alter the inherent dependence of the entire global economy on oil.

Argument III: Rise in CPI indicates successful liquidation of the deflation risk.

Rebuttal: Deflation is being used as a part of the shell game to create a climate of public opinion where monetary expansion will be regarded as benevolent. The resulting inflation is under reported and being promoted as a necessary evil. Direct and oblique references to the Great Depression era are usually enough to send a deflationary chill through people's spines.

In our present financial setup, deflation – monetary contraction – results when debt is completely repaid or when there are foreclosures following a default. It can also result when people stop spending as a result of loss of faith in the economy. Incomes and prices fall during deflation, *but debt does not* – it either remains constant or increases unless repaid.

Two specious arguments are advanced to demonstrate the toxicity of deflation for our economy:

- Anticipation of falling prices due to deflation will cause people to stop spending. This will reduce demand and de-stimulate production. The price of cell phones, computers, and digital cameras falls continuously, but they are still purchased. Falling oil and gas prices will spell nothing but sunshine for the economy.

- Falling incomes in deflationary times will erode corporate profits, leading to lower investment, production, and employment. But cost also declines during deflation and balances falling income. Yes, debt remains constant, but we all know of the special treatment in the name of stimulus and bailout packages for corporations.

By the time the veil over inflation is lifted and its true, ugly face is revealed to the people, it will be too late. By then we will already be in the hyperinflation stage, when the confidence in money is eroded at a faster rate than money can be printed.

Argument IV: An enormous increase in productivity will mean higher and sustained growth, lower inflation, and lower unemployment.

Rebuttal: There is no real productivity growth in our economy – manipulation of statistics and growth data only gives an appearance of an increase in productivity. Since the 1980s, our economy has been bubble-driven and the easy money that comes with bubbles has made us forget this real driver of the economic engine. Prudent savers make up only a microscopic minority.

Productivity is measured as the amount of output given per unit input. The input can be in terms of labor or time. When less input is required per unit production of output, productivity is more. This transforms into higher utilization of all factors of production in areas like land, labor, capital, and enterprise and brings down cost and time of production, leading to sustained economic growth, lower inflation, and higher employment.

Much of the productivity growth argument is premised on two plausibly deceptive phenomena:

- Rapid strides made by computer technology in the past 15 to 20 years. There has been an advance, but this has not improved industrial productivity by much. This is because manufacturing of computers is a large industry in America. It is not important how efficiently computers are made, but how their use improves efficiency of other production processes.
- Labor costs per unit production have declined because

manufacturing is increasingly outsourced to economies where cheap labor is available. Such productivity appreciation actually increases unemployment in the U.S. and makes us more vulnerable to oil shock inflation, as the outsourced production has to be shipped in.

This outsourcing reduces the savings rate in America because unemployed Americans cannot save. Increased imports of such outsourced production accentuates our current account deficit.

The combined effect of development in communication technology and a shift of purchasing power to Europe and Asia is increasing the debt and deficit in the U.S. economy. The confidence in the U.S. economy is the key reason we are able to continue *despite burgeoning debts and deficits*. This can't go on forever, and when foreign investors wake up to this reality and pull out of our economy, we will descend straight into the abyss.

Argument V: Robust growth in the GDP indicates a healthy economy.

Rebuttal: The GDP is only a rough indicator of economic progress and was never intended to be a measure of social well-being. Official figures of quarterly growth of GDP are adjusted for inflation – growth due to inflation is subtracted from total growth. The inflation index used for this purpose is the CPI, the limitations of which we have already discussed.

The GDP is the sum total of the monetary value of goods and services bought and sold within the geographic boundaries of a country-economy in a certain period – usually one year. It includes the total of all government, investment, and consumer spending, subtracting the difference between exports and imports.

A slightly better measure is the GNP, the value of all goods and services produced by the citizens of a nation in one year irrespective of their location. The GNP is the GDP plus the value of production of overseas Americans, minus the value of production by foreign nationals within the U.S. borders. In fact, the GDP evolved from the GNP – the latter was used to measure wartime production capacity during World War II.

GDP comes with the following limitations:

- Every monetary transaction is included in GDP irrespective of its benevolence or malevolence. GDP calculations include nonproductive costs such as those incurred on disaster relief, defense, crime prevention, excessive resource extraction, cleaning toxic wastes, and other such activities.

  Again, debt contracted from foreign lenders is included in the GDP despite the fact that increasing debt is a major economic issue, especially for posterity.

- The GDP excludes all of those functions where money does not change hands, such as domestic responsibilities like running households and caring for family members in the house. If those duties were performed by housekeepers, nurses, or nannies, there would be monetary transactions to include in the GDP.

- Statistical manipulation is a part of the GDP figures, as well. For example, if $1 billion worth of calculators are purchased that have a computing power three times that of earlier calculators in the same base year, sales worth $3 billion are included in the GDP.

Over 70% of our GDP is a result of consumption. Components that produce real wealth, such as mining and manufacturing are negligible. Affluent or excessive consumption, coupled with lower savings is the reason for our tremendous debt and deficit. But all of those issues get swept under the carpet every time officials publish *doctored* economic statistics.

Argument VI: Consumers have faith in the economy, and their spending drives the economy.

Rebuttal: Confidence based on a shaky foundation is bound to crack eventually. Such confidence is also a result of the deliberate stage management of economy-related figures by the officials. People believe the economic picture to be rosy even in the future, and they spend as if there is no tomorrow.

Another reason for heavy spending is the hold of materialism over the minds of American consumers. For quite some time now, we measure a person's worth by what he owns, not by what he does. Plus, we are bombarded by advertisers twenty-four hours a day who create the false impression of a requirement for products and services that we do not really need – and most certainly not in the quantities advertised.

Yes, slowdowns start when people do not spend or invest in the anticipation of economically hard times – a result of them losing faith in the economy. But then, increased spending cannot be taken as a measure of economic well-being, particularly when we are spending borrowed money while high-paying manufacturing jobs are being replaced by low payment service jobs.

Chapter 8 – Why The Gold Standard Will Return

"Time is money."

- Benjamin Franklin, U.S. Founding Father

We certainly are living in financially interesting times. The current financial system faces an impending fall of momentous proportions. This fall is a result of internal contradictions that will mature as the system eventually fails to find ways and means to deal with the current crisis.

It was not always so. Under the classical gold standard, sanity prevailed in the economic world for quite some time. This standard provided the necessary financial stability for traders and entrepreneurs to design and implement long term business plans. With breathing space and peace of mind, many positive outcomes were possible.

Although rulers have debased currency to finance wars before, the advent of the first war on the global scale changed everything – such currency debasement was made permanent. Slowly but surely, degeneration spread to all areas of life so much so that, today, not being extravagant means being a bore. Effects of careful perception management, wouldn't you say?

Under the present financial structure, only the symptoms of economic woes can be addressed. The disease beneath goes unaddressed, and powerful vested interests will be hurt. The weight of the symptom treatment eventually causes the body to feel the full blast of the disorder. This is precisely what will happen: a total collapse of the financial system.

Smart people always heed the first signs of an approaching storm and prepare for it in advance. As the bubbles in the global economy finally stop inhaling the oxygen supplied to it by the life support system of central banks under the express commands of our governments, the financial world will shatter like never before.

And then, as has always been the case since the first recorded grade inflation in 407 BC in Athens, gold and silver will rise as people lose confidence in all other investment avenues. Considering the consistently deceptive tendencies of bankers, it is better to have actual physical gold and silver in your hands; ownership certificates mean little when issued by unethical con men.

Planet Earth in Bubbleland

Fiat money can be seen as a sweet and intoxicating wine. It is also very addictive for those who get to operate the control levers on the printing machines. Under a fiat money system, there is absolutely no limitation on the power of the central banks that operate at the request of governments to print money. Now, all the authorities have to do in order to deal with a funds shortage is to simply print money.

Charging exorbitant interest on loans is the other problem. If the debt has to be completely repaid, the money supply has to expand continuously. How else will the borrower find the money to pay back the interest in addition to the borrowed principal? Under the gold standard, debt was contracted for 100 years at low interest; this was the real interest rate or the cost of using other person's capital.

Under the system of fractional reserve banking (FRB), money is created every time a debt is issued. FRB is the practice of maintaining reserves that are a small fraction of the total debt issued by that bank. A bank is required to maintain 10% reserves, creating nine times the money it holds as reserves. Money and debt, therefore, mean one and the same and the total money in an economy is the total credit issued in that economy.

The money supply has to be continuously increased or else this system comes to a standstill, or even collapses. But when money is additionally created, it loses its value or purchasing power because its supply increases. This is inflation or the growth of money supply that we understand as *price rise*.

Because inflation is an ever-present feature under the current financial structure, lenders charge an extra rate of interest called an inflation premium. Borrowers benefit from inflation because by the time they return the agreed amount (principal plus interest) it has lost some value due to continuous monetary growth. Inflation premium then fuels even more inflation that, in turn, necessitates a greater inflation premium, and the vicious spiral continues.

Again, debt is contracted on the assumption that the financial *tomorrow* will be better than the financial *present*. How else can the borrower repay? Because money and debt expand continuously and concurrently under the present financial system, the future actually worsens. Every time a new cent, dime, dollar, and pound is created, public debt increases. Government's income comes through taxation – meaning it is the people who finally repay the public debt.

When government increases the money supply, false signals are sent to the markets, causing lower-than-market rates of interest. Investment funds are thus readily available and promote speculative or misdirected investment in those asset classes where the expectation of growth is based more on perception than on the performance of that asset class. Such investments are called bubbles.

Another reason for the growth of bubbles is that people seek more lucrative investment avenues as inflation quickly erodes the worth of their savings. This misdirection is eventually corrected by the government or by the market, as restraints are placed on the free expansion of money leading to deflation. Meanwhile, governments prolong and aggravate the eventual correction by printing money and guaranteeing loans that again misdirect investment.

Real long term economic growth can be achieved only with a genuine increase in productivity that comes through reliable currency, savings, low interest rates and minimal taxes. Advances in technology and business management models, as well as a positive government outlook toward the economy, also facilitate productivity augmentation.

Bubbles are the antithesis of real economic growth because such growth is more a result of inflation than of an increase in productivity; the growth is illusory. Furthermore, bubble-led growth is jobless and invites the financial doomsday – sooner or later.

Once a bubble is formed in an economy where this fundamental driver of growth is absent, weak, or neglected, it has to be consistently fed and fattened through the inflationary expansion of money supply. Slowly, the percentage of inflation in economic growth increases at the cost of a real increase in productivity and production.

All bubbles burst because they are not based on a concrete foundation. If they pop immediately, there is some inconvenience. If artificially sustained, they explode violently. They inspire fraudulent companies and deceptive investment schemes that only intend to cash in on the passing hype. When such rackets are busted, the flow of investment funds dries up, and the bubble pops.

Even otherwise, some honest companies will find it difficult to satisfy the heightened return expectations of their investors. Some of these honest companies will also go bankrupt despite their positive intentions. Now markets operate largely on sentiment, and once confidence is lost, the entire bubble edifice starts to crumble under its own weight.

If money is created with debt, it is extinguished when the loan is repaid or when there is a foreclosure following a default. Contraction of the money supply starts when bubbles pop and there are defaults. Such monetary contraction is called deflation. Now, debt remains constant or increases unless repaid under any economic condition.

Under the present financial mechanism, central banks respond to contractions by increasing the money supply. This response is premised on the usually observed phenomenon of an increase in consumer spending when extra money is available. Demand for production of goods and services is created, and this brings the economy back on track.

Such reasoning is also the logic behind increased government spending during economic slowdowns. The expenditure is targeted toward public infrastructure such as dams, roads, bridges, and railroads ports. Apart from the financial angle, these projects also enhance the quality of life of the people and improve the efficiency of factors of production like land, labor, capital, and enterprise in that economy.

In conditions of free capitalism, when the production of goods and services expands at a faster rate than the rate at which money expands, monetary growth is not inflationary. The same is true if people hoard the extra printed money instead of spend, due to lack of confidence in the economy. Free capitalism is largely absent and growing money supplies are usually inflationary, as they are utilized for non-productive expenditures and more investment into bubbles.

Apart from countering economic slowdowns through bailout packages or increased public expenditures, governments inflate money to finance wars and welfare programs, increase its borrowings, and to maintain bubbles. Under quantitative easing (QE), the Fed purchases government bonds with freshly printed money. Reduction of taxes, interest rates, and reserve ratios also expands money.

Central banks are the prime beneficiaries of this process because it does not cost them much to print money. But they do get to earn interest by lending out freshly printed money. Governments, corporations, and other large banks who use this money before it enters circulation and loses value due to excessive supply, are the second order beneficiaries.

Wealthier sections profit from inflation as the prices of their assets, including stocks, bonds, commodities, and real estate, are pushed up. Hikes in food prices hit the poor sections of Americans very hard, for they spend most of their income on food. On the other side, deflations cause foreclosures and people lose belongings they spent their life's honest, hard work to accumulate.

It seems the people can choose only between the bad and the terrible. But we too are responsible. As voters, we have never asked the right questions and, therefore, have never received the right answers. We aggravate the situation by heavy spending and little saving. If we allow ourselves to be taken in, don't we deserve this? After all, it has been said that the price of liberty is eternal vigilance.

Philosophy aside, as an individual what you can do to protect yourself is to invest in gold and silver. As the bubbles start to pop and central banks print paper money hordes, the purchasing power of money will drop and people will lose confidence in most asset classes other than precious metals. *Precious metals* means the actual physical gold and silver, not paper certificates of ownership.

Virtuous Full Gold Standard

The creators of America, the land of opportunity, were fully aware of the problems and self-perpetuation tendencies of fiat money not backed by any solid reserves of precious metals. Criminal cousins of fiat money go by the name of fractional reserve banking, and excessive interest on debt were also known to them.

The powerful banking lobby wanted to grip the economy in its vice-like, yet invisible hand. Provisions in the Constitution represented a balance between the centralizing tendencies of the Federalist bankers and the liberal anti-Federalists, who largely represented the working class farmers.

Nevertheless, the anti-Federalists succeeded in striking a balance, and their provisions were based on biblical principles of ethics and morality. All this was not merely ideological, though. There were many economic merits of an undiluted gold standard, making it possible for investors to maintain some financial and economic ethics.

Economic integrity of this standard is based on two inherent characteristics of gold. One, **gold maintains its stable value** over considerable durations simply because its unit is precisely codified in terms of weight. This enables reasonably accurate economic calculations. Secondly, **governments cannot print gold,** making the money supply in the economy fairly constant. Therefore, we have:

- **Broad Stability of Prices** as inflation is kept under check in a system that does not permit arbitrary magnification of the money stock. This provides a certain peace of mind to most of the entities in the economy.

  Prices are not rigid under a gold standard, but vary within a narrow range as gold flows in and out of the economy for balance of payment of international trade. Such adjustments also occur to accommodate the increased production of gold.

  Increased money supply lends purchasing power to people and creates demand for production of goods and services that stimulates the economy and boosts employment. However, this process is inflationary and in the later stages increases unemployment and causes a drop in real incomes i.e. inflation-adjusted incomes.

- **Incentive for Savings**. With inflation, the purchasing power of savings deteriorates quickly and eliminates the motivation behind savings. Inflation can also lead people to invest their funds in risky, speculative ventures that can foster bubbles.

  Price stability guarantees a return on savings. A 3% (interest rates are low in a gold standard) annual interest rate on savings of $100 will provide $3 net returns to the depositor. In a fiat money regime, even a 9% interest return will be useless if the inflation rate is 11%, and inflation is a permanent feature under the irredeemable paper standard.

  Now, savings are used as capital for entrepreneurs, and when savings increase, the cost of borrowing is cut down, and so are the costs of production. This is the exact opposite of what happens with the inflation premium charged under the present financial structure.

- **Low Interest Rates** are maintained over the long term as the **real interest rate** is low, only **3% to 5%** because there is no **inflation premium** charged in the gold standard. It is not charged because there is *no inflation*.

  The inflation premium is the extra interest rate charged by lenders as a compensation for expected price rise, and is usually greater than the actual rate of inflation. It increases with decreasing confidence in the central bank and government of that economy.

  Borrowers benefit from inflation as the amount that they are supposed to return is able to purchase fewer goods and services at the time of repayment than it could at the time when the debt was contracted.

  A landslide of actions can occur. The inflation premium addresses this potential problem for the lender, but makes capital expensive, which in turn makes production more expensive, thereby adding to the inflation. Inflation further fuels the rise of the inflation premium, and the downward spiral continues.

- **Long Term Finance** is enabled, as there is faith in the constancy of the value of money over a considerable duration. This encourages savings, lowers interest rates, and guarantees the lender of a net income. With returns *guaranteed,* lenders are ready to issue easy and inexpensive credit.

  Gold standard bonds were typically sold for 100 years at a 4% to 5% annual rate of interest. If this is revived, the now-moribund financial debt markets in the U.S. will be, too. And all this can be done without subsidies, corporate loan guarantees, or deceptive welfare schemes sponsored through inflationary printing of money.

- **Controlled Debt:** the government does not have the authority to print money, which only adds to the debt. Remember, under the present financial system, debt and money are twins: when one is born, so is the other. Naturally, the government cannot run up huge debts and deficits through subsidies, welfare schemes, and loan waivers that it struggles to pay back.

  Absence of inflation sets up the structure correctly, beginning at the very foundation and obviates all wasteful expenditures.

- **Full Employment** is possible with a sound monetary system, market-determined wages, and maximum economic growth. Populist policies that fix *higher-than-market-rate-wages* increase corporate debt. Government then has to subsidize these corporations through assistance packages, sponsored inevitably by inflationary money printing.

  Is it not better to earn $100 that will maintain value than to make $125 that will be effectively worth $75 in a matter of months? Continuing wage controls will only increase prices, decrease real income, and, later, increase unemployment as the economy heads further into slowdown. In the absence of employment, high wages are meaningless.

- **Economic Growth without Monetary Expansion** as inflation is checked through non-expansion of money. Genuine economic growth is a consequence of productivity appreciation via savings, reliable currency, low interest rates, and minimal taxes.

Most importantly, the inflation-deflation boom-bust cycle and the typical government response that perpetuates this problem are avoided. Government's market intervention through monetary expansion and guaranteeing large loans misdirects investment like a bubble and all its cancerous effects.

Gold standard with an intervention-free market directs investment into economically productive sectors only. Only rational investors succeed, and no bailouts or subsidies are needed. Typically, money supply grows at about 2% per year, prices adjust automatically, and credit information flows freely.

Effectively, the classical gold standard provided the long term peace of mind and breathing space for the entrepreneur, the investor, the lender, and the people at large. All this lent serenity and sobriety to the entire global economy. Needless to say, this was welcomed by everyone except, of course, the power hungry.

A Revival of Monetary Gold

Monetary systems change every thirty to forty years or so. The classical gold standard era lasted for around 35 years between 1878 and between 1913 and 1914. Then came the diluted gold exchange standard that tottered through the two global armed conflicts and the greatest economic depression the world had witnessed until then.

As if to emphasize the ascendancy of the U.S. on the global political and economic stage, the Bretton Woods System made the U.S. dollar a reserve global currency between 1944 and 1971. Excessive printing of dollars to finance the Vietnam War and President Johnson's costly Great Society Programs crumbled international confidence in the worth of the dollar, and President Nixon was forced to cut off the gold connection in 1971.

Thereafter, the dollar suffered momentous decline. The Managed

Float System was devised through the Jamaica Agreement in 1973. Through the Agreement, central banks were permitted to intervene in the foreign exchange markets only if the value of the currency fluctuated beyond a reasonable margin. The moderating influence of gold over the financial structure, however, was lost.

The 1980s began the age of bubbles in the American economy. Bubbles are a result of excessive speculative and misguided investment in certain asset classes. Rationalism and sobriety are forgotten while a mass hysteria is witnessed as people invest blindly in these assets on the expectation of a rise in prices. It is mainly the hysteria itself that contributes to the rise.

All bubbles burst. However, once formed they have to be sustained by the furious printing of money by the authorities. Government intervention through credit guarantees and bailouts and stimulus packages for corporations also result in artificial support for bubbles as the market determines the direction of investment through such actions of the government.

Contraction or even non-expansion of money causes decline and cessation of investments into bubbles that then pop with disastrous economic consequences. The problem is that prolonging the inevitable only makes it more catastrophic. Across the globe, central banks are pumping trillions into the global bubble economy to maintain the facade of growth.

Now, the intensity of an economic disaster resulting from the burst of bubbles is directly proportional to the time and effort – including money printing and interventions – taken to artificially prolong the eventual, inevitable demise. This is precisely what lies ahead. Eventually, hyperinflation will result from the printing overdrive and destroy faith in paper currencies.

A real increase in productivity is the true path toward sustained economic growth. This is the exact opposite of bubble-led growth. Most importantly, it does not make people used to easy money the way bubbles do. Such easy money eventually eliminates the incentive for hard work, smart work, and innovation and can cause stagnation and even decline of the society and civilization.

Gold and its little brother silver will be looked upon as reliable investment classes as other asset classes lose their paper-currency-based sheen. Because the impending crisis will be of unprecedentedly gigantic proportions, the loss of faith in paper money will also be similarly colossal. Naturally, faith in precious metals will witness a balancing upswing.

This will spark discussions on the merits of the monetary function of these precious metals. Whatever is used as money should serve three principal requirements:

- Store of value.
- Medium of exchange.
- Unit of account or divisibility.

With paper money eroding itself with every new issue of notes, the monetary function of these precious metals that can store and augment value can be revived. Then again, gold and silver are widely acceptable as a medium of exchange, and acceptability is an important criterion for any entity to be accepted as money.

When we consider the third requirement of divisibility, silver assumes a certain degree of superiority. Its price is lower in comparison to gold, and this was the reason silver coins were used for low value transactions in the days of coin money. Things are a bit different these days. When gold is revived as money, people won't shop around with gold coins.

In a gold-based future, reliable depositories such as Brink's and ECB will team up with Visa and MasterCard to create gold deposit accounts. Credit cards of such accounts will be used for payments. Only the ownership of the amount of gold required to settle the bill will be changed. This amount will be based on the exchange ratio between gold and the currency in which the bill is charged.

Public pressure is a very potent force, especially in democracies. When the people realize the merits of the use of gold as money, governments will have no choice but to follow suit. Yes, they will resist and shamelessly unleash propaganda to counter the merits of paper money. But in the end, they will have to fall in line.

The Gold and Silver Leap of Faith

It goes without saying that a revival of the monetary utility of gold will make central banks scramble for gold. Then, the price of gold will go to astronomical heights. Already, the investment demand for gold is shooting up with people losing faith in other assets that derive their worth from paper money supplies. The use of gold as money will multiply this demand.

It takes time for gold to be mined and purified. Despite the increased demand, the supply will not increase immediately, causing the price to go even higher. Then, people will turn to silver investments. Used primarily as an industrial metal, the industrial demand of silver will decrease due to economic slowdown, but investment demand will surpass industrial demand by many folds at this juncture.

Un-affordability of gold will cause a surge in the demand and price of silver. As the economy revives after the peak of the impending crisis, the industrial demand for silver will strengthen even more and continue to further augment its price. Eventually this will create a silver bubble that may overshadow the gold bubble. All bubbles pop, though, and so will these – but that is far away.

Chapter 9 – Disaster Management: Have A Plan, Thrive

"Every problem always creates an opportunity of equal magnitude."

- Dr. Alan P. Chan

Bubbles are tumors that spread financial toxins through the entire economic body. The global economy is dotted with malignant bubbles just waiting to pop. We are sitting on a dormant financial volcano of unprecedentedly high intensity, which will activate and cause momentous destruction on the global economic landscape.

In a way, the impending bubble will be a blessing in disguise. One, it will prompt a change in the present financial structure being heavily biased in favor of heavyweight, vested interests. Second, shrewd investors can make heaps of real money if they transfer their wealth into those asset classes that can not only store value, but also cause it to appreciate.

Being shrewd would require the investor to be able to understand the intricacies of the macroeconomic picture from a long term perspective. This foresight has to be combined with the sagacity to understand the '*all is well on the economic front*' fraud actively propagated by the official machinery.

As has always been the case throughout history, gold and silver appreciate when the economy goes into the doldrums. Under the present financial structure, which supports a bubble economy, the only thing officials can do to fight economic slowdowns is to print more money – causing gold and silver to rise in direct relation to the currency being printed.

Other commodities will also rise, but they will be more inconsistent. While the global slowdown will exert a downward pull on their demand and their prices, the fall of the dollar will make commodities expensive *inside the U.S.* in terms of dollars. This apparent contradiction will add to the volatility of commodities other than precious metals.

In the immediate beginning of the chaos, even gold and silver will be volatile. The golden bubble will rise from the destruction of the present bubble age. This bubble will also collapse, for all bubbles pop. But its time will come about a decade from now. Until then, there is plenty of money to be made.

Adversity can benefit the optimist who views difficulties as opportunities. As the connected bubbles in the linked global economy pop one by one in a domino effect, the dollar will plunge to never before known depths. The easy money made available to Americans by the bubble economy since the 1980s will vanish, and these good old days will quickly become a thing of the past.

This is precisely where a scrupulous and opportunistic investor can make a fortune in real, non-bubble money with smart thinking and timed action. Although the path is treacherous and requires vision to grasp the long term macroeconomic picture, it also takes instinctive guile to call the bluff being diligently cultivated by the official propaganda machinery.

Profits in Perilous Times

For the proactive and savvy investor, the impending collapse of bubbles and the dollar create great opportunities to make huge sums of real or non-bubble money. This won't come anywhere near to the enormous sums of bubble money made since the bubble age began in the 1980s. Nevertheless, a golden opportunity does exist.

In the past three decades, we have developed a taste for free flowing, easy bubble money. All we had to do was purchase stocks and sit in our houses and wait. The bubbles in these sectors would automatically appreciate the value of these assets. In fact, many hedge fund managers advised their clients to purchase *any* index funds without the application of any judgment whatsoever.

Not anymore. The financial landscape is quickly changing and will require smart thinking combined with some bold investment decisions in order to make money. Forget about augmentation of your wealth, *an informed and hands-on approach will be necessary* even to hold on to whatever wealth you have accumulated so far.

Most investors made it big by swimming against the tide – by purchasing stock of diminishing value that was being rapidly sold off. This strategy was based on the assumption that the bust will be followed by a boom, as is most always the case under the present financial structure *if this structure has not reached the tipping point.*

Traditional rationale of investment – the traditional theory of *buy and hold* – works well when the bubbles in the economy are on the rise. It can also work when there is a veritable increase in productivity, since that is one of the fundamental drivers of economic growth that promotes continuing growth.

But traditional rationale does not work when economic growth occurs largely on account of bubbles, when the bubbles are about to burst, and when continuous expansion of the monetary supplies has led the financial system to the brink of disaster. Make no mistake, we are on the edge of the financial cliff. The fall is only a matter of time.

But this is exactly where a fortune can be made. There are three things that need to be remembered:

- The **Macroeconomic Picture** has to form the contextual background for any investment decision. The bubbles in the U.S. economy, like those in stocks, real estate, private debt, consumer spending, dollars, and government spending are about to collapse. When they do, other linked bubbles across global economies will fall.

  Investment in any of these bubbles, therefore, would amount to financial suicide. Traditional rationale shows us that the purchase of any of these asset classes when their prices are falling will not apply this time, because they will not rise for a long, long time.

- The **Long Term Perspective** is necessary. Unusual political developments and actions by governments can have short term repercussions in the market. Remember, markets work largely on sentiment and expectation, and even economically insignificant events can affect them because investors expect them to.

In the short term, markets are like voting machines where investor hysteria can trigger massive and unwarranted price fluctuations similar to what happened in 2008 when the stimulus package and interest rate cuts were announced. Over the long term, however, markets behave like a scale, as it eventually will strike a balance.

- **Fundamental and Informed Opposition to Traditional Rationale** dictates avoiding and limiting purchases of any of the bubbling asset classes when they start to lose value rapidly after the collapse begins. They won't rise again for quite some time. If you already possess such assets, it is better to offload them while you can still find buyers.

Such a basic understanding will insulate you from wrong counsel by fellow investors, investment managers, and by the media. Fellow investors might be naïve and living in denial, while the others might have their interests linked with these bubbles and without impartiality, they push positive publicity to bubble economies.

Primarily, the opportunity to make money will come from investment that profits from:

- **The Falling Stock Market.**

- **The Depreciating Dollar.**

Presently, we are in the phase when returns can be made from falling stocks. Shortly afterward, the dollar bubble will also explode, as other linked bubbles pop and present the opportunity to make considerable gains.

From December 2012, the Fed has started to print $85 billion per month, $45 billion of which will be used for the purchase of Treasury securities. When this money enters the market, investors get funds but cannot purchase these safely regarded Treasuries because these have already been bought. Investment then goes into stocks, and the stock markets boom. This can go on only so long, as investors *trust* stocks.

Again, falling stock markets will also cause the dollar to depreciate, as foreign investors will no longer be interested in converting their currencies into dollars for investment in stocks, something that will reduce the demand for dollars. Therefore, investment in falling stocks overlaps investment in the dollar, and these two phenomena cannot be completely separated.

A declining stock market offers the following investment channels:

- **Shorting with Long-term Equity AnticiPation Securities (LEAPS)** is a good investment strategy if you are comfortable dealing with options. LEAPS are long term stock options that allow shorting for a one- or two-year period. This duration automatically rules out losses from short term volatility.

  Options are contracts that allow the holder to buy or sell an agreed amount of stock at the specified price before the option expires. The holder, however, has the alternative of not honoring the purchase or sale, hence these contracts are called options.

  Shorting or Short Selling is the stock trading technique to make returns from an expected fall in stock prices. The holder of the stock sells it on the agreement to purchase it later. If prices fall, the original holder benefits from the difference between the high selling price and low purchase price.

- **Bear Funds** are an inverse ETF, whose value varies in the opposite direction of the index or benchmark that it tracks. Bear funds include mutual funds and hedge funds and apply shorting to make a quick buck from falling markets. These funds are not as lucrative as LEAPS, but are simpler. They are effective only over the short term.

  ETFs combine the merits of index funds and mutual funds. Like index funds, these consist of all types of securities that are a part of the underlying index, such as the S&P 500. Their value mimics the performance of the index. ETFs are less expensive to administer than index funds, and are more liquid than mutual funds.

Most hedge funds bet on traditional rationale that is on the verge of obsolescence, at least for the time being. These funds have a bright outlook if they understand the macroeconomic picture and the long term investment scenario; they are able to take more calculated gambles and cast their lot with their clients by charging lesser management fees and making money only when they perform.

Once highly regarded for being the reserve currency of the world, the dollar is way past its prime. Foreign investment into the bubbling U.S. economy and deliberate dampening of their own currencies by countries that export to the U.S. are the principal causes of the dollar maintaining its value. This can't go on forever. The dollar's pop will offer the following opportunities:

- **Purchase of Euros**, as this currency will rise in relation to the dollar and is the easiest to trade, compared to many other currencies that also appreciate in relation to the dollar. Euro government bonds are a reliable method for the purchase of euros.

  Gold and silver is moving in tune with the euro and, therefore, investment in gold indirectly amounts to investment in euros. Even otherwise, gold and silver always rises in relation to the currency that is being printed in wholesale proportions, such as the dollar.

- **Shorting Bonds** through ETFs is a long-term strategy for seasoned and sophisticated investors who do not panic due to the volatility of those ETFs that short fixed income bonds, such as Treasury bonds.

  The value of fixed income bonds falls when interest rates rise; the market expects lesser investment into these, due to higher interest rates decreasing the money supply. *Double shorting* is also available with these ETFs: if the underlying index falls by 5%, the value of the ETF goes up by 10%.

Capricious Commodities and the Golden Exception

Apparently contradictory forces will be at play in the commodity market in the U.S. and will add to the volatility of this already fickle asset class. Three types of demands are always in operation for commodities: industrial demand, investment demand, and speculative demand. The last variety – speculative demand – waxes and wanes when the other two demands are respectively expected to grow and to fall.

The falling dollar will make these commodities expensive *in terms of dollars*. On the other hand, global economic slowdown will reduce the industrial demand for commodities and bring down their price in non-dollar terms. This will be the aforementioned apparent contradiction, but it is illusory because it will be dollar-specific.

A depreciated dollar will make U.S. exports cheaper. And because good returns can be made through export, these exportable goods will be made costly even in the domestic U.S. market. Commodities such as **lumber** and copper are used as capital goods, and the slowdown will reduce their global demand.

U.S. coal will be in great demand for power production and so will grain. However, the global demand for beef will fall with the slowdown, and since grain is used to feed cattle, grain can fall as well. Again, the price of grain depends on the grain-based ethanol requirements in gasoline. High prices of grain can drive down these requirements and add another dimension to its price volatility.

Copper, nickel, zinc and other such metals are in plentiful demand for industrial use, but are not looked upon as investments. Popping bubbles will ensure industrial slowdown and dry up demand. This is especially true for copper, which appreciated with industrial demand from the export-oriented economy in China. As always, expectations of the copper rise prompted speculative demand. Now, both of these demands have come down.

Prices of oil and gas will be high in the U.S., but low in other economies. Oil and gas are sources of energy, and their demand grows along with economic growth. Such a demand is driven by two factors. The first is that increased production of goods and services requires more energy. The second is that the affluence ushered in by growing economies promotes a high consumption lifestyle.

Oil prices surged recently from the demand created by booming Asian and other economies that exported to a spendthrift U.S. economy. As the bubbles burst and the U.S. economy slows down, so will these exporter economies. But because the dollar will fall, oil and gas will be expensive in terms of the dollar in the U.S. until the imbalance in global trade is corrected.

Gold and silver will, however, be an honorable exception for the simple reason that demand for it will be driven by the desire of the people to store monetary value in an entity that will not lose its value. On the contrary, demand for other commodities is driven by their commercial application that depends on the state of the economy and expected effects of certain developments.

Gold and silver will then be a class in itself, and the investment demand for them will rise abundantly. Demand for jewelry might fall as jewelry is a *discretionary good,* but the investment demand for gold will keep its prices high and cause it to go higher. Discretionary goods are those items not essential for survival. These are purchased for prestige or luxury, and their demand goes down when the economy slows down.

Here is a list of why gold and silver will be a highly sought after investment:

- **Trusted Asset**: As the connected bubbles in the linked global economy pop in a chain reaction, people will lose confidence in most other asset classes and look for safe investment assets, such as gold, that can store monetary value over a longer duration.

- **Inflation Hedge**: Gold always rises in an economy where there is inflation or currency depreciation; this has been observed since the first recorded grade inflation in Athens in 407 B.C.

- **Size of the Gold and Silver Market**: The global gold market is very small in relation to the stock and bond market. Any shift of capital from the latter into the former will cause huge price appreciation.

- **Production Limitations**: The total amount of gold and silver in the world is limited, and the production cannot be easily and quickly increased. Therefore, demand will always outpace supply in the near future.

- **Windfall Gains from Dollar Fall**: Gold and silver offers a great opportunity to American investors to benefit from the falling dollar if they invest in precious metals, for they will rise in relation to the dollar and offer a secure hedge for wealth.

- **Simplicity**: It is easier to purchase gold and silver than it is to purchase stocks and bonds. Once other asset classes lose their appeal, the simple process to purchase these precious metals will further add to its attraction as an investment.

- **Acceptability:** Gold and silver is much more acceptable as an investment asset in regions like Asia and the Middle East than it is in the U.S. This fact will amplify the demand for gold in the aftermath of the dollar's decline.

- **Tax Evasion Tactic**: Tax rates will be hiked to mop up excess liquidity that was deliberately created in order to fight a potential slowdown. In combination with dropping incomes, this will create an environment for *tax avoidance.*

  Possession of physical gold has always been looked at from this angle as well, for it is difficult for authorities to trace physical gold and silver. Although such illegal behavior is not advisable, the demand for physicals will be driven up by the desire of many to possess precious metals in order to evade taxation.

In the long term, markets always behave like a weighing machine that strikes a balance. Monetary expansion always causes precious metals, chiefly gold, to rise in value for all the mentioned reasons. Power hungry governments and bankers detest gold and silver precisely for its noble character: they cannot bend it.

Every time gold is given step-motherly treatment and its price is sought to be regulated without due regard to the market forces at play, gold prices actually do the opposite. In the economic history of U.S., gold has demonstrated the balancing act on two separate occasions:

- When the private ownership of gold was made illegal in 1933, gold rose and the value of gold reserves equaled and even exceeded the value of money in circulation.

- After the requirement of gold reserves was eliminated in 1971, hordes of dollars were printed. They lost value and gold appreciated. Again, the value of gold reserves equaled and exceeded the total money in circulation between 1980 and 1981.

Silver is both an industrial and investment metal. Popping bubbles will cause its demand and its price to fall, initially. It will rise later as the supply of investment gold starts to dwindle in light of a thumping demand, because silver has always been treated as a secondary store of monetary value – after gold.

Platinum is another precious metal with a dual purpose, but it is chiefly used as an industrial metal for catalytic converters in automobiles. As the bubbles pop, the automobile sector will slow down and dampen platinum's price. This price will not rise for a long time – probably not until the automobile industry is revived. Platinum is not looked upon as an investment metal, so it is better to stay away from it.

Dealing in commodities will be equivalent to dealing in the inconsistent dollar. Except for gold and, to some extent silver, commodity trading will require you to be opportunistic, but only if you are good enough to have a clear view of the long-term macroeconomic picture, the instinct to grasp subtle implications, and the confidence to act. There are no cast iron guarantees, though.

As the current bubbles suffer an inglorious fall, a golden bubble will rise from the ashes. All bubbles pop, and the new one will, as well. But that day is far off. Considering that the present bubble age has lasted more than any other such period before, the product of its destruction – the golden bubble – will endure longer. In the meantime, you could find the key to a whole chest of golden treasures. All you have to do is take the plunge.

Other Investments

Whole life insurance that invests in stocks and real estate will not do well. Hybrid life insurance policies, a combination of whole and term life insurance, won't do well for the same reason. Term life insurance is the cheapest life insurance, and is not a genuine investment. The real cost of premiums as well as pay offs will decline under the assault from raging inflation. Popping bubbles may also cause your insurer to go bust. Keep your eyes open.

Term life insurance is the original form of life insurance and covers the life or health of the insured for a fixed, specified duration of time. Whole life insurance provides damages in case the life or limb of the insured are damaged during his entire lifetime.

Another investment category is **collectibles**, like pieces of sculpture, paintings, or historical artifices. These will crash in value as their owners start to sell them to raise money. That will be the time to buy if you have the means and the desire. If you own them and look upon them as investments only, now is the time to sell.

Investment grade **diamonds** will go up as the dollar collapses and the euro rises, since diamonds can be easily sold for euros, so their fortunes are *linked* with euros. Diamonds used for jewelry will fall as the demand for jewelry – again, a discretionary purchase – falls with the economy as it goes further down the spiral.

Specter of Big Government?

Gold and silver lovers are wary that skyrocketing prices of those precious metals may cause covert manipulations of gold prices by governments and a possible repeat of the 1933 ban on private ownership of gold. A falling dollar causes gold to appreciate and makes U.S. Treasury securities less attractive to investors, thereby robbing the government of a lucrative source of funds.

There are two ways for a government to maneuver gold prices:

- **Sales of Gold by Central Banks**, which is on the decline. China is boosting its gold reserves through the purchase of gold from the market. Both these factors have a positive, upward effect on the price of gold.

Then again, the **Central Bank Gold Agreement-3** is in operation between June 2009 and June 2014. It limits the total annual sale of gold by central banks to 400 tons with a maximum of 2,000 tons over the five-year period. Central banks also spread out such sales in order to prevent price volatility. Nineteen central banks are a part of this agreement, and this restricts the scope for manipulative sales and their effects.

Such sales by central banks are decreasing as even vocal opponents of gold may be privately worried of the revival of monetary function of gold. Boosting gold reserves, therefore, becomes necessary and China is already purchasing gold. These factors cause gold to rise.

- **Currency Rate Fluctuations** in the foreign exchange (forex) market affect gold prices as inflating the dollar depresses both gold and euros. These dealings are in tune with the Jamaica Agreement of 1973 that permits central bank intervention in the forex markets to prevent wild fluctuations in the exchange rate of currencies.

  However, such operations are targeted towards currency. Their effect on gold is a sort of collateral damage. Again, the effect of these transactions on gold price is limited and does not last long.

If private ownership of gold were to be banned, prices will go up and defeat the very objective behind such a restriction. Only middle income gold investors who cannot purchase gold from abroad will be affected, and this would create a black market for gold. Most of the demand for gold comes from outside the U.S., so the price is determined largely outside the U.S. Finally, the sizable amount of gold in circulation makes such a ban impractical.

Gold & Silver Pop

Around eight to ten years from today, the gold and silver bubble will start to pop, but slowly, for the same reason that bubbles in stocks, bonds, real estate and other commodities will be collapsing a little while from now, resulting in a loss of investor confidence. Remember, markets operate on sentiment and expectation more than on anything else.

By then, other asset classes will evolve out of their instability and show their ability to provide returns. Some resistance will be witnessed as gold investors argue that gold has an intrinsic value that other assets do not. However, these asset classes also possess a certain worth of their own, and once capital moves from gold to these assets, the gold bubble will start to go bust.

And because this imminent gold-silver bubble will most likely be the largest bubble ever, bigger than those we are living in at present, the final pop will probably be the most violent explosion ever witnessed in financial markets. Until then, you can link your fortunes with skyrocketing precious metals.

Again, the same strategy can be repeated: if you can profit from the present popping bubbles, you can do the same from the burst of the gold bubble in another decade. Wealth is shifted from an overvalued asset class to an undervalued one.

Bubbles get formed in overvalued asset classes like those assets that command a greater price than they really should. This is an effect of speculative investment because the investors expect, rightly or wrongly, that asset class to rise in value. Such investment further adds to the value of the asset class.

Price to Earnings (P/E) Ratio is a great way to measure if an asset class is overvalued. It measures the price of the share to the earnings of the company and also indicates the number of years the investor is ready to wait to recover their investment. It has an average value of 12. Anything below is undervalued and anything above is overvalued. A P/E ratio of over 18 indicates a bubble.

There is no point to invest in overvalued classes, because it is expensive. Investors will have to wait a number of years to recover their investment and, if it is a bubble, the expected high returns which make him ignore the time and cost overruns never materialize. All assets usually move from being overvalued to undervalued and *again* to overvalued.

Investment into undervalued asset classes is profitable if they are expected to go up. Again, picking the right undervalued class requires a firm comprehension of the long term macroeconomic developments. For example, gold is the right undervalued class at present. When asset bubbles start to burst, these assets will also be undervalued. But they won't be the right investment choice, for they will not rise in the near future.

Around a decade from now, however, these assets *or most of them* will be the correct undervalued class to invest in. This will also be the time when gold will be overvalued and the gold bubble will be on the verge of a collapse. Chances of another repeat of this undervalued or overvalued cycle are very real.

As always, luck will be a determinant of success. Those who hold physical gold and silver today for cultural reasons or for tax evasion will see a rise. But they can lose, too, when in another ten years or so, the gold bubble pops and they still hold onto their gold. Luck in itself can take you only this far – a combination of judgment and skill is also needed.

After the dollar bubble pops, investment into the U.S. economy will be very cheap for non-American investors. They will need only small amounts of their own currencies to purchase vast amounts of our dollars to invest into dollar denominated assets here in the U.S.

Cycles operate everywhere... in nature, as well as in finance and economics.

Timing the Great Wealth Transfer: Now and Later

This might sound like doomsday prophecy, but the approaching crisis will sack and burn the current global financial system. As always, it is difficult to predict the precise time when any financial crisis makes its full presence felt because there are a host of interrelated factors governing the outcome.

Because all bubbles pop, the gold and silver bubble will also burst. Again, the timing cannot be predicted accurately, but a broad range of timing can be guesstimated. This will be somewhere eight to ten years from now. You have to shift your wealth from gold and silver into other asset classes when these precious metals are near their top.

Now, currency is a very poor measure of the value of gold and silver, or any other asset class for the simple reason that the purchasing power of currency keeps on changing with changing economic cycles. Currency can measure price, not the value. This is important when determining if gold and silver are near their peak.

If we go into a deflation, the price of gold could go up as high as $2,500 or $5,000 per ounce. On the contrary, if we go into an inflation situation, this price might go to $10,000 an ounce or more. In the case of hyperinflation, this may go to billions or even trillions of dollars.

With currency notes being printed furiously by major central banks, the value or the purchasing power of all major currencies is going down. The point is that currency cannot be a measure of the peak value of gold or silver. Therefore, we need a better measure of value – indicators that can quantify the purchasing power.

Dow to Gold Ratio or the ratio of the total number of points on the Dow index to the price of one ounce of gold in dollars is one such measure. The Dow index is a stock market index that represents the trading performance of thirty large publicly owned companies based in the United States. This ratio averages around four.

When the economy booms, this ratio increases as gold is not perceived to be a better asset or a better store of monetary value as compared to stocks, bonds, or real estate. During market crashes, the value of the ratio comes near unity – when the ratio reaches one – due to falling index and rising gold. The higher this ratio was before the crash, the lower it goes after the crash.

Just before the famous market crash of 1929, the Dow-Gold ratio was 18. It slipped to 2 in 1932. In 1966, this ratio measured 28. From there it descended to 1 as gold rose after its connection with dollars was cut in 1971. With the dot-com boom, the Dow-Gold ratio went up to 45. It is coming down and is at 8.35 as of February 2013.

Considering the correlation between previous highs and lows, this time the ratio might touch 0.5, or half. If the economy deflates, it might only go down to a value of 2. Hyperinflation, however, can take this to 0.1 or even less. Again, this emphasizes the non-rigid nature of the likely situation; you can't fix a point and say this is the peak.

Because we are primarily interested in knowing the top value of gold and silver, the Dow-Gold or the Dow-Silver ratio puts things in the reverse as it measures stocks in terms of gold and silver. What we need is a ratio that measures gold and silver in terms of stock. The way to arrive at such a ratio is to reverse the Dow-Gold ratio.

What we then get is the purchasing power of gold and silver as the *value* of these precious metals – the amount of shares they can purchase. Since the dawn of the great bubble age in the American economy in the early 1980s, the **Gold-Dow Ratio** and the **Silver-Dow Ratio** are on the decline, meaning a continuous erosion of the purchasing power of these metals.

These metals are starting to rise now and will do so for quite some time to come. Silver is more scarce than gold and as supply of investment gold dwindles due to huge demand, people will turn to silver. This will pull its price to higher levels. And because silver finds application in industry, people from the industrial world will be ready to shell out whatever it takes to get their hands on silver. The silver bubble may eventually overshadow the gold bubble.

Similarly, **Gold and Silver Measured in Real Estate** is another indicator of the top value of gold and silver. Real estate is now still in a bubble, being artificially supported by the Fed and its printing presses. Like all bubbles, this too will pop the way it did between 2007 and 2008. And when it does, gold and silver will be able to purchase more and more of the falling real estate.

A good way to detect a housing bubble is the mortgage-rent ratio. This compares the total cost of purchasing a home to the total cost of renting a similar property. In the U.S., this ratio has an average value of between 1 and 1.05. It climbs up during real estate booms and bubbles and falls when these bubbles pop.

Back in 1989, this ratio went up to 1.25 and fell to 0.9 by the mid-nineties. In the pre-2007 era, described by many as the largest real estate bubble in history, this ratio went up to an insane value of 1.85 to 1.95. It came down to 1.25 in 2010. Because the fall below the mean value is proportional to the rise above the mean, this time the ratio will plunge deeper.

And when that happens, the price of real estate will fall, fall, and fall. Needless to say, gold and silver will rise in comparison. Again, how deep this ratio will go or how to judge the precise moment when gold and silver have topped is something that depends on a host of other factors.

These developments have to be seen in the broader context of how currencies behave – the value of the dollar and other main currencies such as the euro and pound – the exchange rates between these – and the value of bonds. If currencies fail and there is a more than realistic chance of this happening, the price of gold and silver will rise to astronomical levels.

Also, this time the demand for gold and silver will be more than it was back during the 1970s when these metals were also on the rise. The price of these metals will, therefore, break new ceilings due to the following causes:

- Today, more people can participate in such trades. In the 1970s only Americans and West Europeans could do so, and the price of gold was set mainly on the Commodities Exchange in the U.S. and the London Metals Exchange. Russia, Africa, and the entire population in Asia were left out.

- These days, people are more willing to invest than be satisfied with deposits in banks. Communication has improved, and the world is more connected than ever before. Information travels fast and investors in one part of the world can easily trade in markets located in other, distant areas.

- As compared to the 1970s, people today possess greater purchasing power.

- A currency crisis may occur in view of over-printing to sustain the bubbles in the economy. Each time a new dollar, pound, euro, cent, or dime is created, its purchasing power falls and so does its worth in the eyes of the people. Investors will, therefore, increasingly turn to gold and silver.

In the Final Analysis

After a careful consideration of all the above information, ownership of physical gold and silver that is never traded should be considered. This will be a hedge against financially uncertain times. After that need is filled, you can think about ownership of mining stocks.

Physical gold and silver can be stored both at home and at offshore locations. There is some safety in geographical diversity. Stocks of Australian, Canadian, and South African mining companies are better than their American counterparts and most of the investment into mining stocks has to go into large producer companies with reserves and a sound working culture.

Again, stocks of exploration companies should be avoided because such companies are not into production and do not maintain reserves of precious metals. Their prospecting activities may or may not be successful, and it is better to adopt a careful approach with them.

Gold and silver form the undervalued class at present and will break many price records in the time to come. The stocks of companies are a more profitable option that also happens to be more risky. Also, you have to hold your purchase-happy hands for some time before investment into these becomes a viable option.

Please remember, there are those amongst us who prefer to be comfortable; more risk adverse folks should stick with continuous involvement in their market positions, if they do not mind that extra measure of risk. For them the advice of 'high-physical-gold-percentage – low-stock-percentage' is more applicable.

A meticulously thought out plan of action that incorporates the big picture at the macroeconomic level and your temperament is the best way forward. This plan should also be organic and has to evolve with changing times, for conditions in the market are never constant.

In order to get to the top, you have to ride on top of that cycle. You invest in an undervalued class and watch it grow. When it gets near its top, you sell it and invest in another undervalued class and the cycle continues. As of now, gold and silver are the undervalued assets, while real estate and most other stocks and bonds are overvalued.

After the aforementioned eight to ten years, gold and silver will be overvalued, for there will be a gold and, probably, a larger silver bubble in existence. The overvalued assets of today may be the undervalued asset classes of this period. Then, it will be time to shift wealth into such undervalued assets. Until then, enjoy the gold and silver ride.

Temperament Issues

The way you think is the single most important determinant of what you make of yourself. Critical thinking is necessary to survive and profit from the financial storm that is on the horizon. This attitude is essential for success – anywhere and everywhere. It's up to you to decide to set yourself apart as part of the thinking class, or be a part of the shouting rabble.

Fiscal rationalism helps you understand the fundamentals of the market and the wider economy. You have your own analytical skills for making investment decisions and are not affected by manipulative tactics inspired by the vested interests. This way, you do not allow strangers to chart the course of your life at the cost of your interests.

Peace of mind truly is priceless. Its importance in life cannot be quantified in terms of money alone. Money is a means to that end, but not the *end in itself*. After all, the aim of this book is to safeguard and augment your finances so you can get some peace. It will be imperative, then, to devise a plan that suits your temperament or else the plan itself can destroy your tranquility.

Your **risk tolerance** will be the starting point. There is absolutely no merit in adopting a risky investment approach if you are not comfortable with high risk. Generally speaking, a moderate level of risk that balances well with possible gains is a better approach. And when in doubt, err on the side of caution.

Then comes the issue of your **level of involvement** – whether you are comfortable with frequent sales and purchases or prefer to purchase early and wait for longer durations. Those who adopt the former path are traders who try to buy low and sell high in the shorter and medium duration. The latter are investors who are in for the longer term.

Traders are bound to slip on their chosen path. This is because there will eventually come a time when the apparent high point where the trader sells his stock is not the real summit, just a flat period before the stock takes off again. Then, the trader has to wait for the next cycle. You never know if you will be around, financially and physically, when the next one arrives.

Another problem with the trader strategy is the amount of time and involvement. It is huge and is, therefore, recommended only for those who have the time and don't mind frequent trading operations. No approach in a dynamic market comes with a cast-iron guarantee of success, but with the trader path, there is greater chance of returns being lesser than the invested time, money, and energy.

Investors with a high level of emotional intelligence (EI) adopt the latter course of action. Such individuals understand the market and the broader economy and are confident enough to go against the apparent trend; they are bold enough to buy when stocks are falling and sane enough not to hold for too long, when stocks are on the rise.

High EI investors know how much to save and invest as opposed to consumption expenses and are well aware of the limits of any approach including novel and risky strategies. Their portfolio represents balance, *a manifestation of their moderate psychology*. Most importantly, they can identify an undervalued asset and act appropriately before most others do.

The Plan

Once you identify yourself, you can frame a **Dynamic Plan of Action** based on diligent research and investigation. This plan has to be modified in case the original was not appropriate. Changes will also be needed in order to fine tune and adjust it to the changing situation. The plan of action will involve delimitation of:

I. Definitive Goals, such as ownership of *X ounces of gold* or *Y ounces of silver* or *Z acres of land*. The goal cannot be unclear such as, say, *making of lot of money*. It has to be categorical, within the limits of possibility, and measurable.

If you do not define your final goals, you are likely to waver in your beliefs and, therefore, in your actions. Such knee jerk reactions and unplanned changes will cause a lot of anxiety and stress and increase the chances of making unwise decisions.

II. Strategy has to be outlined after gleaning a proper understanding of the market, the broader economy, and the cycles therein. Investment has to be directed into the asset class expected to be the top performer in the coming cycle. This requires foresight that, again, is based on an understanding of the fundamentals, research, and instinct.

It was in the early 1980s when the great bubble age began in the American economy. The size and inherent strength of our economy had inspired and facilitated the making of easy money – all you had to do was mindlessly invest in certain assets. The rising bubbles would automatically magnify the investments.

This bubble era started to decline from the year 2000 onward. All through the bubble age, gold and silver were on the decline because people turn to these stores of monetary value only when things get tough. Currently things are just starting to go down that path, and there is only one way the price of these precious metals is headed – upward.

Previously, booms were shortly followed by busts and the cycle continued. We stand on the threshold of a groundbreaking change in the global financial system. It is a change that will introduce a paradigm shift in its operations. This time, when stocks, bonds, real estate, and most other commodities go down, they will not rise for a long time.

In reference to cycles, gold and silver will rise consistently and considerably for at least another eight to ten years. This will be the gold and silver bubble. Like all other bubbles, these too will eventually pop after the mentioned eight to ten years. Until then, they offer a smooth and lucrative ride for shrewd investors.

And when they fall, other asset classes like stocks, bonds, real estate, and other commodities will rise. Just before this happens, it will be time to shift wealth from these precious metals to the *expected-to-rise* among the other asset classes.

III. Tactic involves implementation of the understanding developed when the original strategy was chalked out. Investment in collapsing asset classes – as was the case earlier, to benefit from the rise in the boom that would follow – will not work this time. Not in the immediate future, at least.

Gold and silver always rise during economically tumultuous times, as people lose faith in most other investment avenues. The surge in demand will have a similar effect on their price. There is no reason they won't rise this time. With so much money being created, it is no wonder people are already losing faith in paper money.

As gold climbs very high under pull from immense demand, availability will fall. Even otherwise, the prices of gold will make purchasing it more than difficult. Then, people will turn to silver. What makes silver more attractive is its current price is not very high – its chief demand for now is of the industrial variety, and investment demands will over take industrial demand due to gold being too expensive for most people to invest in.

This very industrial application will cause the price of silver to jump as the economy starts to recover, bit by bit. Revived industrial activity will recreate the demand for silver, and many in the industrial world will be ready to spend a fortune to acquire this essential material.

Then again, you have to decide which form of these precious metals you would like to purchase – physical metals, ETFs, or precious metals left with depositories. Stocks of gold and silver mining companies are another investment option. All these alternatives have their own merits and demerits and are discussed in a subsequent section of this chapter.

Teamwork

Investment is a team game. If you have been in the investment field for some time, you will know how one situation can be looked upon from almost innumerable points of view. Again, the likely effects of economic and political developments on market sentiment can be infinite. Considering different views can take your team close to the comprehensive, big picture.

But then, there is always another side to the coin. Two heads are better than one so long as too many cooks don't spoil the broth. The best way to have a team is to take advice from a few genuinely good newsletters recommended to you by investor friends and acquaintances who are as informed, sane, and experienced as yourself, if not more.

Apart from newsletters, there are good books on investment and websites that specialize in precious metals and their price trends. They also provide fairly accurate advice. However, information on where to find such sources is not readily available. You have to hunt for them and compare their counsel with your own informed analysis. This is the best way to shortlist the sources. It requires due diligence, though.

Building Noah's Ark, Individually and Collectively

There is an inherent link between the economy, energy, and the environment. The economic engine is driven by energy resources that are found in the environment. Today's model of economic growth is based on consumerism: the consumption of more and more goods and services. This leads to greater extraction of natural resources and produces more waste.

Resources are supplied by the environment, which also assimilates wastes. Resources are limited and so is the absorption capacity of nature. When the rate of accumulation of wastes is greater than the rate at which they can be broken down, the environment fails to execute its all important function of maintenance of life on this planet. Such is the toxic contradiction between Mother Nature and today's economic model. *And no one beats nature.*

Bubble economy compels the authorities to keep on printing money or bail out banks and industries in times of financial stress. Such market interventions misdirect investment and maintain the bubbles that eventually collapse. These interventions are temporary and, worse, designed to maintain the status quo. But then, everything is about to change. How long can the old system be artificially extended?

In order to deal with the impending financial bubble pop we need to follow a roughly four step sequential process. And, there will be some courses of action to which a person cannot resort to on his own

– cooperation from the community will be essential. This financial storm may turn out to be a blessing in disguise, for the age old community spirit may be revived as the accumulated poisons in the present system are finally neutralized.

These four steps are:

- **Commit to Act** by accepting that a financial bubble pop is *a fait accompli,* it is only a matter of when. Living in denial won't help at all for the illusory world will fall like the proverbial castle built out of thin air.

- **Self-Assessment** to understand your current finances and what they need to be in order to deal with the approaching crisis. This will also require an estimate of the gravity of the brewing financial blizzard.

- **To-Do List** will be infinite as you will want to address everything and anything that you expect to happen.

- **Prioritization of the List** so that you have a viable plan of action. You also need to be realistic in admission of what you can take care of individually and what can be addressed as a group. The sooner you acknowledge your own limitations, the better will be your response in dealing with them.

This approaching storm can be in the form of financial structure breakdown, protracted recession, or a collapse of all government services. Within a year or so, a banking crisis can unfold as the artificially sustained credit and housing bubble pops. A little later, petroleum supplies may collapse and add to the inflation. Baby boomer retirement will add to the woes as we proceed towards national insolvency and maybe towards a new monetary system *not* based on fiat money.

Again, the intensity of these possible outcomes is a matter of debate. This means we have to assume a certain possibility with certain intensity and then design our disaster management plan. Since banking and finance is central to the current situation, let us assume a failure of the banking system as the starting point.

Skeptics might argue that all these possibilities are hypothetical and things will go on like before. That would amount to living in denial. Isn't it better to be prepared? That way, even if things go on as before, *you don't lose anything*. Except you spent the preparation time and locked your funds into some investment.

Preparing for an eventuality that does not occur is a lot better than witnessing your financial ruin by not preparing for the crisis that does occur. And the crisis will hit us. If you don't prepare, you will live with a sense of self-disgust for quite some time – you were right about your concerns, but did not take the necessary precautions for that concern. So long as the potential cost of not taking action is far greater than taking such action, the latter is justified.

The second step of financial self-assessment has to factor in your current and future needs compared with your present and future income, and all forms of assets that you possess. This will give you a fair idea of where you stand in relation to the future. As you jot down your needs, you will discover dependency on many things we take for granted.

In order to compile the to-do list, you need to make certain assumptions again. First, how early will the crisis hit us? We have already assumed a timeline and the most likely outcome – that of a banking system collapse as the housing and the debt collapses.

Second, the possibilities need to be judged on their probability and intensity. If a certain possibility is highly probable and will damage finances considerably, it needs to be in the list. Low-probability-high-intensity events will also make it to this list, but occupy the second rung. High-probability-low-impact possibilities can be quickly and inexpensively addressed. The low-probability-low-impact scenarios can be skipped altogether.

A banking and financial system collapse is a high-probability-high-intensity event likely to hit us in the immediate future. We can similarly calculate the possibility and impact for the food distribution network, cuts in government spending, and collapse of the dollar. If you sit down with people who understand these financial intricacies, the list will be virtually endless.

Finally, you have to prioritize the list. Things that you can do by yourself without much expense and without external assistance will be at the top of the list. Withdrawing cash out of banks and distributing your bank deposits with various banks can be the starting point as a hedge against bank failures and forced bank holidays to prevent bank runs.

Investment in gold, silver, and other precious metals would be the next in order. You can do this by yourself, but only after having enough cash to address the day to day requirements. The hard part – significant lifestyle changes, acquisition of new skills, or new forms of employment – comes later.

Things you cannot do on your own and possibilities that no one can do anything to hedge against have to be addressed at the community level by a professional or left alone. At the community level, you can design savings plans with common deposits and common returns. Again, precious metals are a stellar asset to put your money into.

Emotional Intelligence and Investor Behavior

Emotional Intelligence (EI) is the ability to perceive, evaluate, and control emotions – that of oneself and of others. EI enables a person to better understand himself or herself, as well as others, and achieve better cooperation while working together. In investment management, EI is important as it permits the investor to maintain a calm demeanor and think rationally when everyone else is doing the opposite.

Being emotionally intelligent is different from *being emotional* or *being in touch with one's emotions*; instead, it is the ability to recognize and apply emotions profitably. If we adopt this definition of EI, then even an emotional response that turns out to be profitable can be said to be an emotionally intelligent one.

Those with high EI do not trade too frequently, and they use low-cost fund options. Such people have a clear idea of how much to save and invest vis-à-vis how much to consume, the degree of active management, the limits of risky or novel strategies, and the concentration of the portfolio. They are able to overcome fear and buy when the stocks are falling. When stocks are on the rise, they wisely control their own greed and do not hold for too long.

Hard evidence of emotionally intelligent people making good investors comes from the book **'Emotional Intelligence and Investor Behavior'** by John Ameriks, Tanja Wranik, and Peter Salovey. They surveyed numerous investors and arrived at the conclusion that investors who scored highly in EI tests are more likely to perform better with investments.

In the present situation, an emotionally intelligent investor has to choose the correct investment avenue. We have discussed how government intervention through QE and loan guarantees misdirects investment and forms bubbles. All such diversions are corrected by the market and, therefore, all bubbles pop.

Bubbles in the U.S. economy will explode violently. Other bubbles in the world economy are inherently linked with these bubbles, and they too will burst. Then, there would be no point in purchasing stocks, since they would never rise. Precious metals remain the safe choice for the sane, emotionally intelligent investor.

Gold and Silver Investment

In order to understand the dynamics of gold and silver prices, we need to know the difference between things that people own. Broadly speaking, we buy two kinds of things:

- **Consumables** are things that we continuously need for consumption. These include most of the essential commodities, rather than luxuries. Because they are continuously used up, consumables have to be periodically purchased.

  Water, milk, bread, electricity, and gasoline are examples of consumables. Furniture, televisions, computers, cell phones, and other appliances that we discard after some duration can also be classified as consumables.

- **Collectables** are things that are not really essential for survival. These are expensive and collected as a hobby or as a mark of prestige. Collectibles are purchased only when the buyer has enough money available after spending on consumables.

> Vintage cars, fine wines, historical artifacts, classic paintings, postage stamps, first edition books, things formerly owned by famous personalities, diamonds, gold silver, stocks, bonds, real estate and the like are collectibles.

The price of a consumable is the sum of its manufacturing cost and the profit that the market allows the manufacturer to make, usually 1-10%. Collectibles fetch a much higher price – their price equals the manufacturing cost plus the scarcity premium, which can also be called the extra charge levied on account of a huge demand supply gap. It makes a great demand but shows an extremely limited supply.

Markets do not allow a long term scarcity premium for consumables. Supply disruptions due to strikes or natural disasters can lead to the levy of such premiums for short durations. There are a large number of suppliers, and the competition between them ensures that there is no long term shortage because suppliers have a vested interest to meet the demand. Suppliers make profit by increasing sales, not charging premiums.

Stocks of companies that are expected to do well can be classified as collectibles. During a bubble, stocks of companies that deal in some asset class acquire an unbelievable premium because there are too many people chasing a small amount of a stock. With time, this premium comes down. By then, if the company has not increased its strength through its assets and profits high, stock prices are not maintained and the stocks may sell for a discount, resulting in a negative premium.

Like markets, collectibles and consumables are a product of sentiment – there can be no logical explanation as to why people want to collect paintings or ancient artifacts. Precious metals and gemstones such as pearls, rubies, diamonds, sapphires, and emeralds are natural collectibles.

Gold is a special collectible. Its majestic aura has been untouched for 6,000 years. It cannot be synthetically made and it is almost impossible to fake. Yes, it can be diluted to some extent. But the changes can be easily identified with machines. Adding to the price of gold will be its acceptability. Other collectibles, such as postage stamps or fine wine, cannot be used as a mode of payment, but gold can be.

As for scarcity, gold supplies are limited and its production cannot be quickly and easily increased. This means the demand for gold will always exceed its supply. Annual demand for gold is around 4,000 tons, while supply from the mines and recycling is 2,900 tons. Production from mines is expected to go down when gold begins selling at just above the cost of production.

Covert gold sales by central banks of the Western world were widely believed to be holding down the price of gold. Gold and dollars move in the opposite direction. With the appreciation of gold, non-U.S. investors find dollar denominated U.S. Treasury securities less attractive. This attraction is the reason the U.S. economy trudges on despite huge deficits and debts.

Our trading partners, as well as foreign investors, have a stake in maintenance of the high value of the dollar, hence the participation of other central banks in this venture. This cannot go on forever, as the gold reserves are limited. The price of gold will rise. Interestingly, you can profit from this development by buying gold at low prices.

Apart from such covert sales, authorities have successfully implanted the fractional reserve banking model in gold ownership. Large investment banks can actually sell gold ownership certificates of the gold that they do not possess, as we shall see in the subsequent section. As the current crisis worsens, the demand for physical gold will rise. The crisis had destroyed even the last iota of trust people had in certain investment bankers and their accomplices.

Silver is the junior cousin of gold and has always been looked upon as a secondary store of monetary value in times of economic distress. In the last half century, silver has been used for a variety of industrial applications. In fact, around 90% of silver is used for industrial applications – such use makes it a consumable.

As the global economic slowdown retards industrial activity, the demand for silver and its price will fall. That would be the time to buy it, and the supply of gold is limited. As investors find it increasingly difficult to obtain physical gold, they will turn to silver, and the stocks of silver are also limited. This will be when the demand and price for silver will *skyrocket*.

Rising gold and silver have to be seen in the background of the conversion of the dollar from a collectible to a consumable. For a very long time, the dollar was the reserve currency of the world. Under the Bretton Woods Mechanism, many central banks maintained dollar reserves, not gold reserves.

It does not cost much to print dollars. It was the high demand for the dollar that added a massive scarcity premium to its value.

In order to fight the apparent threat of deflation, the Fed is working overtime to operate its dollar printing presses. With so many dollars floating around, there will be no scarcity premium attached to the dollar, and its value will erode thick and fast.

Cash backed by gold had value because people knew it was virtual gold they were exchanging. Un-backed fiat money is like a title deed of a non-existing house. Under such conditions, paper money will finally demonstrate its intrinsic value – that of paper – and people may use it as a fuel source, as it was during the 1923 hyperinflation in Weimar, Germany.

In times of economic distress, people look to shift their wealth into asset classes that can store or amplify monetary value. Without doubt, gold and, later, silver will be these assets. And do not worry about their slightly rising prices. Invest in them. The real ascent is yet to make its presence felt.

The Consolidation

Unprecedentedly fluid situations require unprecedented measures. And when prevention is just not in the cards, dealing with the situation head on is the only alternative. The entire global financial system is on the brink of a disaster like the world has never seen. The sooner you realize this, the better, because the earlier and more effective will be your response.

We are on the verge of a financial system revolution, one that will introduce radical changes in the manner in which this mechanism operates. As investors, we need to get out of the market cycle psychology. Before now, slowdowns were followed by booms. It made sense to purchase falling stock during slowdowns, for it would rise with the boom. Not anymore.

This is easier said than done. Since the 1980s, we have all gotten used to easy bubble money. All we had to do was purchase stocks, bonds, real estate, and other commodities and wait. Rising bubbles would take the price up with them. When on the ascent, they created a lot of non-real wealth. Going downhill, they will liquidate their creation, if not more. All bubbles pop.

Wealth created by bubbles is illusory because it is not based on a genuine increase in productivity, the real, long term driver of economic growth. It was made from speculation and hyped expectation, a very shaky foundation. Markets work on fickle sentiments and when investor perception turns *anti-bubble,* right or wrong, the bubbles collapse.

At present, our economy is composed of six bubbles – stocks, real estate, private debt, consumer spending, dollars, and government debt. These are symbiotically linked with numerous other bubbles in the global economy. Globalization ensures a two-way connection between these bubbles. And when one collapses, so will the others.

Once bubbles get formed in an economy where productivity improvement is absent, neglected, or limited, they have to be sustained because their burst slows the economy down. Credit guarantees for corporations and banks by the government, fiscal stimulus, bailout packages, and monetary expansion provide such sustenance. However, such measures not only prolong the inevitable pop, but actually make the future burst more intense.

Public memory is short, agreed. But the memories of the dot-com and housing bubble crashes must be still fresh. The entire global economy is bubbling with interlinked speculative investments, and when one bubble starts to go down, so will the rest. This time, the market slowdown will not be followed by revival; instead, it will take us where we have never been before.

Do not bother to check with investment advisors. Their counsel is based on the buy-and-hold traditional rationale that works well in rising bubble economies such as the one we had for the past 30 years. It also works in economies with continuous productivity improvement.

Traditional rationale fails in a crashing bubble economy when prices fall, fall, and fall.

Most financial advocates get paid for roping in investors, and investors will put their funds on the line only if they expect the economy to do well. Yes, there are a few objective advisors, but they remain exceptions. These 'experts' couldn't predict the present slowdown. What, then, will make them see the coming storm?

You can avoid getting caught in the falling bubble trap by following two main rules, but nothing is a cakewalk. The imminent crisis will be a precarious and slippery one, and will require you to be on guard. Complicating the situation will be the perception manipulation machinery let loose by the authorities in active collaboration with the media. These rules are:

I. Until the Dollar Bubble Pops between now to next few years, investment by all prospective investors, domestic and foreign, should stay way from all stocks and real estate, U.S. or foreign. The same applies for investment property, such as real estate held for investment purposes only.

Other bubbles in the U.S. economy will also pop with the dollar bubble. It is difficult to predict the exact timing of such a collapse because the inflated dollar will not really fall unless foreign investors and our trading partners decide to pull the plug.

Stocks and real estate have yet to hit the real bottom. If you plan to sell your stocks, talk to your accountant, since you may be able to spread out the sale over a period of time and use tax law to your advantage. Most importantly, do not interpret a short-lived rally in stocks or real estate as a sign of recovery. There will only be a fall in the longer term. As of now, wealth needs to be shifted from these assets into cash and, later, into gold and silver.

Inflation benefits the debtor since the value of the sum to be repaid has eroded. The sum is still the one agreed at the time the debt was contracted, but its purchasing power has come down considerably. The hyperinflation that occurs after the bubbles collapse will effectively liquidate your loans if you have a fixed rate mortgage at a reasonably low rate and make enough to pay back the mortgage.

In case you have already signed a mortgage, refinance it to a low and fixed rate with a term of 30 to 40 years. Adjustable rate mortgages see an upward revision of the lending rate during inflationary times. If you are confident you can pay the installment after the bubbles have collapsed, do not rush to pay back the mortgage – inflation is on its way to help you.

An even more aggressive option is to raise loans with your house as collateral and invest the proceeds into gold and silver. This requires you to be really confident about your repayment abilities. There is a risk of default and eviction. Eviction can be postponed by applying for mortgage assistance and foreclosure bailout plans that governments usually offer during financial distresses.

In normal times, it takes one year for banks to evict mortgage defaulters. This duration will increase during the crisis, as the government helps defaulters keep their houses, at least for the time being. Such tactics are for the thick-skinned among us who don't mind fighting daily turf wars with bankers and authorities.

II. No Long-Term Bonds and Fixed Rate Investments will be worth little, as inflation will knock the value out of their returns. When the dollar and government debt bubbles finally pop, foreign investors will pull out of our economy. This will create a shortage of capital and increase lending rates. Authorities will have to increase monetary supply.

Also, monetary expansion is usually inflationary. Considering the magnitude of the collapse, the Fed will have to print twenty-four/seven in order to fight the resultant slowdown. Runaway inflation will mean fixed rate investments – such as long term bonds – are worth nothing more than the piece of paper used to represent them.

Inflation benefits the borrower and hurts the creditor. Bonds are issued by the borrower – either the government or a corporation – and the purchaser is the creditor. If you end up with these, your position will be equivalent to that of the bank that gives you a fixed rate mortgage and loses out due to inflation, as mentioned earlier.

Right before the collapse of the dollar and government debt bubbles, gold and silver will be excellent avenues to move your wealth into.

Just before these bubbles are fully punctured, short term investment entities such as money markets and short term government bonds can slightly hold and augment your wealth. However, these have to be disposed off before the full pop.

Keep these in mind over the upcoming 2013 to 2023 period. This will be when the last of the six American bubbles, the government debt bubble, collapses with foreign investors pulling out and our trading partners refusing to play ball anymore. The precise timing cannot be stated with accuracy, as markets operate on sentiment. It will take only one major pullout or some event that triggers a negative chain reaction.

Counter Psychological Inertia

Thirty years is more than a generation, and old habits die hard. If you were a young investor back in the early 1980s and made a fortune from investment in stocks, bonds, and real estate, you will not like this analysis. What is even worse, the suggested alternative investment avenues are not looked upon favorably by other investors. But then, this is how fortunes are made. Even while you were basking in the shiny days of bubbleland, you knew deep inside something was amiss; this was too easy a way to make money. Or were you completely taken by the glamour or style, which made you overlook the sobering substance?

Be that as it may, financial times are changing fast, and if you do not keep up with them, you will end up a relic of the bygone, bubble era. Wanting a return of the bubble times is wishful thinking. Like a seasoned surfer who knows how to stay atop every coming wave, you can cash in on the coming financial wave. Otherwise, you can drown. The choice is yours.

Trust & Faith

Sentiments and perceptions are an integral part of stock market operations. The preceding discussion may appear to be right, wrong, or somewhere in between. As an investor, you can follow it completely or partially. You can even write it off as nonsense and remain pessimistic. Unprecedented situations require foresight. Whining is for losers.

Your Potential Plan

- Conversion of adjustable rate mortgages and other loans into fixed rate ones.
- Don't rush to pay off any fixed rate debt.
- Focus on paying off all variable rate credit cards.
- Shifting to a lower expense lifestyle.
- Sell collectibles and jewelry other than gold and silver jewelry.
- Ensure continuity of employment; don't quit your job until you have another one safely in the bag.

Economic crises lead many to **bankruptcy**. If you feel the need for it, swallow your pride and declare bankruptcy. There will be many others doing the same. But before you do so, you will do well to shift sizable chunks of your wealth into trust funds for your children. The timing of this shift has to be checked with your lawyer, because doing so just before you declare bankruptcy can legally amount to *fraud*.

Profiting from Collapse

As has been repeatedly mentioned in the preceding chapters, transfer of wealth from stocks, bonds, real estate, and other commodities into cash and then into gold and silver is the most advisable alternative.

Gold is a unique collectible in that it has continued to allure us for at least 6,000 years. The price of a collectible is the sum of its production cost and its scarcity premium. The latter far exceeds the former and is the extra price it commands in view of the demand being much larger than the supply. Vintage cars, fine wines, art pieces, historical artifacts, first edition books, stocks, bonds, real estate, gold, and silver are examples of some collectibles.

The opposite of collectibles, consumables are those items that we *consume continuously*. These include essential items such as water, milk, bread, gasoline, and electricity. TVs, cell phones, computers, furniture, and other appliances that we discard after some time are also consumables. Their price is the cost of production plus a profit margin allowed by markets.

In the near future, the demand for gold will go up, and so will its price. The following are the reasons for this expectation:

A. Relink to Gold: Despite the recent rally, gold prices have not reached the level they should have, because gold no longer functions as money. Therefore, no monetary premium in the form of additional pricing due to its use as money has been added to its existing value as a pure commodity. Soon, however, this function of gold will be revived, and that will add to its demand.

Gold has been used as money – coin money and monetary reserves – from as early as 2,500 B.C. because it serves two important functions of anything used as money. It is an efficient store of value, and it is acceptable as a medium of exchange. Once refined, gold remains on this planet. It does not rust or even tarnish. We discontinued the dollar and gold reserves link in 1971.

The dollar moves in the opposite direction of gold. U.S. Treasury securities are denominated in dollars and are still regarded as an attractive investment. When gold rises and the dollar falls, these securities become less attractive to foreign investors. Such inflow of funds is the reason our economy continues to trudge along, despite massive debts and deficits.

Another facet in the love-hate relationship between the dollar and gold is the role of our trading partners and exporters. As mentioned before, these partners tacitly collaborate to maintain the value of the dollar because it keeps their exports inexpensive and, therefore, cheaper. Such actions also keep the funds flowing in.

Our current debt is around $16 trillion. Unfunded liabilities go to about $87 trillion. Instead of fixing the basics, we make a show of fixing the symptoms – we print money to cover these and other gaps. As of December 2012, the Fed is printing $85 billion a month for the purchase of U.S. Treasuries and to stimulate the housing sector. *No wonder the dollar is losing value.*

Anything in excess is bad, and two wrongs do not make a right. Shaky monetary foundations create the mess of ever-increasing debt, both public and private. The pressures of a bubble economy necessitate continuous and inflationary monetary expansion that eats up the value of hard earned savings.

We aggravate matters by a shopaholic, high consumption lifestyle by buying the consumerist argument that has been carefully cultivated by the powers that be. Again, we refuse to understand this structure that holds us in perpetual debt while we spread our shameless hands before the government asking for subsidies. Governments oblige by inflationary creation of money.

Global confidence in fiat money is also on the decline. Runaway decline in the confidence in fiat currency creates the climate of opinion, and technology provides the means for the positive revolution. The earlier problem of divisibility of gold and silver will be eliminated by online transactions. Earlier, low denomination *buy and sell* had to be settled with copper and nickel coins and added to the complications of the transaction.

Such overwhelming public preference for gold will make them and, later, their governments adhere to a gold standard. This will spike the demand for gold and, therefore, its price. And once the preference for gold overwhelms the preference for dollars, other currencies will follow the fall from grace. The revival of gold's monetary function will surge its demand.

In all systems of governance, and especially in democracies, public pressure, right or wrong, is a very potent force. Isn't that the reason financially unsustainable and apparently welfare-oriented programs continue with assistance from inflationary money printing presses? Every time authorities try to subjugate gold or cheat on it, it does the opposite. This is what happened in 1934 and between 1980 and 1981, under immense pressure of public demand.

During earlier crises, many countries used the dollar instead of their currency. That will no longer be the case as the ills of fiat money will finally be exposed in the light of a better alternative. Sure, governments will resist the revival of the gold standard because it requires fiscal prudence and discipline they are reluctant to adhere to.

With its monetary function revived and fiat money falling in public estimation, central banks and governments around the world will go on a gold purchasing spree or gold repatriation from the U.S. (just like Germany did in January 2013) in order to reassure people of the money being backed by something concrete. Dollar reserves won't mean anything when the dollar itself is being accused of fraud. This will add to the price of gold and silver.

B. Limited Supply: In public perception, monetary policy became a potent instrument for regulation of money and credit in the 1980s, when Paul Volcker, then Fed Chairman, declared a so-called war on inflation. Interestingly, this decade saw the cat and mouse game between minor inflation and minor deflation and, to the informed observer, demonstrated the limitations of monetary policy.

By then, such cycles were considered a part of our financial existence. And so was un-backed, irredeemable paper money. People forgot why gold became money in the first place and placed blind faith in the ability of the central bankers to deal with financial exigencies. Gold, therefore, fell in popular estimation and there wasn't any demand for gold as a monetary or investment entity. Lesser demand means lesser price.

Other assets continued to do well from the 1980s, and this sped up the overall gold fall. Falling prices meant it was no longer economical to mine gold, and many such companies stopped or suspended mining activities. As other commodities lose their appeal in the aftermath of the approaching crisis, investment demand for gold and silver will hit the skies and so will their price.

Historically, gold production has expanded by an average of around 2% per year, meaning it will continue to be scarce. It cannot be printed, as money can, and it represents the real effort. The cost of printing a $1 note and a $100 note might be same. But it takes 100 times the effort to find, mine, and refine a 100-ounce gold bar, compared to a 1-ounce gold ingot.

C. Market Trades will further add to gold prices. With gold on the rise, mining companies will start to sell off those securities they purchased as a safety measure against the possible fall of gold. Such positions move in the reverse direction of gold. Naturally, such sales will decrease their price and provide the upward fillip to gold.

Carry trade is the practice of borrowing at low interest rates and investing the proceeds into high-return investments. Borrowing non-interest-paying gold, selling it, and investing these returns into interest-paying debt instruments has been the prime carry trade in international markets.

With gold prices moving up, gold will command interest and counter the debt instruments that are losing out, and such trade will lose steam. Central banks around the world had loaned out their gold. Very few of these borrowers will be able to return the borrowed gold due to disruption in the main form of carry trade. Central banks will then have to purchase the very gold they loaned, and this will again cause *price appreciation of gold.*

Traditionally, Wall Street investment managers included gold and gold mining shares as an asset class in investment portfolios. The practice was discontinued in the 1990s, and between 2005 and 2006, the total market capitalization of all publicly traded gold stock was the lowest of all the 30 stocks represented by the Dow Index. Hedging abilities of derivatives reduced the allure of gold as a hedge. The fall of gold and gold mining stock in 1987 hit the proverbial nail in the golden coffin.

Back in 1987, many investment portfolios included gold, and the fall affected most asset classes. Also, gold had been in decline from 1980. The crashing stock market will demonstrate that the hedging value of derivatives is only as good as the paying ability of the counterparty. Numerous silent vultures are waiting for the collapse to start the purchase of gold. The prices are headed only our way.

Chapter 10 – Traditional Investments Will Fail

"Gold still represents the ultimate form of payment in the world. Fiat money in extremis is accepted by nobody. Gold is always accepted."

- Dr. Alan Greenspan - Former US Federal Reserve Chairman

In order to make our discussions sound like sane advice and not like tales from a doomsday thriller, we'll undertake a discussion of why and how asset classes other than gold and silver will lose heavily during and after the crisis that will shortly hit us. This will put everything in a better perspective and hopefully enable better understanding.

Many things will change with this crisis. One of the first things will be the people's perception about looking at credit ratings, even by top-class credit rating agencies. These ratings are based on past performance, and they make a relatively easy anticipation of future economic conditions. They will not work this time, much the same way they did work not in the case of Lehman Brothers.

Markets work on sentiment more than on anything else. This is because investment is based on certain assumptions for the future. When certain developments appear to affect these assumptions, investors react, and this reaction causes many rises and falls in the market. We also attempt to link the role of perception in shaping the future course of the market.

The Falling Stock of Stocks

A stock is a certificate that makes the holder an owner of a certain fraction of the company. When you purchase stocks, you are essentially buying the company's future earnings. Stock value goes up if the company makes profits. Stock holders can also vote on decisions that affect the future of the company. The more stock they own, the more voting power they have.

Stocks were not always the most preferred option of American and overseas investors, both individual and institutional. Before stocks there were bonds, and before bonds there was gold. Stocks captured the investor imagination in the early part of the 20th century and went from strength to strength, albeit with a few hiccups.

For the past fifty years, especially between 1980 and 2000, the Dow Jones Industrial Average was augmented by a thunderous 1,000%. For this same period, the growth of the GDP was a more modest 260%. Contrast this fantastic rise to the Dow's moderate 300% rise between 1928 and 1982.

By now you must have guessed that this phenomenal rise is in fact a bubble – excessive, speculative, and misdirected investment into a certain asset class. Bubbles attract investment because the underlying asset is expected to rise and this expectation is not based on concrete performance of the asset class, but only on speculation.

If you want to stay in a bubble, active management of the portfolio is needed. Understanding traditional rationale and the recent history of stocks is essential for active management of an investment portfolio that contains stocks. We would, however, advise you to refrain from such active management, for it is fraught with grave perils.

Before the 1920s, investors evaluated stocks on the basis of the dividend paid. The buy-low, sell-high model of capital gains evolved in the 1920s. This model made the stock market more speculative and trading increased. In six years, the Dow increased fourfold but crashed in October 1929, halting speculation. Three more years were, however, needed for it to reach a historic low.

After the crash, stocks became unpopular particularly as the Securities and Exchange Commission checked manipulative and unethical behavior. Stocks regained popularity in the 1950s and 1960s, followed by a bust in the 1970s due to recession and inflation. The 1980s saw their revival.

Stock Valuation

Problems start when the value of the stock is not connected with the performance of the company. This disconnect can be created by perception through the active and manipulative use of media. A bubble results when people are ready to pay such high prices and are ready to borrow in order to make such a purchase or investment.

Price to Earnings (P/E) Ratio is the most widely used measure for stock valuation. It is the ratio of the market value of a share divided by the earnings per share (EPS). If a company's share is presently trading at, for example, $60, and earnings per share over the last 12 months have been $5, the P/E ratio for the stock is 12 ($60/$5).

While earnings are a measure of the profits made or the net income of the company, revenue represents the gross income of the company – the amount of money made by it through the sale of goods and services *before* deduction of all expenses. EPS is the total annual earnings of a company divided by the number of shares issued by that company in that year.

Implied in the P/E ratio is that multiple of the company's EPS the investor is willing to pay at present in order to purchase the company's stock. It also indicates the number of years the investor is ready to wait to recover his investment. If this number is large, it means there is a bubble. *Remember, a purchase of stock represents buying the company's future income.*

The future is uncertain. The company's earnings may fall, the economy might slow down, or the stock market might value these earnings with downward revision – all of which lower the value of stock. During economic downturns, price also goes down and so do earnings.

What the future value of the company will be and what is the current equivalent (the stock price) of that uncertain future value can only be estimated, not pinpointed. This uncertainty of stock values makes the market dependent on investor psychology or sentiment, as different investors foresee different possibilities.

During bubbles, all that the investors look for is the rising price of stock. If it is going up, they want to join the bandwagon without due regard to any rational indicators. Even otherwise, it is not easy to define future earnings.

Price to Revenue Ratio can be another measure. However, if a company is unable to convert revenue into earnings, it means there is something seriously wrong with the management that bodes ill for the future health of the company. The investment might never pay off. By ignoring the net earnings, you are also overvaluing the company.

Book Value or Liquidation Value is the value of the company's assets, not its earnings or revenues. This can be a reasonable measure of the company's wealth, and the share price can be compared to this value in case the company owns considerable assets, but does not manage them very well.

Private Company Valuation or the valuation of a private company – a company that does not trade its stock publicly on stock exchanges – is significantly lower than for public companies. Typically, private companies trade at four to six times their earnings such as the 15 to 20 range for public companies.

This lower valuation is called *liquidity discount* or *marketability discount*, and it exists because private companies are not as easy to sell or liquidate as public companies. Also, many private companies are purchased with borrowed money, and buyers don't want to wait for four to six years to repay the debt.

Presently, liquidity discount is much higher because private companies are not participating in the stock market bubble. This makes them safer from the point of view of investment. Furthermore, such private company valuation is more realistic and more sober than bubble valuations.

Most financial analysts are stock salesmen. Most of these analysts are employed by firms that make money by getting people to invest into stocks and bonds. They cannot be expected to provide objective analysis. Over 95% of financial analysts still provide the buy-and-hold advice based on traditional rationale.

Independent and objective analysts who try to advise differently will be sacked by their firms. If these are analysts with considerable reputations, Wall Street and the financial media, both of which have a vested interest in maintenance of the investment fund flow into stocks, will move in to destroy their credibility and ostracize them from the financial world.

Non-independent analysts will provide the counter argument that they have used valuation techniques as described earlier. The speculative element in even honest use of these indicators has already been noted. Furthermore, these techniques are more or less based on the traditional rationale of buy-and-hold.

Traditional logic mandates a waiting period after the purchase of stock. The economy and, therefore, the stock market are expected to grow in the medium and the long term. This growth will augment the value of the purchased stocks, and when they are at or near their peak, they have to be sold. The profit is the difference between the buying price and the selling price.

Such logic is based on two assumptions. One, there is a natural growth rate for all economies, but there is no such thing as a natural growth rate. Any sustained growth eventually comes from productivity improvement; that, too, is not natural, but a result of improvements in technology, business models, and government policies for business.

The second assumption behind the logic is that we are not in a bubble, for all bubbles eventually pop and bring down the value of stock. It works well when bubbles are on the rise, not when they fall, as holding on to falling stock is futile. Since the 1980s, the entire global economy is bubbling and these are about to pop with an unprecedentedly loud explosion.

In the long term, a company's growth cannot be greater than the overall GDP growth. Between 1980 and 2000, the Dow grew by over 1,000% despite economic growth of only 260%. This means the growth of stocks of most companies and, by extension, the stock market is headed for a prolonged downturn.

More Appropriate Valuation

At the root of this problem of bubbles is faulty valuation heavily based on assumptions about the future –the earnings of the company, the state of the economy, and interest rates. All these assumptions are highly subjective. The mainstream sections among financial analysts, their employer firms, Wall Street, and financial media can be always found on the deceptively optimistic end of such assumptions.

Three General Rules of Stock Purchasing:

- Buy at a discount to the stock's intrinsic value so even if the market falls slightly, you are not in the red. This is the margin of safety.
- Find ways to profit from the inevitable volatility. One such method is diversification.
- Understand your investment style and plan accordingly – whether you are willing to learn on your own and actively involve yourself, or you need professional assistance. In both cases, you will need to be cognizant of genuine valuation techniques.

Markets operate on sentiment, but sentiments are subject to change. Yes, the process is slow. But eventually people will come out of their bubble view. This understanding will be accelerated when the interconnected bubbles in the linked global economy start to explode in a chain reaction.

Tragedy of the Stock Collapse

Aided by rising bubbles, people have been used to making money from stocks for more than a generation. Old habits die hard. People will hold on to stocks and look upon downturns as temporary phases. Then again, there are those who purchase during falling prices on the expectation of a rise in the near future.

When the markets around the globe declined by 40% in 2008, the Fed printed huge sums of money and our government went on a borrowing spree to boost the markets. Again, powerful vested interests had undertaken manipulative trading in order to keep the markets afloat or to make it fall. For these reasons, the stock market won't crash immediately, but in *stages*.

But because bubbles are driven by investor sentiment and hysteria, they can fall as quickly as they can rise. A trigger for the collapse of bubbles in our and the rest of the global economy may come from a slowdown of the Chinese economy, aggravation of the European debt crisis, or Israeli aggression against Iran.

Eventually, inflation on account of overprinting of money will drive up interest rates and dry the funds inflow into these bubbles. As money printing and inflation start to rise, the time lag between printing and inflation will come down. Such printing will also start to decrease, which is effective for boosting the stock market and leading to the prolonged fall of stock prices.

Domestic investors will be worried about rising inflation and rising interest rates eating up their returns. Foreign investors will be alarmed by the falling dollar as inflation forges ahead. Foreign investment funds are a major reason we can operate despite trebling debts and deficits. When overseas investors withdraw, the real downward slide will begin.

Unlike bonds, stocks are brothers-in-arms that rise and fall together. The intensity of the rise and fall may vary, but the overall direction is the same. If you already own stock, consider selling it gradually and invest into physical gold and silver.

No Love for Bonds?

Bonds were the preferred investment avenue for Americans before stock and after gold. Bonds are a loan debt that can be bought or sold on the bond market, and they offer a fixed amount of returns. When a company issues bonds, it contracts debt from the purchaser or investor. However, the creditors are not fixed entities, as bonds can be traded.

Again, bonds do not make the holder a fractional owner of the company the way stocks do, they only make him a creditor. If the company goes bankrupt, stock holders are launched in the frontline to face the cannons of loss. Bond holders come next.

Dividends or earnings from holding shares can be at a fixed rate of interest (preferred rate) or at a variable rate (common dividend). Usually, returns from holding fixed-interest bonds are fixed because the percentage of interest remains constant and is calculated on the basis of the principal or the original price of the bond, regardless of the changing value of the bond.

Depending on who the borrower or the issuer is, bonds can be United

States Treasury Bonds, savings bonds by the federal government, municipal bonds by state and local governments, corporate bonds by private companies, certificates of deposit by private financial institutions, or mortgage-backed-securities by government sponsored agencies.

Yields on bonds are always changing because of the changing market price of bonds. Those differences are a result of a function of three factors. Again, as with all things related to markets, investor sentiment based on the perception of future developments plays a pivotal role. These factors:

- **Interest Rate Risk:** If interest rates go up or are perceived to go up after the bond was issued, bond prices of these old bonds will fall because fresh bonds will fetch higher returns. Depreciated bonds fetch lower capital gains. The reverse happens if interest rates fall or are expected to fall.

- **Credit Risk** is the perceived risk associated with the creditworthiness of the borrower. The more creditworthy a borrower is or the more creditworthy his market reputation is, the lower the interest rates. Borrowers with weaker credit reputations have to pay greater interest rates.

  Bond prices will go up if the creditworthiness of the borrower goes up after the bonds were issued. Likewise, prices will fall if his reputation is dented.

- **Time Risk** is the sum of the above two risks in that the greater the time until maturity, the greater the interest risk and the credit risk. Investment for a longer duration means the funds of the lender are locked in for a longer period, hence larger returns in the form of higher interest rates; lower bond prices are demanded.

  If interest rates are expected to go down over the long term, however, the reverse happens when longer term bonds fetch lower interest rates and command higher prices.

Changing Bond Landscape

Traditionally, bonds are regarded as safer, although less lucrative than stock, for the following reasons:

- **Repayment of Principal**, the sum for which the bond was originally issued at maturity, is guaranteed by the bond issuer, unlike any issuer of stock.

- **Bond holders are paid before stockholders**. This is particularly beneficial if the creditworthiness of the borrower or issuer goes down over the period of the bond or if the issuer were to go bankrupt.

- **Bonds are backed by the assets of the issuers**. Public bonds are backed by governments who can raise taxes to make payments, while private bonds are backed by the assets of the private entity.

When the oncoming financial bubble pops, central banks will print money to fight the effects of falling bubbles. Rising inflation will cause a rise in interest rates and bonds will lose value. Because investors do not expect this, they will lose heavily and dent the perception of safety associated with bonds.

Three connected changes in early 1980s made bonds attractive again after the lull since the 1960s. These were:

- Expectation of lowering interest rates increased the price of bonds that increased capital gains from them.

- Relaxed government regulations allowed banks to issue increasing numbers of bonds.

- Tremendous deficits made the government issue more bonds. At the same time, there was an increase in corporate debt, consumer debt, and mortgage debt.

People and investors believe that the good part of the last thirty years will continue. They also blindly trust their government to find a way out of any situation, the way they did by purchasing bad mortgages and printing money to deal with the mortgage crisis, here and in Europe. Again, living in denial is always easier. But that is about to change.

Generally, interest rates are 2% to 3% above the rate of inflation. The massive printing of money will eventually cause inflation to rise tremendously. Interest rates will rise even higher and bonds will lose their allure. Governments can deal with the situation by heavily printing money and by borrowing. These boost the economy only in the short term.

Finally, even these measures will no longer be possible, as they trigger inflation that cause interest rates to go higher and bonds to lose out. Inflation also means a fall in the value of dollar. Rising interest rates on bonds mean that the government will never be able to repay the principal. And it can pay the interest only by further borrowing and that only further increases inflation.

This is where the vicious cycle of bonds will be complete, as medicine turns toxic and the diseased body can no longer take in even one more dose. The dollar and government debt bubble will explode, and we will face the full blast of the financial storm.

Fall in Installments

Living in the past and in blissful denial of the present *coupled with a blind faith in the ability of the government to play savior of last resort* will mean that the bond market does not collapse immediately. When the government prints money and borrows more, the markets respond positively, temporarily.

We have noted how the time lag between money printing and inflation decreases with the increasing printing of money. As this starts to happen, all the reasons for people's faith in bonds will be liquidated. And yes, deep down inside, even average investors know that something is amiss. They just don't admit it, not even to themselves.

Bonds issued by borrowers with lower creditworthiness will be the first to fall. Companies will be liquidated, and no one will purchase bonds or stocks. Already reeling under decreased tax revenues due to unemployment and expenses for bailouts, pensions, insurance, and debt obligations, the government will no longer will able to print money or borrow to ease the suffering.

Traditionally, this is when the Treasury asks the Fed to purchase its bonds by printing money, something that will not be possible in the light of runaway inflation. When U.S. Treasury bonds issued by the most solid debtor, the U.S. government, themselves become non-creditworthy, what happens to the lesser bonds?

Unreal Estate

Real estate witnessed sustained growth in the 19th and the 20th centuries due to an increase in demand for land. Supply of land is limited because the total amount of land on earth cannot be increased. Until the 19th century, people lived on farms and relied on available resources for most needs.

Demand increased in the 19th and 20th century because the following interlinked drivers of genuine growth of real estate growth were at work:

- **Population Growth** put increasing pressure on land.
- **Urban Migration** due to changes in economic structure from agrarian to industrial. Along with increase in population, this put the limited land within city limits under increased demand.
- **Wage Increases** due to technological and economic changes left people with more to spend on houses than ever before, creating additional demand for real estate.

With increased congestion in cities, people started to purchase vacation homes, and this further added to the demand for real estate. Real estate cooled down slightly in the 1970s due to raging inflation, but picked up again in the 1980s as the economy started to boom and mortgage rates came down, making it easier to purchase real estate.

This was also the start of the bubble age when cheap credit fuelled a spending bubble. Demand for real estate boomed and so did the prices. Home owners now refinanced their mortgages using the increased price of their houses to get even more loans for even more spending and, maybe, the purchase of more real estate.

Banks and other lenders willingly obliged. The rising real estate market not only attracted huge investment from people's own funds, but many individual investors borrowed from banks – from other people's hard-earned savings – to invest into this galloping bubble. Earlier, such leverage was available to large institutional investors only. The bubble hysteria was on.

Such a feedback loop of inflation enabled people to spend money that was not hard earned, but simply a result of appreciation of the assets held by them. The worst part of this was the gradual elimination of the incentive for hard work, since some people found that they could live lavishly without productive effort.

Lying underneath the economic boom was the menace of inflation. This meant that while real wages or wages after adjustment for inflation did not increase, people were increasingly getting used to easy money and a spendthrift lifestyle. Using their homes to take out equity, homeowners were going on a buying spree for depreciating assets or things that give no real intrinsic returns, such as installing a swimming pool or getting that new flat screen TV. Other bubbles were at work, too, and fattening each other.

All bubbles pop and this one did between 2007 and 2008 for the simple reason that none of the fundamental drivers were at work. Government intervention has managed to re-inject some life into it, but that won't last forever. Many investment advisors will still promote real estate because they feel low interest rates creating easy credit will last forever. They won't.

Printing money and the purchasing of bad mortgages from banks and other lenders is inherently inflationary. These measures boost the market for short durations only, and therefore have to be repeated. We have noted before that the time lag between money printing and resultant inflation will decrease with increased money printing.

Slowly at first and galloping later, inflation will assume huge proportions. Interest rates will go up automatically, and this will make mortgages expensive. This is where the vicious cycle gets completed and the symptom-treatment medicine is no longer effective to prevent the full manifestation of the disease.

Traditional investment advisors will argue that the continuous increase in population creates a sustained demand for land. This is not entirely correct. More efficient use of land can be ensured by governments through policy intervention and offering incentives.

There have been periods in the past when growth in real estate was either limited or even negative. Therefore, there is no such thing as natural growth in real estate unless fundamental drivers are at work. And how can real estate keep rising when the real income of people has not been rising? The collapsing interlinked bubble's collapse will reduce employment and people will not be able to buy homes with then-expensive mortgages.

What accentuates bubble blindness regarding real estate is its two-centuries-long rise with only a few hiccups along the way. Two hundred years is around seven to eight generations. At least four to five of these must have seen land transforming those from rags to riches. But then, the approaching storm is set to change many things, including the steadfast belief in land.

Denial is Always Easier

First of all, admit there is a problem that is going to get worse, not better. Do this after taking a complete view of the macroeconomic picture. Living in denial and in the bubble-land of the past is no good. All things evolve with time. If you don't pay attention to the changes, you will make a bubble era relic out of yourself.

Strictly from the financial point of view, the prices are going to go down and will hit the bottom, and stay there for the next decade or so. There might be a slight rise in the days to come, as another round of money printing props up the bubble, but the long term trend is a sustained drop.

In case you consider retaining the primary house, consider the following:

- Convert all outstanding mortgages to fixed rate mortgages. The approaching crisis will come with inflation and drastically reduce the value of what you repay (not the amount). Avoid all kinds of adjustable rate mortgages that increase their rates with inflation and preclude your profit from inflation.

- Make only the minimum possible installment payment, as inflation is on the way to help you in lowering the value of actual payment; let the bank take more market risks than you.

- Whatever happens, do not borrow with your house as collateral if you intend to use the proceeds for living expenses and not for investment. Falling value of the home may leave you cashless and homeless. Unless you use it to buy physical gold and silver.

If falling real estate prices make the mortgage more expensive than the primary home that is also the collateral, check if you qualify for a government mortgage refinance program. Even if you don't, fight foreclosure legally, as sometimes there are lapses in loan agreements. The government usually helps people keep their homes during financial distresses.

Otherwise, it takes almost 1-2+ years on an average for eviction to be legally implemented, and banks are not too enthusiastic about foreclosures as it adds the responsibility of selling the foreclosed property. Negotiation with legal help, therefore, can be a way to deal with such situations.

However, now is a good time to buy a primary residence if you do not possess one and if you can get a fixed rate mortgage. This is because the interest rates on mortgages are low and will only go up in the near future. Besides, when inflation hits, your low fied interest mortgage will disappear in relation.

Income producing rental properties are temporarily up because people have lost homes in foreclosure, they cannot get mortgages, or they are waiting for the decline of real estate prices to make purchases. This phase won't last forever. Rents will fall with falling real estate prices and weak to no job growth. Such as Las Vega's rental real estate market in December 2012.

Farmlands that produce income from crops or livestock can be retained. With inflation set to go higher, the prices of agricultural commodities will also rise and fetch good returns. The falling dollar will also make exports of such produce lucrative, despite inflation. However, credit and inputs will be expensive, and government support for farms will decline.

Remember, there is a cost of doing nothing, not only in terms of loss of value of the real estate, but because you could have used the proceeds to invest into those assets that will go up during and after the crisis – *physical gold and silver*, for example.

Life Insurance

Like most of our beliefs, the faith in whole life insurance and annuities comes from the past when, before government insured depositor's money in banks through the Federal Deposit Insurance Corporation (FDIC), banks were not that safe. These purchases were regarded safer than bonds and it was believed that these pay even if the insurer goes bankrupt.

Whole Life Insurance policy remains in force for the entire life of the insured. Premiums have to be paid every year (generally) into the policy and when the insurer dies, the named beneficiaries are paid the tax free benefit. Such policies relax the insured, as he is covered for life and is sure of his beneficiaries receiving the benefits.

Such long term insurance acts as a forced savings account, and the insured can procure a loan against his accumulations in this policy. Unlike term life insurance, the amount of the premium does not increase despite an increase in the insured's age. Term insurance provides benefits only if death occurs within the period of coverage. Whole life insurance is more expensive, though.

Annuities are contracts between the insured and the insurer, wherein the insured pays a lump sum or a series of installments in return for periodic payments, starting immediately or later. Annuities are more popular with pension funds where the insured does not withdraw until he reaches the statutory retirement age.

After retirement, the investor is paid fixed sums periodically until he dies. Payment is continued even if the accumulated deposits and interests are exhausted, for the purpose of annuities is to prevent senior citizens from outliving their income. Withdrawals from this fund are taxed as general income, but not as capital gains.

Proceeds from annuities are invested into some assets – like bonds or stocks – and these investments are insured. Therefore, annuities are investments with some degree of insurance protection for the investments. Purchase of insurance for these investments makes them more expensive than if funds were merely invested. It also lowers returns, but does add a layer of safety.

Whole life insurance is more of an investment than insurance. Annuities also combine investments with insurance. The problem is that these cannot be safer than the assets they invest into and the insurance they provide for these investments. Any kind of insurance covers a short list of dangers and works only if conditions do not get too bad.

Insurance companies have done well by selling these policies. Whole life insurance provides the long term funds, and the benefits paid back to the insured are only a fraction of what the company makes through investment of these premiums. Annuities allow the company to sell investments as well as insurance.

Must people regards whole life insurance and annuities as safe for the reasons mentioned below. These arrangements also make whole life insurance and annuities expensive, and the added expense comes from the policyholder's pocket. The arrangements include:

- Insurance is provided by some of the best-rated insurance companies in U.S. that have weathered many a financial storm.

- Many of these companies use reinsurance and have large reserves to address contingencies. Reinsurance is the purchase of insurance by an insurance company from another insurer to spread out risk.

- State governments maintain a fund out of tax on premiums to serve as buffer and the federal government can always play savior of last resort.

These policies are reasonably safe in normal times, as in distressing ones. But can it survive a real crisis wave in the financial world? The main assumption is based on relatively low interest rates. The upcoming crisis will cause a rise in inflation, in interest rates and bonds, along with stocks, and real estate will get a body blow.

These policies are heavily dependent on bonds and, to some extent, on stocks and real estate, they will fall along with these asset classes. We have already noted how inflation and rising interest rates will consume the markets for bond, stocks, and real estate. Whole life insurers have reserves and they will do better than annuities, but only for a while.

No company is too big to fail – AIG is a good example – for insurance companies will not honor their obligations by liquidating their assets. They maintain a sensitive balance between inflows and outflows and the moment this turns negative, they will suspend payments. And if by some miraculous chance they pay their dues, raging inflation will already have eaten up their value.

All this at a time when the government itself is in a huge financial mess and cannot print or borrow money anymore due to the runaway inflation it causes. Unemployment means low tax revenues and the super power on this planet will finally plead helplessness. *May God be with us all.*

Checking Out

Consider checking out before rising interest rates decimate income from bonds. Move into term life insurance; it makes more sense if you are young and the breadwinner in your family. It is also less expensive and does not tie you up for life. Alternatively, you can borrow against your accumulations in the whole life insurance policy and use the proceeds for investment into physical gold and silver. Do not use such borrowing for consumption. Since such loans are never repaid, they are subtracted from the death benefit.

For annuities, there is a penalty for premature withdrawal, but it is a lot better than losing everything. Such a penalty is lower if you are closer to the statutory retirement age.

Long Term Care (LTC) Insurance is not a good policy to have unless you are above 60 years of age and in poor health. **Disability Insurance** is good for the time being, but not during and after the crisis. Inflation adjustment is provided, but that is not sufficient. However, usually employers provide this insurance and it does not cost you anything.

As deductive reasoning suggests, as most asset classes are eroded by inflation and rising interest rates, people will start to turn to the age old hedges against inflation and financially hard times – gold and silver. Again, as we have done throughout this book, we recommend investment mostly into physical gold. If you don't hold it, you don't own it.

Chapter 11 – Paper Gold: ETFs, Mining Stocks, and Derivatives

"Money isn't the most important thing in life, but it's reasonably close to oxygen on the 'gotta have it' scale."

- Zig Ziglar, American Author & Motivational Speaker

Gold and silver can be owned in their physical form, as Gold ETFs, as stocks of companies that are into mining of these precious metals, and as commodity futures. Each type of ownership has some merits and some limitations. Some of these limitations are surmountable.

Physical ownership is the safest way to be in possession of these metals. It is the basic form, and unless the price of physical gold and silver goes up, the prices of other forms like ETFs and mining stocks will not appreciate. They possess their own intrinsic value that more or less persists in all kinds of economic conditions.

Types of Paper Gold and Silver

ETFs

ETFs stand for exchange traded funds. Instead of tracing the performance of an individual company, these track the price of a market index such as the Dow or the S&P 500. These can also be designed to follow the price of a commodity such as gold, silver, or even oil. These are the simplest ways to invest in precious metals because they have ticker symbols just like stocks and can be purchased from any stock trading platforms, even on your smart phone, but not the safest.

Here's the catch: large investment banks can issue ETFs for gold and silver that they do not actually possess. This is because they are legally entitled to issue ETFs, for example, for 300 tons of gold or silver when they have only, say, only 100 tons of these metals. If you ask for the physical delivery, you may get only a fraction of what you have purchased, or *may not get any at all.*

Legally, ETFs are an unsecured bond, a debenture. Holders of ETFs become general creditors, not owners. They will lose their investment if the ETF manager goes bankrupt. As the crisis explodes, most assets will fall. ETF issuers deal in other assets too and rising precious metals will not immediately compensate other falling assets. ETF managers have a good reason to go bust.

Mining Stock

Keep in mind that if you invest in mining companies *you are still only investing in paper assets.*

Owning mining stock offers leverage because a 5% increase in the price of gold and silver can cause the price of stock of mining companies to rise by *more than 5%*. The reverse is also true, and can prove lethal; during the crisis and in the immediate aftermath, the prices of even gold and silver are expected to be very volatile.

Apart from this, there is the possibility of the closure of mines due to different reasons, such as labor strikes, accounting scandals, corporate scams, mismanagement, and regulatory action. Mines in conflict zones, particularly those in Africa, can be closed down anytime and some countries may nationalize mines as gold and silver prices go sky high.

Then again, there is the question of which companies to invest into. Stocks of exploration companies are risky, as these may or not actually strike gold or silver. Companies that are into production and possess huge reserves of these precious metals can be a safe bet, but these are not immune from the aforementioned general mining-related problems.

Purchase of stock of mining companies will be counterproductive in the near future as all stocks will fall with the stock market debacle. Later, when the gold and silver bubble starts to rise and shine, such stock can be looked upon as an investment asset. By then, the stock bubble will have deflated, allowing you to pick up such stock at low prices. At the moment, however, *pure gold and silver is safer.*

Leveraging gold investments or borrowing in order to invest in gold by purchasing gold on the margin is not recommended in the near future because gold will be highly volatile. Short term price drops may cause the lender bank or broker to try to fleece the investor, even if the investor's long term estimation of gold price turns out to be correct at a later date.

Once the dollar bubble bursts and the gold and silver bubble starts to rise, leverage can be considered as volatility will decrease and precious metals will demonstrate a sustained rise. However, the accurate timing of such a rise cannot be estimated, and it is better to adopt a safe and steady approach for precious metals investment, one that does not involve leverage or involves very little of it.

One plus is that lower capital gains tax is imposed on income from stock and not on precious metals stored as collectibles. Physical precious metals, collectible or otherwise, are also difficult to trace.

Purchase on the Margin

This is purchasing with an initial payment that is a fraction of the total cost of the investment or the purchase. The rest of the funds are borrowed from a bank or the broker who handles such investment. The purchased investment serves as the collateral.

If the price of the investment goes up by a certain percentage, the gains go up by more than this percentage increase in investment. *This lends leverage.* With every such increase in the value of investment, however, the leverage decreases and becomes zero when the loan is completely repaid. This means that leverage decreases as your investment rises.

On the way down, losses are also amplified, and the broker will deduct the losses from the investment that serves as the collateral. When the value of the investment goes below a certain point, the broker will demand a deposit into the failing account which he will then foreclose. Such a vehicle is a fair weather friend who is prejudiced even during good times.

Brokerage fees and the broker's exorbitant interest on the loan further add to the expenses. For precious metals, storage fees are charged. Even gold and silver will be highly volatile during and just after the crisis. Purchase of gold and silver investments on the margin can lead to foreclosure due to short term falls even if the price rises in the long run.

Futures and Options

These provide immense leverage to those who can play the game and win it, too. These are not for the novice, nor for the faint hearted. An essential feature of these trades is the changeability of rules – if the goalposts are themselves shifted, where should the rookie aim?

Futures are contracts that promise to deliver a certain amount of a particular commodity at a fixed date in the future at an agreed price. Options are future contracts where the agreed trade can be cancelled by the buyer or the seller. Uncertainty regarding future prices makes these contracts, especially options, highly speculative and risky, but also very lucrative.

As gold and silver start to demonstrate sustained and humungous rise after the crisis, there is a chance that the developments on 1980 are repeated. It was between 1980 and 1981, when despite depleted volumes, the value of gold reserves surpassed the value of the amount of money in circulation simply because people lost faith in dollars and shifted to gold and silver.

Then, the Commodities Exchange (COMEX) and the Commodities Future Trading Commission (CFTC) capped the price of silver and prohibited creation of new futures contracts allowing for implementation of existing future contracts only. With no new buyers, the prices could only go down. Contrast this with the raging rally of physical gold and silver.

With rising gold and silver, many will insist on the actual delivery of physical precious metals from future contracts. Default will then be unavoidable on the commodities exchange, particularly regarding silver. As the hunt for physical silver begins, its prices will only rise from then on.

In 1998, when Warren Buffet insisted on delivery of 127.7 million ounces of silver from his future contracts instead of settling for cash, silver almost doubled. Silver for immediate delivery rose even further. This phenomenon, wherein a commodity costs more for delivery today than later, is called *backwardation*.

And when default becomes inevitable, COMEX and CFTC will change the rules again. The point is, with ETFs, margins, futures, options, pools, and certificates, you play the game where the rules are decided by someone else, rules that are subject to change without prior notice. You will get played. You do not play the game, because you cannot... at least as a beginner.

Pool Accounts and Certificate Programs in Gold and Silver

In reality, these are a Ponzi scheme full of deceptive exercises. People believe the managers of these schemes purchase gold and silver with the money they pay. Instead, they use the money to pay for their own investments.

These are inexpensive and easy to operate. We all like to avoid complications and therein lies the trap. After all, the devil is always in the details. They are cheap because they don't impose a storage charge – because they are not storing anything. This is the precise litmus test. If no storage fees are being levied, these programs are deceptive.

Digital Bullion Trading Exchanges

These offer a limited trading platform. Precious metals are stored by these exchanges, and interested traders have to create accounts with them. After funds are transferred into these accounts and identity is verified, the trader can buy and sell bullion with other traders of that exchange.

An inherent limitation of such exchanges is their partial isolation from the global markets. Trading is conducted only between the traders who list themselves on the exchange, not with the traders on the connected financial markets of the world. Prices on these exchanges can, therefore, be different from those on other financial markets.

Digital Precious Metal Currency

This is an online method to trade in gold, silver, and some prime global currencies. Companies that offer these services operate around the clock all 365 days of the year, and trading is very convenient. Plus, the fees are reasonable, making this activity inexpensive.

Accounts with these companies are a combination of a bank account, bullion storage account, currency trading account, and a payment system. You can hold currencies such as U.S. dollars, euros, pounds, and Canadian dollars in these accounts and the interest is comparable to those paid on savings accounts.

For holding gold and silver, fees are charged at competitive rates. A combination of currencies and precious metals can also be held in these accounts. Trading is conducted between precious metals and these currencies and also between different currencies. The metals in your account belong *only to you*.

Individual Retirement Accounts (IRA)

Your IRA accounts can hold gold and silver, through allocated storage. You will need to open such an account with a manager allowing such investment and trading. After this is completed, most dealers of precious metals will comply with your order and your purchased metals will be held by a custodian, usually a bank, in allocated storage. Trading then becomes convenient.

Beware of Paper Gold

Unlike physical gold, which is within your reach at all times, these are all a part of the financial system, and can be wrongfully taken away from you. Most importantly, their value is largely independent of anyone else.

ETFs and mining stocks respectively depend on the performance of the market index and the company, while the value of cash depends on how much the government prints of it.

Admittedly, ETFs are the simplest way to invest in gold. Their flexibility and simplicity are a major attraction. But, as always, there is a murky underbelly. Investment banks can operate on fractional reserves while issuing gold ETFs. They can issue gold ETFs worth, for example, 3 tons of gold when they possess only 1 ton of physical gold. This dilutes the amount you can actually get your hands on, if you can ever get them on, that is.

Again, gold ETFs are legally treated as debentures or unsecured loans. If the ETF issuer goes bankrupt, the ETF holder will be treated as a general creditor, not a rightful owner. ETF issuers invest in other asset classes, as well. When the crisis hits us, the gains from gold and silver will not immediately and fully balance the losses due to other asset classes. They have a good reason to go bust.

Again, the capital gains tax levied on returns from ownership of such ETF and stock is lower than that imposed on precious metals owned as collectibles. However, precious metals are difficult to trace and their sale and purchase is largely *outside the financial system*. This means that their ownership can remain undeclared and taxes can be evaded.

Politicians will, as always, jump in with the tide of popular opinion. After all, this will divert people's attention from their failures as politicians. Imposition of taxes on windfall gains will make the loser majority feel happy, even if they don't gain anything from this envious exercise.

As a smart investor, you should not be deterred from stock ownership by this possible development. You might have to shell out a few extra bucks, but you will retain most of the returns. Most importantly, you get to learn about the market operations that, if applied correctly, can be the source of unspoken riches.

Argument for Owning Physical Gold

Physical ownership is the safest way to own these metals, and here is a list of the reasons why:

- It represents the most basic form of these metals. Unless these are purchased, the price of other forms – mining stock, gold ETFs, or gold with depositories – will not rise. With increased purchases of mining stock, the supply of these metals would increase and actually depress their prices.

- Physical gold and silver have maintained their allure across centuries. They never fail because they have an intrinsic value, a value of their own that they carry even when not used as money. This makes them money in themselves.

- Independence is the hallmark of physical gold and silver. Sadly, this is the precise feature that makes many authorities detest them. Such independence ensures that:

  - Their performance is not dependent on someone or something else – values of stocks, bonds, ETFs, and derivatives depend on the performance by the issuer, while cash is similarly dependent on the government and its money printing presses.

  - These are completely private and not a part of the financial-political system, a system that will hoodwink you at the drop of the hat the way it does with the values of cash, stocks, bonds, real estate, and other assets.

  - In order to transfer the ownership of physical gold and silver, the financial system is not necessary – they can be directly sold or purchased.

  - They maintain their broad value during inflation, deflation, war, disasters, political and economic crises, and the like.

- Even small amounts of stored physical gold and silver can total up to huge values.

- The spread – the difference between the bid price and the ask price – is very low in the case of gold and silver, as opposed to high spreads for trade involving diamonds or collector coins.

  Bid price is the price a potential buyer is ready to pay and ask price is the price at which the present owner is ready to sell.

- Uniformity of gold and silver ensures that any two units of these metals are similar, unlike diamonds or collector coins that require an expert to certify their value.

Minimum Risk Investment Strategy

Invest in physical forms of gold and silver ownership for the distribution of the investment risk. Physically owned gold and silver can be stored at home. It can also be stored in segregated vaults and allocated vaults throughout the country and abroad for safety in geographical diversity.

Gold ETFs can be used as an investment vehicle only if you intend to hold gold for short durations. Considering the crux of the preceding discussion, longer term possession of gold and silver will be more profitable and more soothing for your nerves. Those who want to play it extremely safe should possess only the physical forms, and hyper-risk lovers should deal only in stock.

Chapter 12 – Owning Physical Gold & Silver: Types and Storage

"Although gold and silver are not by nature money, money is by nature gold and silver."

- Karl Marx, Great Economist, Founding Father of Marxism

Physical gold and silver ownership is the best method to invest in precious metals, if you take the necessary precautions. Even a small, strong box can hold gold worth a lot, and if this safe deposit vault is located in the strong room of a bank, there isn't much to worry about. As always, it is better not to let the word of your ownership of physical precious metals spread too far.

Types of Physical Gold and Silver

Physical gold and silver can be in the form of:

- **Bullion** – precious metals in their bulk form as bars or coins. If these coins are issued by countries, they are legal tender. It is illegal to deny their acceptance as money, as a medium of exchange. Examples of such legal tender coins include Canadian Maple Leaf (24K), American Gold Eagle (only 22K, non-pure), South African Krugerrand (24K), and Chinese Gold Panda (24K).

  World renowned banks and minters also mint their own pure 999.9 fine 24K gold and 999.9 fine silver bars, which are just as authentic and as easy to sell as government coins. These can be sold at a lower premium, as well, because they are not minted by the government. These minters include PAMP Suisse, Johnson Matthey, Engelhard, A-Mark and NTR.

  The metallic or bullion value of such bars and coins depends on weight and purity, and it is greater than the nominal value represented by their use as currency coins. This is the best form of physical ownership of precious metals.

These days, bullion can be purchased online and over the telephone. It is important that you verify the authenticity and integrity of the bullion dealer before you do business with him.

- **Junk Silver** includes silver coins minted before 1968 that are 90% pure. These are legal tender, less prone to confiscation than bullion, and their metallic value is greater than their nominal value.

  Junk silver will be sold for a discount because it has different levels of purity and needs to be further refined. When the rates of silver go up, everyone will want to sell it. If more junk silver is sold, refineries will not be able to process all of it, then demand for this variety of silver will come down and so will its price – the way it did between 1979 and 1981.

- **Numismatic Coins** are attractive and considered collectibles because they are so rare. Their price is known, as numismatic value is based on their condition and scarcity. From the point of view of acceptability and for their storage at home, U.S. Eagles, both gold and silver, are the most advisable. They look official with 'United States of America' and 'one troy ounce of gold' or 'one troy ounce of silver' printed over them and are available in one ounce increments.

  For the purpose of investment, purchase of *0.999 fine silver* is the best alternative. This is investment grade silver required by the industry, and the industry will be ready to pay huge sums for it as demand surges but supplies dwindle due to insufficient mining in the recent past.

  Such coins are designated MS-65, with MS meaning Mint State and 65 meaning numerical grade. This grade varies between 60 and 70, with 70 meaning a coin in the perfect condition. Stay focused and stay away from these, as our objective is to invest in the intrinsic value of physical gold and silver, not their numismatic value. These are attractive as collectibles only. The value of collectibles usually comes down during financial crises as people sell them to raise some money. Avoid numismatics unless you are an art lover.

Storage of Physical Gold and Silver

Storage is the primary issue with physical gold and silver. It can be a constant source of worry if stored at home. If it is deposited in the safe deposit vaults of banks, you risk its exposure to a very meddlesome and unfair financial system. Furthermore, banks may be closed indefinitely in times of a crisis right when you can make the most out of such gold, the way they were shut down for a week after the 9/11 tragedy.

Again, bank insurance and FDIC insurance does not cover safe deposit vaults and there have been cases when safe deposit boxes have been misplaced when branches of even reputed banks have changed location. Storage with normal banks, therefore, is fraught with grave and avoidable risks.

Gold and silver have a high value density, and even small volumes of pure forms of these metals have a very high value. Very little space is needed for their storage unless you own huge volumes – then you would be a billionaire and afford specialist protection and this entire discussion will be irrelevant from your point of view.

If you are not the nervous type, you can store these at home in a specially designed and cleverly concealed bolted down safe. In conjunction with keeping such possessions a closely guarded secret, this becomes a very effective ploy. If no one knows you store such valuables at home, the chances of a burglary are minimized.

You can insure these metals stored inside your house, and such meticulous arrangements might even earn you an insurance discount, but it will add to the list of people who know your ownership of gold and its storage in your own home. The objective behind insurance is to reduce risk, not to create conditions that increase it.

Storage at Home

Storage options for the physical form of these precious metals depend on your risk tolerance. Storage at home is the most convenient, although it may not be the safest. In times of emergencies – such as the aftermath of 9/11, when electronic banking transactions and banks remained closed – precious metals stored at home can turn into proverbial gold mines as its demand climbs up.

A quality safe is a good way to hold precious metals for home storage. For best results, hide your safe well. Consider placing it in the wall behind a large picture, portrait, or make it accessible through a false, invisible door located inside a cupboard. The other face of this wall has to be inside the house.

Such meticulous arrangements for storage will also make you eligible for insurance discounts. It is better not to let anyone outside your close inner circle know that you store precious metals at home, and care needs to be taken whether or not you even tell them the exact location. Little space is required for gold, but silver will need much more room and you can afford to be choosy about the location.

Safe Deposit Boxes at Banks

This is a common storage method that people regard as very safe and very convenient, but it may not always be so. Consider this:

- Bank's insurance or FDIC insurance does *not* cover safe deposit boxes.

- A week after the 9/11 attack, operations at banks, stock markets, and ATMs were discontinued. Gold and silver respectively rose by 9% and 11%, but couldn't be retrieved if deposited with banks. However, precious metal dealers operated in that week, and those who had stored gold and silver in their homes cashed in.

- Cases have been reported when the safe deposit boxes of people with reputed banks have gone missing when branch locations are changed. After all, the banks are dealing with someone else's money. You can't expect them to be diligent beyond a certain point.

Storing precious metals with banks is like placing private wealth at the disposal of public agencies such as the government and the financial system – the reputation of both of whom is not very respectable, to say the least.

Storage Accounts or **Depositories**

Different levels of security are available and the owner can take physical control of the deposited metals at any time. Such gold and silver becomes a part of vault system, which simplifies purchase and sale. Different levels of security include:

- **Segregated Vault Storage** by reliable depositories such as Brink's is the best option in this regard. Your possessions are carefully checked and noted on official papers under videotaped surveillance. These are then marked and placed inside containers with your name and account number. The containers are sealed and then placed inside vaults.

  If you take physical possession of the deposited valuables even ten years later, the same gold and silver you deposited will be returned. Of course, you can take possession anytime. Most importantly, you retain ownership of your possessions even if the depository goes bust, closes down, or experiences a change in ownership.

  Being a part of the vault system, such gold can be easily and quickly sold. Similarly, you can conveniently purchase gold and silver that is a part of the vault system. Such trading does not require quality recertification. Purchase on the margin with fractional initial payment is allowed.

  Top depositories such as Brink's are outside the banking system and the laws that govern it. Brink's closes down only one day in a year, Christmas Day, and did not shut down in the week after 9/11.

- **Allocated Vault Storage** is the second-best level of security, as your ownership of a certain amount and certain quality of gold and silver is guaranteed, but you are not allocated any particular bars or coins of such metals, as is done in segregated vault storage.

- **Depositories** are another way to invest in precious metals. After the purchase paperwork is completed, depositories keep the precious metals with a separate legal entity. The buyer legally owns the precious metals even if the depository goes bankrupt, and the physicals can be physically shipped to the owner at any time. These charge higher commissions than gold ETF dealers and allow the purchase of gold on the margin.

In the interest of financial security, do not let anyone beyond your core family know that you have physical gold and silver stored in your house, if you choose that option.

How High Will Gold and Silver Go?

A peek into the recent financial history will give us a rough idea of the heights to which gold can rise and how silver follows. There is always an element of approximation in such estimates, as markets work largely on sentiment and it is difficult to predict the precise intensity of such sentiments, even if the general direction can be judged. These projections are, therefore, ballpark figures.

Under the Bretton Woods System, gold was artificially pegged at $35 an ounce. Despite the covert sale of gold to prevent its appreciation, the dollar suffered erosion due to massive printing undertaken to sponsor the Vietnam War and President Lyndon Johnson's Great Society Programs.

Two devaluations in the early Nixon years took gold to $38 and later to $42 dollars an ounce. Finally, in 1971, the connection between dollars and gold reserves was permanently cut as international confidence in the dollar was plunging fast. By 1980, gold rallied to an all-time high of $877. A similar bull rush will take it to somewhere in north of $5,000 an ounce.

Unsurprisingly, 1980 was also the year when the value of depleted gold reserves equaled and later exceeded the total money in circulation in our economy. This just goes to show how the will of the people asserts itself. When they lose faith in currency, people turn to this time-tested store of monetary value.

Another way to arrive at the approximate price of gold is to look at its relation to the Dow index. When the Dow index gallops in boom times, the value of each point on the index is a multiple of the dollar price of one ounce of gold. And when the index crashes, each point on the Dow becomes almost equal to the dollar price of one ounce of gold.

In the boom of 1920s and in 1966, the Dow was worth more than 20 ounces of gold. When the index crashed, it became equal to one ounce of gold. The highest point of the Dow came in 2002, when it was worth 44 ounces of gold. Calculated from this angle, gold would rise to around $12,000 an ounce. People always turn to gold in times of distress.

Back in 1966, the price of gold was not free to migrate in tune with market forces, since it was artificially pegged at $35 an ounce. That is no longer the case. With gold free to move up and down, this time the rise will be as good as unhindered and, therefore, will scale new heights. All you have to do is to cast your lot with it before it goes up.

Silver is the little brother of gold, and its price waxes and wanes with that of gold. Primarily, it is used as an industrial metal. Its application as an investment metal is secondary to that of gold, after its industrial demand has been satisfied. The ratio of gold to silver price averaged 47 in the 20th century. This will rise and then fall in the upcoming period.

As the bubbles pop and slow down the global economy and industrial production, the industrial demand for silver will fall. This will be the time to purchase as much silver as possible. Production and supply of gold is limited. As investors find it increasingly difficult to get their hands on gold, they will turn to silver, causing its price to top.

Despite its rise as an investment metal, the monetary function of silver may not be revived. Earlier silver coins were preferred for low value transactions – having gold coins for such transactions would reduce their size to tiny, almost invisible pellets. With online money transfers based on gold deposit accounts as mentioned earlier, this limitation of gold is eliminated.

Natural Pushback

It is a trait of power hungry people to challenge the rule of law. Economically, this violation manifests in an inclination for the paper standard and a deep seated detestation for the gold standard. Financial intricacies ensure that people can be swindled easily, even in democracies, through careful use of the media to shape public perceptions.

Gold and silver has never failed, but men and governments have. The rule of law and the sovereignty of people can better exist under a gold standard than under the paper variety. This decentralization has proved to be the undoing of the gold standard.

But then, no one can play God for long. As the current crisis worsens progressively, its own internal contradictions will become apparent, slowly but surely. Economic plight has triggered many a revolution before, and there is no reason to believe this won't happen again. Perhaps then we will see the financial wheel come full circle. Until then, be ready and invest carefully.

Chapter 13 – Common Objections to Precious Metals Investing

"Nothing will ever be attempted if all possible objections must be first overcome."

- Samuel Johnson, English Poet

Our present financial system is based on shaky, unstable foundations. This is one of the reasons we witness cyclic booms and busts. The structure is so faulted that any measures initiated for the remedy of a dilemma just cannot go beyond the redressal of the visible manifestations. The greater malaise that lies underneath is left untreated.

Now, however, we are very close to the breaking point, for a never-before-known amount of money has been pumped into the global economy to merely treat the symptoms of the underlying disease. This time around, the bust will shake the very fundamentals of the entire global economy and trigger radical changes in the way the financial system operates.

Gold and silver have always served as a hedge against economically uncertain times. Because of the unprecedented intensity of the coming storm, the loss of faith for paper money and asset classes based on it will be so great that people will call for a revival of the temperate and sober classical gold standard.

With the monetary function of gold revived, the demand for gold will shoot up and so will its price. Modern electronic fund transfers that enable low value transactions will preclude the revival of monetary function of silver. Nevertheless, the short supply of gold and astronomical gold prices will create demand for investment silver.

However, you cannot merely invest in *any* form of gold and let the market forces do the rest for you. A nuanced, sophisticated approach is necessary for appropriate investment decisions. Such understanding also protects you from falling prey to fraudulent investment managers and false propaganda let loose by those with a vested interest against the rise of gold and silver.

The Delusionists

Success in such precarious times is not guaranteed. However, such a plan in conjunction with confidence, patience, and the *ability to keep your head when everyone else around you is losing theirs* can help you at least survive, if not thrive. How well you handle the crisis depends on your ability – innate and acquired.

You will need to efficiently avoid the misguidance unleashed by the envious, the scheming, the ignorant, and the big-mouthed-loose-talkers. This requires determination and conceptual clarity. Firmness will counter the suspicions you have about your judgment – suspicions created by the unfolding situation. However, there is a fine line between being firm and being rigid.

Many delusionists have a vested interest in creating a deceptively optimistic situation. Such professional con men can be found in government, administration, banking, finance, industry, and media. Such manipulation prevents a buildup of public anger against the public authorities and their undue favors to industrial captains. It also maintains the inflow of foreign investment.

If people lose confidence in the economy, there will be bank runs followed by a partial collapse of the banking system. The financial sector needs people to invest in order for the sector to survive, and people won't invest unless they are confident in the economy. The media becomes a necessary tool in this grand forgery and so do *hired economists* and *pliant financial experts*.

Even experienced technical analysts can get only their predictions right about 60% of the time. Fundamentals, however, are right 100% of the time. This is not to say that no technical analysts know the fundamentals. There are objective counselors among them, but those kind of honest advisors remain exceptions. The following examples will put things in a better perspective:

- Between 2004 and 2005, many would have told you to invest in real estate, since that market was bubbling due to the Fed's cheap money policy unleashed in order to counter the effects of the dot-com bust. Housing popped in late 2007, and real estate investors were left high, dry, and very frustrated.

Meanwhile, the rest of the financial world gasped as the crisis spread elsewhere through mortgage backed securities. The Fed printed $200 billion in March 2008 to bail out the financial industry. Such printing continues with increased vigor, and every new dollar depreciates all existing dollars, including those in your wallet and banks.

These financial packages come from the taxpayer's money, and common people are made to pay for errors by big business, banks, and governments. It can be said that socialization of losses and privatization of profits is already underway.

- Base metals such as lead, nickel, and zinc began to outperform precious metals in 2006 and 2007, and many would have advised you on these being better investments than precious metals. But when the trudging economy slows down the industry, the demand and price for these metals naturally comes down. Precisely the reverse happens with gold and silver.

Common Objections to Gold and Silver Investment

Apart from the manipulation of public perception through the use of media, pliant economists, and manageable financial specialists, supporters of precious metals are also afraid of **market manipulations by the authorities to dampen gold and silver** prices.

At the root of the official dislike for gold is the movement of gold and the dollar in opposite directions. A decline in confidence in the dollar and assets denominated in dollars causes people to shift to gold. If confidence in the dollar declines, investment funds from abroad dry up steadily, something the authorities want to avoid at all costs.

Prohibition of private ownership of gold is another apprehensive possibility for the lovers of these precious metals. Such a drastic measure was implemented in America in 1933 as the country struggled with the crippling effects of the Great Depression. This time around, the possibility of a repeat of this measure is highly unlikely because:

- Prices of gold will shoot up and negate the very objective behind such a prohibition – maintenance of the lucrative aura around U.S. Treasury securities for foreign investors that keeps the inflow of foreign investment funds intact.

- Prices of gold are largely determined outside the U.S., as the demand for gold is mainly based outside the U.S., particularly in Asia where gold is highly sought after and is a part of the lifestyle.

- Only a small section of investors, like those with middle level incomes who cannot invest in overseas gold, will be affected by such a ban. What this effectively means is the demand will not reduce by much and, therefore, prices will continue to remain high.

- Although Americans are not culturally inclined towards gold like Asian buyers, physical gold is owned by many across the country. Practically, it becomes virtually impossible to implement such a ban. If a ban is imposed, it's almost guaranteed that a huge black market for gold will be created and, again, defeat the very purpose.

If we are placed on the Gold Standard tomorrow.

Under this standard, the value of the total money in circulation is equal to the value of maintained gold reserves. National currencies are defined in terms of weight of gold. This provides stable exchange ratios between currencies. For example, if the price of one ounce of gold is $100 in the U.S. and £50 in Britain, £1 equals $2.

Being a tangible quantity with real value, one ounce of gold provides a stable exchange standard and keeps the total amount of money in the economy reasonably steady. This prevents depreciation of the money and inspires confidence in it. Money supply and prices are not rigid or fixed in this standard, but vary within a narrow range without being volatile.

Because the purchasing power of currencies and the exchange ratios between them are stable in the long term, businesses and traders get the breathing space to design and implement long term commercial plans. Buying and selling is stabilized in national and international markets. Despite occasional booms and busts, net inflation in this period – between 1878 and 1913 – was near zero.

Economic equilibrium and international balance of payments (BOP) are automatically maintained under this standard. A booming economy has more gold and, therefore, more money. This allows that economy to import more. Since payment is made in gold, such gold outflow contracts the money supply. This leads to deflation and economic slowdown.

Falling money supply decreases imports and prices. This brings down production costs and makes export of goods cheaper. Demand for goods from this economy rises, and gold flows back into the economy and allows an increase of money supply. The value of gold-based currency keeps changing within a close range with changes in the amount of gold reserves.

Because international trade payments are settled through transfer of gold, inflation cannot be exported. If imports are paid through printing of money, this money soon loses its value in the domestic and international markets. Inflation, therefore, gets exported the way it was from the U.S. during the Vietnam War. Such toxic export is not possible under the gold standard.

Objections to Gold Standard

Now that we have discussed the possibility of the revival of monetary gold, we also need to know precisely why the authorities dislike the gold standard. Their dislike is based on the supreme hate for gold, which does not toe their line. Similar to the propaganda against gold and silver, you can also expect to hear fairy tales against the gold standard.

It must also be remembered that the gold standard works best in combination with minimum government intervention in the market so that market forces are free to determine investments and wages, proper tax policies, and a balanced budget with minimum subsidies. In itself, it cannot counter bad economic policies, irrational tax policies, and populist labor laws.

I. The Limited Supply of Gold argument is premised on the practice of maintaining gold reserves of a value that equals the value of money in circulation under the classical gold standard. Calculation of the amount of required balancing gold must have been based on the price of gold when it was not doing very well.

This contention ignores a rational yet not-so-obvious *difference between the volume and the value of gold* and the tendency of gold and silver to rise during economic hard times. Some very sound counter arguments can be put forth, such as:

- When the financial storm that is presently in the making explodes, the prices of gold and silver are headed towards outer space, not merely for the sky. Such a rise in prices will more than balance the amount of money in circulation.

  On two occasions in our history, the total value of gold reserves has come from behind and overtaken the value of money in circulation. The first time was in 1934, after the private ownership of gold was banned in 1933. Again between 1980 and 1981, the same was observed as even the diluted gold standard was eliminated in 1971.

  The gold rally of 1980-81 is the principal counter to the argument of gold supplies being insufficient *in value*. This was observed despite gold reserves being depleted due to foreign nations – especially France – making a run for the gold reserves with the Fed due to a severe trust deficit in the dollar. It was the people's eternal love affair with gold that caused gold to forge ahead.

  Ever since the first recorded grade inflation in Athens in 407 B.C., gold has appreciated when people have lost confidence in money. Relentless money printing by major central banks is causing currency depreciation. Gold and silver will rise as a consequence, and even low volume reserves will exceed the value of monetary supplies.

  It will be worthwhile to mention here a pre-independence development of 1764. Parliament banned the issue of fresh currency notes to stop the havoc wreaked by irredeemable and un-backed fiat money. Gradual withdrawal of these notes from circulation was also mandated. Except for Rhode Island, all of the colonies fell in line.

There was a brief period that required adjustment to the replacement of one system of money by another. After that period, there followed a prosperous era for production and trade until the Continental currency experiment of the Revolutionary War again destroyed faith in currency.

Although the cancellation of fiat money around 1764 was limited in scope and area, it goes to show that a revival of a more sound system of money is possible. In the present era, this will not be possible without strong and creative leadership backed by the pressure of an informed and rational public opinion.

- At the end of 2011, there were around 171,300 tons, or 6 billion ounces, of gold on this planet. Around the same time, official gold holdings with central banks across the globe amounted to only 16% of the total gold stock above the ground.

  Once extracted from mines, gold remains where it is. It does not even tarnish, much less rust. The above statistics for the *volume* of gold are not very large, agreed. Precisely this non-large volume will cause the price of gold to explode as demand becomes a multiple of supply.

  A return to the gold standard would be necessary to restore public confidence in money. Unless backed by a concrete asset, people will not trust paper notes. Then, central banks would need to acquire more gold, causing its price to rise further. Forget about shortage, the value of gold reserves will be many times the monetary circulation.

- Even when gold is not doing very well, the exchange ratio between gold and currency can be changed within limits in order to strike a balance between gold reserves and monetary supply.

- Under a gold standard, price levels remain very low and,

therefore, eliminate the necessity for having large amounts of money in circulation. A car worth, say, $10,000 under a paper standard can be purchased in $500 under a gold standard.

II. The Gold Standard Causes Panics and Crashes the way it did in the 19th century, particularly in its latter half, is another deceptive contention. By 1878, the then-major economies had migrated to the classical gold standard where 100% reserves were maintained by banks in gold. Before this year, most economies used a bimetallic system of currency.

These panics of the 19th century and crashes were more a result of government intervention in the banking systems, such as allowing banks to suspend redemption in specie and prohibition of branch and interstate banking. Other reasons included fractional reserves, wildcat banking, issue of greenbacks, and the National Banking system.

III. The Gold Standard Causes Inflation is probably the most ironic and irrational of all the expositions voiced against the gold standard. This is because prices have consistently risen since 1971, when the connection between dollars and gold reserves was permanently cut.

Perfect short term price stability has never been achieved anywhere. If we compare the price levels under the gold standard and the paper standard, the glaring differences are immediately visible: the average change in consumer prices under gold was zero. The most continuous inflation under gold was an estimated 2.4% per year observed between 1902 and 1907.

Annual variations in wholesale price indexes 1879-1914 were considerable because this index accorded greater importance to price-volatile farm commodities and crude materials than is done at present.

Stability under the gold standard ensured low interest rates on bonds for a longer duration. Average maturity of new corporations has fallen from over 37 years between 1900 and 1904 to 20 years more recently, between 1968 and 1972. Longer durations and lower rates are a measure of the faith placed in the financial-monetary system by the lenders.

In 1913, the Federal Reserve was established. This was also the year the gold standard was diluted to the gold exchange standard. Between 1846 and 1913, the consumer price index increased by only 10%. This increase goes up to 625% in the 1913 to 1980 period. The acceleration was more pronounced after 1971.

For 100 years, between 1833 and 1933, wholesale prices rose by 0.9% only. The U.S. was taken off the domestic gold standard in 1933. In just ten years, after all links to gold were severed in 1971, this index went up by 259%. The charge of gold standard causing inflation is more than laughable.

IV. Gold is Subject to Speculative Price Changes is another specious argument advocated against gold. This contention turns reality on its head; gold rises because people distrust currency notes under the paper standard. Gold witnessed speculative investment in the years following 1971 because paper currency depreciated fast. The same awaits a repeat.

If we had been on a gold standard, the value of currencies would have been stable and there would not have been any speculation. The real speculation was about the value of the dollar, which caused speculative investments into gold after 1971. Similar developments will be repeated on the global landscape, as central banks work overtime with their currency printers.

V. The Gold Standard Benefits Gold Producers who can place a veto on international financial and trade transactions by withholding or dumping gold. Under the gold standard, payments for international trade are made in gold and this maintains a balance of payments, prevents wild fluctuation in prices, and eliminates the possibility of export of inflation.

What this argument ignores is that if we were in a gold standard, it would be in everyone's interest to maintain stability. Engineering short term instability for short term gains will be useless when considering the long term price in respect to economic isolation and suspicion. In a globalized world, the scope for such tactics is very limited.

Such a contention would have had some merit before the dawn of the Central Bank Gold Agreement (CBGA) era in 1999. For the period between 2009 and 2014, it is the third such agreement in operation. The CBGA-3 caps the total sale of gold by signatory central banks to 400 tons per annum or 2,000 tons over the five-year period of the agreement.

This formal restriction brings a semblance of order to the gold market and prevents volatility in gold prices. When the approaching financial storm reaches us, currencies around the world will hit bottom in terms of their purchasing power as people lose confidence in paper money. Central banks are, therefore, expected to shore up their gold supplies.

There are 18 signatories to CBGA-3, including the European Central Bank and central banks of Switzerland, Luxembourg, Germany, France, Italy, Spain, Portugal, Greece, Ireland, Belgium, Finland, Sweden, Austria, The Netherlands, Slovenia, Cyprus, and Malta. Naturally, such a wide group provides stability in the gold market.

Often, challenges are opportunities in disguise. The pessimist will, of course, disagree. The gathering financial storm will throw numerous challenges. While it may be too much to assume that we will be able to deal with all of these, we can certainly prepare ourselves and offer a fight. It's not whether you win or lose, it's how you play the game.

Sooner than later, people will realize the merits of the monetary value of gold. The pressure of public opinion will force our governments to revive the age old gold standard. Regardless of everything else, we have not seen a change in our monetary system in forty years. And when people set their mind on this change, no amount of manipulation will work to sway their opinion.

Chapter 14 – Caution: Things to Watch Out For

"Choose your friends with caution; plan your future with purpose, and frame your life with faith."

- Thomas S. Monson, American Religious Leader

Now that you have acknowledged the inevitable fall of the global bubble economy, also realize that easy money will no longer be available. Falling bubbles across the globe will cause the value of most assets to drop like a pack of falling cards. The situation we are about to face will be worse than what the world has seen so far. Survival and profit will now require understanding, innovation, and adaptation.

Gold and silver will be the safest assets, as they have been throughout the history of economic distress. But that is not enough. You will need to understand the fundamentals in order to take possession of the correct form of these metals and avoid falling in the sweet-looking traps laid out by other forms. Most importantly, you will need to call the bluff of official pronouncements.

Hocus Pocus

At the root of the manipulation of gold and silver prices is the conflict of interest between the dollar and gold – they move in the opposite directions in the market as falling faith in the dollar makes people shift to these ancient hedges. Although the applications of silver are somewhat different than that of gold, any prolonged rally in gold prices also boosts silver.

When the dollar falls, our government, the financial lobby on Wall Street, and our trading partners lose out. The government loses inflow of foreign investment funds into dollar denominated assets in our economy. Wall Street depends on domestic and foreign investment for its profits. Our trading partners can keep their exports cheap only with a strong dollar.

On a broader scale is the dominance of bubbles in the global economy.

If investments into dollar denominated assets dry up, these asset bubbles in our economy will collapse. Their links with other bubbles in other economies around the globe will mean a collapse of the entire global bubble economy.

As of now, there are six bubbles in the U.S. economy: stocks, real estate, private debt, consumer spending, dollar, and government debt. In a globalized world, these are connected with other bubbles in other economies, such as the construction bubble in China, the real estate bubble in Europe, and the commodity export bubble in Canada and Australia.

Sooner or later, all bubbles collapse and make life miserable. The present financial structure allows the treatment of the symptoms of economic problems only. Governments, therefore, artificially sustain bubbles by printing money, lowering interest rates, creating bailout and stimulus packages, and handing out credit guarantees. All this is mainly beneficial for the vested financial interests.

Any treatment of manifestations alone, while neglecting the greater malaise underneath, is bound to be a makeshift arrangement. Such measures only prolong the inevitable and make it more agonizing in the process. In the meantime, pliant personalities from both the journalist and economist professions are hired to paint a bright economic picture.

There was a time when the **financial lobby** included various forms of gold and silver in investment portfolios. With the bubble age that began in the early 1980s, gold and silver lost their allure as stocks, bonds, and real estate gained at the cost of these precious metals. Now, the bubble age is nearing its end and free market forces will boost gold and silver.

But then, Wall Street does not gain much from the appreciation of gold and silver because their portfolios have turned their back on these metals. Furthermore, if the whole truth about the economy is told, people will stop investing into assets other than precious metals and these managers will have nothing to manage.

Again, the present financial system permits redressal of *symptoms only*. The financial lobby, therefore, joins forces with officials in painting a rosy picture of the economy and denounces gold, the now natural enemy of the dollar. The authorities benefit not only because of a strong dollar, but also because this diverts people's focus from official failures.

Sections of the financial media and the economist profession are gainfully employed to this end. The upright among these professions do not vocally oppose such stage management, and their inaction legitimizes the wrong opinions in the eyes of the people. After all, when you shout out lies ten times, they start to appear to be the truth.

Large investment banks play another game with the prices of these metals. They gradually purchase huge amounts of gold and silver through futures contracts. Even before they own these metals, they sell it at once and cause their prices to drop. This sets off a panic among investors who want to get rid of their precious metal possessions.

Naturally, prices go down further. These colossal banks then purchase these metals at the depreciated rates. Despite what they say in public, directly and indirectly, these seasoned financial personalities know about the future rise of gold and silver and are shoring up their reserves to profit from the prospective rally.

As an investor, the first thing you need to do is see through the games played by all the named vested interests. This requires some critical thinking that goes beyond the obvious, but the entire plan is not very difficult – just hold on to your physical precious metals on the understanding that in the next ten years or so, their prices are headed only in the upward direction.

Classic Scams Plague the Journey to the Golden Destination

Now that we have described why strategic-level manipulations are undertaken by the powerful vested interests, we can move ahead and attempt to glimpse the operational-level perils associated with gold and silver investment and how to successfully duck them. This will present the strategic plus tactical-level picture of all the booby traps awaiting you.

Right at the very beginning, two things need to be made absolutely clear:

- Not all operators in the precious metal industry are bad; only a few rotten apples create this false impression. As always, good examples never make great news.

- *Physical* gold and silver that you can access immediately is the safest investment. Other forms of precious metal investments come with some degree of risk.

Let us look at some of the hazards:

1. Numismatics are collector coins that are more the collectible type than the investment type. When the approaching crisis hits us, many will lose a lot of valuable money and those with collectibles will try and find buyers. There will not be many buyers around in economically tough times, so naturally, the price for all collectibles will come down.

In contrast to bullion, whose price depends on the content of metal inside it and the dealer's profit, the value of a numismatic coin depends on the above two factors, plus the numismatic premium, the rarity value. The more unique or older a coin is, the more its rarity premium will be.

Usually, the rarest coins are owned by the wealthiest who can afford not to sell them when the market goes down. For the rest, the state of the economy and the mood of the public determine this component of the price. People will be ready to purchase for such discretionary goods only if they have basic needs covered.

Another aspect of the numismatic premium is its wide variation. While a certain buyer might find a unique trait of the coin attractive and, therefore, want to shell out huge sums for it, the same characteristic can make it unattractive or even repulsive for some other buyer. The element of *subjectivity* in this part of the numismatic coin's value is immense.

Dealer's profit for numismatic coins varies from 15% to 100%. In the case of scammer sellers of numismatics, this can go as high as 1,000%. Contrast this with the 1% to 5% dealer's profit for bullion coins. If you look upon all these coins as investments, you will have to wait for a 15% to 100% increase in the numismatic coin's value in order to merely recover the investment. The corresponding figure for a bullion coin is a more manageable 1% to 5%.

Ambiguity regarding the veracity of numismatic coins means that the pool of buyers for them is fairly limited, and eligible buyers have to be hunted. This naturally reduces the demand for them and also the numismatic premium. Bullion coins, on the other hand, have a ready market and the buyer will only need to check if the metal content is as pure as claimed. Machines are available for such tests.

Numismatic coins are worth collecting only if they are genuinely old or truly rare – like a century-old coin that accidentally remained out of circulation or like those Morgan Silver Dollars that were released by the U.S. Treasury decades after being minted.

Brand new collectibles are not collectibles at all, for they defeat the very purpose of a collection – the rarity value. Also, as we shall see later, the transparent grading slabs can be tampered with for the sale of ungraded coins as graded ones. Such practices destroy the very systematization ushered in by grading services.

Numismatics, therefore, are good only as collectibles or as a hobby, not as an investment. If you develop this hobby, you may find a few genuinely good clubs and coin dealers who can provide you with a wealth of truly rare information. Then, you may be able to convert your hobby into a lucrative trade.

Even if you cannot, the hobby will still make you happy, and there are great chances of not making money on numismatics. The financial woes let loose by the approaching financial storm brings down the value of collectibles as owners try to sell their collectibles to raise money in a market where very few have the means for such a purchase.

2. Frauds and Rackets are a part of the precious metals industry, as with all other industries. Most dealers in this sector are, however, honest, hard-working folks. Creativity is a great gift, and some of the rotten apples in this trade have been so ingenious that they made dramatic news and given a bad name to this entire industry.

In as much as 99% of coin related scams, numismatic coins are involved. This is for many reasons. First is the allure of numismatics with sections of people – particularly family members of the wealthy – who are not so smart. Next, these coins can be linked to a host of periods and personalities in history.

Then again, numismatics are easier to replicate. The metal, design, age, and condition can be built into new coins. Minting techniques were not very advanced a couple of centuries ago, and this also facilitates easy duplication. Faking bullion coins is difficult as the forger will have to duplicate color, density, look, and the ringing sound of gold or silver.

Typical channels employed by fraudsters:

- **Perilous Phone Call Rackets** such as the *nationwide rare numismatic coin scam* unearthed in 2001. More than 1,000 people were defrauded to the tune of $25 million in total, and the ring masters involved six people who jointly owned six corporations for this express purpose.

  Salesmen would aggressively urge people to buy coins that were said to be rare. If the potential customer did not agree, they would give them telephone numbers of 'competitors' who, in fact, were among the remaining five corporations of this ring.

  These so called competitors would then over-valuate the coins, more than what the prospective customer was asked for by the salesman, and lend doctored credibility to these coins. The actual price of the coin, by the way, was only a small fraction of what was charged. Beware of such stage managed credibility builders.

- **Advertisements** in magazines are inherently contradictory to the precious metals sector. This is because the advertisement has to be submitted to the magazine some time before it is actually printed, and the price of precious metals keeps changing. During and after the crisis, it will rise very quickly after initial volatility.

  TV ads are also contradictory, because a precious metals dealer who offers fair price just cannot make enough to support such ads unless he is running a racket. Profits on bullion coins range between 1% and 5%, while those on numismatic coins are in the 15% to 100% range. If the dealer is asking for a commission of more than 100% with numismatics, he is likely to be a phony operator.

- **Commemorative Coins** are similar to numismatic coins in that the genuine ones among them have some collector's value. It is not always possible to check with the authority that is said to have issued these coins, as the issuers of fake commemorative coins name some distant and nebulous authority.

- **Counterfeits** again involve numismatics on almost all occasions. Some are specially designed to be fake coins and are ascribed to a period or personality in the distant past. Many coins are legally minted as reproduction coins and sold as replicas; these become counterfeit when the owner sells them as originals.

  Sophisticated trickery is on in the form of graded counterfeit. The forger gets a genuine coin graded. Later, he expertly removes the transparent slab covering it, and inserts an ungraded coin into it. Remember, the slab has the bar code and other specifications that grade the coin.

  Such slabs can also be purchased online directly from the maker, and the grading details can be printed over it. The slab not only adds to the perception of authenticity of the coin, but prevents minute examination by the buyer; the buyer cannot sense the weight, feel, or sound of the enclosed coin.

3. Repeat of the Nationalization of Gold measure of 1933 is a difficult but not an entirely impossibility. It can be done if people demand gold and silver for payment, something that can happen in the case of hyperinflation – when people lose faith in currency more quickly than the government can print it.

If such a day does arrive, the greatest wealth transfer has already occurred. And if you have physical gold and silver in your possession before such a day, you have already covered this possibility. Now, all that you have to do is sell the gold and silver to the government and invest the proceeds in asset classes that are undervalued at that point in time… real estate, maybe.

The simple logic is that the government makes rules, enforces them, changes them, and bends them. This understanding provides you with another litmus test: if a coin dealer says that a certain variety of coins are 'un-confiscate-able,' he is lying. Even democratically elected governments can turn tyrannical when they want to, especially when adversities make the pretext available.

The following reasons make such a measure counterproductive:

- The ban will cause a surge in gold and then in silver prices and negate the purpose of keeping the prices of these metals under check, which is to maintain the worth of the dollar. In 1934, the value of gold reserves exceeded the value of the monetary base – a direct effect of the 1933 ban – which caused gold prices to surge.

- Most of the demand for gold comes from outside the U.S. Such a ban would, therefore, have limited impact on the worldwide price of gold.

- Again, the ban will only affect those middle income investors who are not able to procure gold and silver from overseas markets. They will not affect the overall demand and, therefore, the price of gold and silver by much.

- Gold-owning private citizens are distributed throughout the country. It will make the imposition of the ban a Herculean if not an impossible task. Again, the black market for gold and silver will be fuelled and further spike their price.

Gold Silver Portfolio

Talk to a qualified financial advisor who is an expert in this area to allocate your portfolio properly. The following is a suggestion on how your gold-silver portfolio can be structured. As always, there is more than one means to achieve the same end. These suggestions are, therefore, only recommendations, not ironclad rules:

- Have physical gold and silver in your possession at home or in safe deposit vaults of banks.

- Have offshore physical gold and silver not in your possession.
- Have gold and silver short stock and options if you are risk adverse and choose to have your physical holdings insured against potential short term turbulence.

Depending on your inclination for risk, total physical gold and silver should make up a decent portion of your portfolio. Remember, this is after gold and silver start to rise consistently after the complete pop of the dollar bubble. Until then, physical gold and silver should be the preferred alternative.

Talking about nationalization of gold or gold mines, the ongoing political turmoil in Zimbabwe raises the risk of nationalization of gold mines, and it is better to stay away from. Private ownership of gold was banned in the United States in 1933 and many gold lovers fear a repeat of such atrocious measures. But such a ban looks doubtful:

- Prices of gold will shoot up and defeat the very purpose of such a ban, keeping the U.S. Treasury securities attractive, which keeps foreign funds flowing in.
- Gold price is largely determined outside the U.S. because the largest demand for gold comes from outside U.S., especially from Asia, which has a cultural affinity for gold.
- Such a ban will only affect a small section of middle income investors, who cannot procure investment gold from overseas. The demand will not drop by much, and prices will continue to be high.
- Considering the fact that ownership of physical gold is dispersed throughout, the consequence of a ban will be a thriving black market for gold.

Even though forbidden gold ownership in this fabled land of opportunity may not be a possibility, taxes on windfall profits of gold and silver companies are a haunting prospect. The meltdown will impart a body blow to the livelihood of many. As gold and silver scale new heights in this upcoming period, all those who convert this crisis into an opportunity will be at the receiving end of the public ire.

Such anger and acrimony is totally unjustified, especially if it's targeted against smart investors and precious metal companies. Is it not the naiveté of the public that created the problem? People don't see it that way. Politicians wanting to make capital out of misplaced and envious anger will cash in by imposing such taxes, so diversifying your holdings internationally will be a great play in this scenario.

With your basic finances in order, you can move toward gains. *Speculation is based on expectation*. The investor does not get paid to own something immediately, but nevertheless makes the purchase on the expectation of higher returns in the future.

Nothing ventured, nothing gained. If at all there was a calculated and hedged gamble worth taking, this is it. Ask any investor who could not get his act together back in the 1970s when gold broke many glass ceilings, and he will tell you that such opportunities knock on your door only once in a generation. You may not be around the second time, *physically* or *financially*.

Finally, and we all know this, but *money is not everything*. In boom times, prosperous conditions can give you the ability to purchase things that make you happy. But that is what money can do, at best – facilitate happiness, not buy it. Happiness is abstract. It cannot be measured, since it has to be felt.

IRS Reporting Requirements

Please consult a professional tax advisor on these matters. Requirements include the following:

- You are not required to report the purchase of any precious metals in any quantity. If you purchase in large quantities and in cash, however, the authorities start to think you are someone who has made money illegally, and you may be taken in for some interrogation.

- Sale of precious metals for a cash value of $10,000 or more must be reported to the IRS by the seller. The emphasis is on the cash, not on the precious metals.

As a seller, it is better not to deal in cash, but in bank wire transfers. The banks and precious metals dealers do not report these, and there are a million such transactions being conducted every day.

- If you sell precious metals back to your dealer, certain items must be reported by the dealer. These include:

    - Krugerrands, Gold Maple Leafs, or Mexican Onzas each of 1-ounce weight in quantities of 25 and above.
    - Gold Bars of 1-kilo (32.15 troy-ounces) weight in quantities of 1 or more.
    - 100-ounce gold bars in quantities of 1 or more.
    - Any size gold bar of 1 kilo or more.
    - Any size silver bar of 1,000 troy ounces or more.
    - Any size platinum bar of 25 troy ounces or more.
    - Any size palladium bar of 100 troy ounces or more.
    - Any combination of 90% silver coins of more than $1,000 face value.

Dealers do not need to follow these requirements when it comes to the purchase of American Gold Eagles, Silver Eagles, less-than-one-ounce gold coins, medallions, foreign coins, and commemorative coins, irrespective of the quantities involved.

However, if you sell gold, silver and other precious metals, you are required to report the sale, as you have made capital gains. All such gains made from the sale of stocks, bonds, and other investments need to be reported. There is a difference between what you need to report and what the dealer must report. Again, always check with your certified tax professional for the most updated requirements.

And because the objective is peace of mind, it is better to follow the IRS rules and consulting a professional will be invaluable in this regard. After all, governments make, implement, amend, and bend rules… but *you* cannot, not for long.

This brings us back to square one: own gold and silver in their physical form only. And store them in a place where you can easily access them any time of the day, any day of the week, any week of the month, and any month of the year. Our banking and financial system has a huge critical flaw. Basically, it is simple: *If you can't hold it, you don't own it.*

About the Author, Dr. Alan P. Chan, Pharm.D

Dr. Alan Chan has been a precious metals investor since 2006. After receiving his doctorate in pharmacy from University of the Pacific, he was involved in start-ups, real estate and private investments.

After the real estate bubble in September 2008 knocked around 75% off his heavily leveraged real estate portfolio and essentially wiped out his pre-construction projects, he was back to square one.

In late 2008, during financial planning due diligence for starting a family with his fiancé (a former Morgan Stanley financial adviser), he discovered the critical flaw in our global financial system and how it causes bubbles and stock market crashes. Since then, Dr. Chan has spent over 4 years researching our financial system and macroeconomics. "The Critical Flaw" focuses specifically on the role our monetary policies have played in bringing about the current and future economic tragedies. Most importantly, he has discovered a saving grace: how gold and silver can help us profit and protect ourselves.

Glossary

Annuities	Contracts between the insured and the insurer wherein the insured pays a lump sum or a series of installments in return for periodic payments starting immediately or later.
Austrian Theory of Business Cycle	Any expansion in credit loaned out by banks creates conditions for a boom-bust or an inflation-deflation supply.
Barter	Trading one good for another.
Bimetallism	An economic system based on gold and silver.
Book Value	The value of the company's assets, not its earnings or revenues.
Bubble	The excessive and speculative investment in an asset or a sector of economy that is expected to rise in value.
Bubblenomics	Bubble based economics.
Bullion	Precious metals in their bulk form as bars or coins.

Certificates of Deposit	Certificates that specify the amount of money deposited by a person with a bank or savings and loan institutions and the duration for which the funds will be with the bank.
Classical Gold Standard	Monetary system in which the standard economic unit of account is a fixed weight of gold.
Commercial Bank Money	Funds held in demand deposits with commercial banks.
Commodity Backed Money	Money that is backed by real commodities like gold and silver, and that can be exchanged for that commodity on demand.
Commodity Money	Uses commodities as a medium of exchange.
Continental	Paper money issued by the Continental Congress.
Currency	The concentrated form of wealth that is used for trading.
Current Account Deficit	The excess of the value of imports over the value of exports.
Deliberate Price Dampening	Done through the futures trading route when the purchase is to be completed at some future date but the still unpurchased commodity can be sold to someone else.

Derivative	A financial instrument whose price and value are derived from the price and value of the asset that underlies them such as stocks, bonds, commodities, currencies, market indexes, and interest rates.
Double Coincidence of Wants	A transaction where both exchangers have what the other person wants and both are ready to exchange at the same time.
Economy	The institutional mechanisms directly and indirectly related to production, distribution, exchange, and consumption of goods and services.
Eurodollar Deposits	Deposits of dollars with a bank outside the United States, either a foreign bank or a foreign branch of an American bank.
Fiat Money	Without intrinsic value but derives its legitimacy from the fact that the government orders people to accept it as money and makes it illegal for anyone to reject its use as a medium of exchange.
Fiduciary Money	Fiat money.
Forex	Abbreviation for foreign exchange.
Fractional Reserve Banking	Where banks retain only a fraction of the total deposits as reserves.
Gold Standard	Monetary system based on gold value.
Gold Exchange Standard	Monetary system based on exchangeability of printed money for gold.
Greenbacks	Money issued during the Civil War.

Gresham's Law	When government compulsorily over-values one money and under-values another, the undervalued money disappears into hoards or leaves the country while the overvalued money floods into circulation.
Gross Domestic Product	It is the sum total of the value of all goods and services produced by all people within the geographical boundaries of an economy-country within a certain period of time.
Gross National Product	The sum total of all goods and services produced by citizens of a nation in certain duration irrespective of their location.
Hyperinflation	Phenomenon when people lose faith in the currency faster than the rate at which new currency is printed.
Inflation	More money in circulation decreases the purchasing power of money, creating a price rise.
International Monetary System	The institutional mechanism that determines the exchange rate among different currencies, facilitates international payments, and accommodates the movements of capital across international borders.
Jobless Growth	The impression of growth without any real increase in the production and productivity of goods and services that creates jobs.
Leverage	The use of debt / loans for finance as against the issue of equity securities.

Monetary Base	The currency in circulation plus the reserve balances and deposits held at the Federal Reserve by banks and other depository institutions.
Monetary System	A system of money in a particular country-economy or in the whole world and the mechanisms employed by a government to control it.
Money	Money is created when loan is obtained, should be extinguished when loan is repaid.
Money Market Deposit Account	Savings accounts that offer a higher rate of interest than usual savings accounts in exchange for *larger-than-usual* deposits from which only a limited number of withdrawals can be made in one month.
Money Supply	Those safe assets that can be used by people, households or businesses, to make payments or as short term investments.
Monometallism	Based on one type of precious metal.
Negotiable Order of Withdrawal Account	Interest paying accounts on which checks can be drawn.
Net Present Value	Method used to calculate the financial position of municipal and state pension funds.
Options	Contracts that allow the holder to buy or sell an agreed amount of stock at the specified price before the option expires.
Participation Rate	The percentage of eligible workers who actually participate in the labor force.

Price to Earnings Ratio	The ratio of the market value of a share divided by the earnings per share.
Redeemable Paper Currency	Backed by deposits of precious metals such as gold and silver and can be exchanged for these precious metals on demand.
Repurchase Agreement	Short-term loan obtained in money markets (vis-à-vis long term capital markets) by a dealer of government securities through the sale of such securities.
Savings Accounts	Demand deposits that pay some interest.
Securitization	Conversion of assets into securities that can be traded in financial markets.
Short Selling	Stock trading technique to make returns from an expected fall in stock prices.
Sovereign Debt	Money or debt owned by a country.
The Taylor Rule	Asks for an increase in lending interest rates with increasing inflation.
Quality of Life	Measured in an economy through harder to quantify terms, like happiness due to peace, freedom, environmental quality, satisfaction, and consumer comfort.
Quantitative Easing	Creation of new money.
Thal	Precursor to the word "dollar"; was minted in a valley in Bohemia.
Wealth	Regarded to possess value in an economic system.

Resources

The websites, books and articles listed below were used as references and source material for this book.

TheCriticalFlaw.com

Private Gold Silver – http://www.PrivateGoldSilver.com

Harvard Business Review. http://hbr.org/

Gold Anti-Trust Action Committee. http://GATA.org

Casey Research. http://CaseyResearch.com

U.S. Government Accountability Office: http://Gao.gov

U.S. Treasury: http://ustreas.gov

Federal Reserve: federalreserve.gov, Statistics: http://federalreserve.gov/releases

Federal Reserve System (all branches), http://federalreserveonline.org

Ron Paul: http://dailypaul.com; http://house.gov/paul; http://ronpaul.org

CPM Group: http://cpmGroup.com

GFMS: http://gfms.co.uk

World Gold Council: http://Gold.org

Silver Institute: http://SilverInstitute.org

Dow Theory Letters: http://DowTheoryLetters.com

Jay Taylor's gold and technology Report: http://MiningStocks.com

Gold Mining Stock Report: http://GoldMiningStockReport.com

http://ShadowStats.com

http://GoldSeek.com

http://SilverSeek.com

http://MarketOracle.com

Understanding LEAPS. Boston, MA: McGraw- Hill, 2003.

"Uncle Sam, Deadbeat Debtor?" New York Times, July 23, 2006. Robert J. Shiller. "The Significance of the Market Portfolio."

Review of Financial Studies, 13(2) (2000): 301–29. Athanasoulis, Stefano, and Robert J. Shiller. "World Income Components: Discovering and Implementing Risk Sharing Opportunities." American Economic Review.

Miami Millions: The Dance of the Dollars in the Great Florida Land Boom of 1925.

The Great Depression of 1990: Why It's Got to Happen, How to Protect Yourself. Ravi Batra *(Author)*

"Fistfuls of Dollars Fuel the M&A Engine." Wall Street Journal.

The Fabulous Decade: Macroeconomic Lessons from the 1990s. Alan S. Blinder *(Author)*, Janet L. Yellen *(Author)*

Rich Dad's Advisors: Guide to Investing In Gold and Silver: Protect Your Financial Future. Michael Maloney

Empire of Debt: The Rise of an Epic Financial Crisis. Will Bonner and Addison Wiggin
Journal of Monetary Economics. "Chairman's Letter to Shareholders." Berkshire Hathaway, Inc.

American Economic Review, How America Lost Its Mind and Money in the Internet Era.

"The Debt Bubble Threatens to Derail Many Baby Boomers' Retirement Plans."

Wall Street Journal, "A Truer Measure of America's Ballooning Deficit."

"Did Pension Plan Accounting Contribute to a Stock Market Bubble?" Washington, D.C. Board of Governors of the Federal Reserve System.

"What Moves Stock Prices?" Journal of Portfolio Management.

The Dollar Crisis: Causes, Consequences, Cures. Richard Duncan.

The Stock Market Crash – and After. New York: Macmillan, 1930. Friedman, Milton.
The Great Crash: 1929, 2nd ed. Boston: Houston Mifflin.

Aftershock: Protect yourself from the next global financial meltdown. David Wiedemer (Author), Robert A. Wiedemer (Author), Cindy S. Spitzer (Author)

"Goldman Sachs: On Top of the World. In Its Taste for Risk, the World's Leading Investment Bank Epitomizes the Modern Financial System."

Manias, Panics and Crashes: A History of Financial Crises. Charles P. Kindleberger (Author).

The End of Globalization: Lessons from the Great Depression. Harold James (Author).

Origins of the Crash: The Great Bubble and Its Undoing. Roger Lowenstein (Author).

"Asset Prices in an Exchange Economy." Econometrica, 46 (1978): 1429–45. Mandel, Michael.

"Bubble, Bubble, Who's in Trouble?" Business Week, June 15, 2006. McGrattan, Ellen R., and Edward C. Prescott.

"Is the Stock Market Overvalued?" Federal Reserve Bank of Minneapolis Quarterly Review, 24 (2000): 20–40. Melzer, Allan H.

"Monetary and Other Explanations of the Start of the Great Depression." Journal of Monetary Economics.

Wall Street to Main Street. Cambridge, U.K.: Cambridge University Press, 1999. Posen,

Adam S.

"It Takes More than a Bubble to Become Japan." Institute for International Economics Working Paper No. 03-9, October 2003. Prechter, Robert R.

At the Crest of the Tidal Wave: A Forecast for the Great Bear Market. Robert R. Prechter (Author).

Conquer the Crash: You Can Survive and Prosper in a Deflationary Depression. Robert R. Prechter (Author).

On Financial Frauds and Their Causes: Investor Overconfidence." American Journal of Economics and Sociology.

Bankruptcy of Our Nation. Jerry Robinson (Author).

"The Great Crash and the Onset of the Great Depression." Quarterly Journal of Economics, 105, (1990): 597–624. Rosenberg, Yuval.

"The Boomer Bust." Fortune, June 19, 2006. Samuelson, Robert J.

"Measuring Bubble Expectations and Investor Confidence." Journal of Psychology and Markets.

The Seven Rules of Wall Street. Summers, Lawrence H., and Victoria P. Summers (Author).

The Coming Collapse of the Dollar and How to Profit from It: Make a Fortune by Investing in Gold and Other Hard Assets. James Turk (Author).